Articulated
Experiences

SUNY series in the Philosophy of the Social Sciences

Lenore Langsdorf, editor

Articulated Experiences

*Toward a Radical Phenomenology of
Contemporary Social Movements*

Peyman Vahabzadeh

State University of New York Press

Cover image: Giuseppe Pellizza da Volpedo, *Il Quarto Stato* (1901), oil on canvas, 283 × 550 cm. Courtesy of Galleria Civica d'Arte Moderna, Milano, Italia.

Published by
State University of New York Press, Albany

For information, address State University of New York Press,
90 State Street, Suite 700, Albany, NY 12207

Production by Judith Block
Marketing by Jennifer Giovani

Library of Congress Cataloging-in-Publication Data

Vahabzadeh, Peyman.
    Articulated experiences : toward a radical phenomenology of contemporary social movements / Peyman Vahabzadeh.
        p. cm. — (SUNY series in the philosophy of the social sciences)
    Includes index.
    ISBN 0-7914-5619-6 (alk. paper) — ISBN 0-7914-5620-X (pbk. : alk. paper)
        1. Social movements. 2. Phenomenology. I. Title. II. Series.

HN13.V34 2002
303.48'4—dc21   2002021675

10 9 8 7 6 5 4 3 2 1

to the memory of
Ahmad-Ali Vahabzadeh (1965–1988)
the experiences his bright lips articulated

Contents

Acknowledgments

Although this text bears my name as its author, it found its current appearance through the intellectual support that I received from Ian Angus, Marilyn Gates, and Jerry Zaslove, to whom I would like to acknowledge my endless gratitude. As well, some of the formulations in this text surfaced in several intriguing exchanges I had with Hossein Fazeli and Azadeh Farahmand with whom I am gratefully immersed in poetry and friendship. Ladan Vahabzadeh and Mario Di Dio also helped me in various ways and I would like to express my appreciation to them.

An earlier version of this text was submitted as my dissertation and I would like to acknowledge my gratitude to the Social Sciences and Humanities Research Council of Canada (SSHRCC) for the Doctoral Fellowship (1998–2000) that financed the research needed for this work. I would like to thank the Inter-Library Loans Division at Simon Fraser University for their admirable efforts in obtaining necessary sources as well as the Department of Sociology and Anthropology of Simon Fraser University for various kinds of support they provided for me. I also thank *Canadian Journal of Sociology* for permission to use an earlier, shorter version of Chapter 2.

My thanks also go to my parents for their lifelong belief in me and for their kind support when time was rather unkind. Finally, this text became possible through the loving support that I received from my wife, Giti, who generously shouldered my share of responsibilities at home, especially in taking care of our son, Emile. I could not have possibly gained the necessary time to complete this text, had it not been for her silent devotion.

But in what is most its own phenomenology is not a school. It is the possibility of thinking, at times changing and only thus persisting, of corresponding to the claim of what is to be thought. If phenomenology is thus experienced and retained, it can disappear as a designation in favor of the matter of thinking whose manifestness remains a mystery.

Martin Heidegger
"My Way to Phenomenology" (82)

To the question, What is to be done? when raised together with the question, What is being? a radical phenomenologist can only respond: dislodge all vestiges of a teleocratic economy from their hideouts—in common sense as much as in ideology—and thereby liberate things from the "ordinary concept" which "captures" them under ultimate representations.

The entry into the event [of Appropriation] is the homecoming from metaphysical errancy, which, for us, children of technology, remains thinkable and doable only as the struggle against the injustice, the hubris, of enforced residence under principial surveillance—whatever form it may take. Such removal would be the politics of "mortals" instead of "rational animals." It carries out the answer to the question, What is to be done at the end of metaphysics?

Reiner Schürmann
Heidegger on Being and Acting (280–81)

CHAPTER 1

What Can New Social Movements Tell About Post-Modernity?

How is it possible to account for the fact that in the heart of an
epochal enclosure... certain practices are possible and even necessary,
which are not possible in others?... How does it happen, in other words,
that a domain of the possible and necessary is instituted, endures for a
time, and then cedes under the effect of a mutation?

Schürmann, "'What Must I Do?' at the End of Metaphysics"[1]

The purpose of this study is to examine whether "new social movements" correspond to the possibility of an epochal transformation. If the postmodern designates the questioning and rejection of foundational thought, and if the new movements, in contrast to the "older" social movements, generally involve nontotalizing, antifoundationalist praxis, then, the question is, can we speak of a certain relationship between the two? Specifically, can we speak of new social movements as movements proper of an imminent post-modern era? This is a noble question in that it requires from us a certain audacity in acknowledging such possibility. And if we welcome such possibility, almost all hitherto social movement theories turn out to be inevitably outmoded, because they tend to theorize new social movements within various foundationalist frameworks. It is precisely this theoretical predicament that informs the inquiry of this text. It necessitates a thorough investigation, in the light of radical phenomenology, of the possibility of whether these movements indicate a new constellation in theory and praxis, and therefore, attest to a possible radical shift, although it may still be in its embryonic stage, in the ways we, the mortals (who "have renounced all ultimate holds"[2]), act out our existence?

1

Thus, the entire project hinges on the question posed in the epigraph to this introductory chapter. Despite the fact—or perhaps precisely because of it—that the current work is a study of, and hopefully a contribution to, the theories about contemporary social movements, due to the nature of its orientation, it situates itself primarily within contemporary social and political thought. It is important to note, as one might expect, that the analysis offered in the following text prepares for a postmetaphysical mode of acting and thinking, which collapses all hitherto perceived philosophico-sociological relationships between theory and practice. As is well known, ever since Aristotle philosophy has effectively played the central role in securing the rational foundations to which the whole of action in a given era should conform. Since the advent and expansion of modernity, sociology has carried out such a derivative conception of practice by not only deciphering, under the banner of sociological theory, the rational foundation(s) of society out of the existing social relations and institutions, but also by offering a specific vision of the future to which modern practices should subscribe. The long-presumed metaphysical-referential identity between theory and practice did not allow ways of perceiving the relationship between theory and practice, thought and action, other than referentiality.[3] By deconstructing such a relationship between theory and practice, which ultimately puts referential and derivative conceptions of action out of operation, a postmetaphysical approach frees thought and action from all metaphysical fetters. It thereby allows us to think a major shift into the post-modern, (that is, an era liberated from the burden of ultimate foundations). This direction will therefore prompt us to investigate and expose, as our point of departure, the referential assumptions prevalent in some of the contemporary social movement theories. As will be shown, such assumptions as human nature, rational/calculating individual, the subject, the agent, and the social structure intimate the modes of thought that belong to an era dominated by metaphysical representations of ultimate foundations.

The central inquiry of this study is pregnant with other questions as well. Arguments for the "newness" of new social movements, as some social movement theorists have already indicated, call for critical examination. Throughout this text I will discuss how the highly connotative, multifaceted, small in appearance yet great in effect, adjective—"new"—poses serious predicaments for theory. Does a mere distinguishing of a set of contemporary practices from other practices—which are nowadays deemed, thanks to insight granted retrospectively, as once dominant—qualify the former as "new"? Or, is it merely the prevalence of certain practices resisting the formerly dominant modes of practice that designates them as "new"? Can we see the celebration of the "new" in the social movement literature as a by-product of the increasing acceptance of the postmodern turn in the social and human sciences? Indeed, how and under what conditions does the "new" become conceivable and intelligible? These questions constitute the major components of the inquiry of this text. As I will show in the following chapters, *articulated experiences* set the content for identities and make the emergence of social imaginaries possible. The movement actor, therefore, receives his or her identity from the destinal path toward a social imaginary. A *genuine* articulation of experiences sets forth a *non-hegemonic, transgressive destiny*, one that defies the limitations that the *hegemonic regimes* impose on action. The great challenge before the new social movements of our day is to free their practices from what I call the *oppressive categorization* of actors by contemporary hegemonic regimes of *technological liberalism*. I will also discuss in the subsequent pages that the waning of *teleocratic* holds over new social movements' practices is indicative of the possible transition toward a postmetaphysical, post-modern era in which the legitimation of *praxis* cannot proceed from *theoria*. As such, this study intends to show what implications the study of contemporary social movements have for contemporary social and political thought. As well, it intends to place these implications in the broader context of a possible *epochal shift* toward a post-modern era in which action is not to secure the rational foundations of society. It will thereby offer an outline for a social theory that is enriched by a postmetaphysical philosophy of the epochal conditions of intelligibility and constellations of truth. Hence the relevance of the now fashionable and popular notion of "postmodern"—a notion that cannot be referred to without having already and adequately established exactly what the "post-" intends to delineate. This study will therefore necessarily move toward a critical elucidation of the "post-" in the post-modern, as resistances against the tedium of universal justifications of action.

The thesis that I intend to develop and defend in this text is that at the reversal of modernity that we are experiencing today, the new social movements allude to the *possibility* of post-modern, nonmetaphysical and nonprincipled modes of thought and action. The passage through the caesurae between epochs is led by experiences that defy the current hegemonic foundations of society, the subject, and agency. That is why the new social movements cannot be adequately and properly understood without asking simultaneously the two questions: "What is 'new' in new social movements?" and "Are we post-modern yet?" The epochal character of this inquiry, therefore, necessitates the development of a social movements theory that is informed by Reiner Schürmann's (Heideggerian) epochal theory.

As such, the current study will not extensively concern itself with how particular modes of identity, antagonism, and resistance emerge as particularities. Rather, while paying heed to such particularities, the study will seek to reveal and elaborate on how these particularities, one way or another, allude to the civilizational crisis of universal models that reign over our time. It will therefore search for commonalities, for what can link humans together in their struggle against various forms of oppression and injustice without appealing to any universalistic and foundational model. Such a theoretical tendency, indeed, will need to critically examine several contemporary forces involving the situating of humanity—namely, capitalism and the state. But for the purpose of maintaining the proper focus of this text on the questions of action and social movements, arguments about these factors will be reduced to those pertaining to social movements in particular, not to society in general.

Radical Phenomenology and Action

To deconstruct action is to uproot it from domination by the idea of finality, the teleocracy where it has been held since Aristotle. . . . Action is not deconstructible in isolation. This is why the first task is that of a phenomenology of epochal principles.

Schürmann, *Heidegger on Being and Acting*[4]

The primary methodological approach of this study is adopted from Reiner Schürmann's radical phenomenology. His pathbreaking, "backward" reading of Heidegger—that is, from the "topology of being," to the "truth of being," to the "meaning of being"[5]—not only ended the "hermeneutical dilemma" of how to interpret Heidegger, but also enabled a political theory based on an astute awareness of the metaphysical epochs whose normative-legislative-predicative principles have been operatively holding fast the West in the past twenty-five centuries. His take on the "hypothesis of metaphysical closure" enjoys a particular emphasis on the anarchic actor and shows his undeniable affiliation with a radical "Left" that is suspicious of all universalistic models. Schürmann offers an anti-humanist, epochal theory that severs all references to metaphysical ultimacies (such as the modern subject) by deconstructing the principles that govern an epoch. As such, he provides a theory that anticipates the possibility of the waning of the principles of modernity and prepares for a passage to the post-modern era characterized by the absence of normative principles. Since Schürmann's theory is itself an expansion of Heidegger's political theory, my reading and application of Heidegger's texts will primarily follow the theoretical contours sketched by Schürmann. This approach provides the context for probing the two major inquiries of this study. First, how are intellectual constellations of such social relations and arrangements as subordination, oppression, rights, and democracy constructed within social movements? Second, based on the directions revealed through the first inquiry, how is an epochal theory of social movements possible?

Radical phenomenology enables us to think our contemporary issues in terms of the epochal constellations of truth. Throughout this text, I use the term *epoch* to designate, following Heidegger and Schürmann, *the self-establishing of an era* in which an interruption sets two different ages (indeed, two different worlds) apart from one another, just as nowadays we separate the medieval era from the modern era. As such, radical phenomenological thinking opens new horizons before a self- and epochally-conscious theory that at each step checks itself in relation to the hypothesis of metaphysical (modern) closure. As a methodological framework, radical (or deconstructive) phenomenology contains the remarkable potential to incorporate various theories into its discourse, while exposing and abandoning their metaphysical assumptions. This is particularly the case with the task, undertaken in this text, of bringing the concept of experience back into a theory that has already undergone the subversive radicalism of French deconstruction. The study will specifically explore various aspects of action within the three planes of analysis that Schürmann identifies: existential, historical, and event-like.[6] These planes of analysis will enable me to bring together the theoretical contributions of deconstruction, postmarxism, Gramsci, and especially the phenomenologically informed political theory of Claude Lefort that make up a crucial component of the theoretical approach of this study. This will hopefully elucidate the reason why I have intentionally bypassed the already established sociological phenomenology (pioneered by Alfred Schutz, Peter Berger, and Thomas Luckmann). The nonmetaphysical approach of epochal theory, of radicalized phenomenology, necessitates a fresh start in order to show the important contributions of a radical phenomenological inquiry to the contemporary social and political thought. This phenomenology, as Reiner Schürmann points out in the epigraph to this section, deconstructs the teleocracy that has dominated action since the dawn of Western philosophy.

We will start to pursue the various facets of the main theoretical concerns of this text in Chapter 2, which investigates how the acknowledged emergence of the "new" movements in social movement theories of Alain Touraine, Alberto Melucci, and Klaus Eder, through their emphasis on identity, marks a paradigm shift in social movement theory. I will shows how these recent theories suffer from assumptions about an ultimate ground that eventually impede them from properly understanding new social movements. Chapter 2 will pave the way for further reflections on the predicaments that new social movements have forced theory to face.

CHAPTER 2

Identity and Contemporary Social Movements

The exponents of this conception of history have consequently only been able to see in history the political actions of princes and States, religious and all sorts of theoretical struggles, and in particular in each historical epoch have had to share the illusion of that epoch. For instance, if an epoch imagines itself to be actuated by purely "political" or "religious" motives, although "religion" and "politics" are only forms of its true motives, the historian accepts this opinion. The "idea," the "conception" of the people in question about their real practice, is transformed into the sole determining, active force, which controls and determines their practice.

Marx and Engels, *The German Ideology*[1]

Social movements are often deemed the manifestations of social crises par excellence. The theoretical literature concerning social movements has clearly undergone major focal and analytical shifts in the past two decades. Such shifts are nowhere more evident than in the coinage and increasing application of the term *new social movements* (especially during the 1980s)—a term that originated with the French sociologist Alain Touraine as well as the Italian sociologist Alberto Melucci. Ironically, the term itself is as widely employed as it is conceptually imprecise. It conveniently bundles together a variety of contemporary social movements under a generic rubric that enables social movement theorists to make quick references to their object(s) of study. In its differentiative function, the term certainly alludes to social and theoretical changes that have rendered some former practices and theories no longer amply pertinent. It also sets apart a new school of theory from older theories. The new movements are therefore "new" only in contrast to the supposedly sweeping political formations such as the workers' movements or liberation/popular fronts. But as one might expect, the distinction between old and new movements does not come without theoretical problems. For one thing, it tends to reify both older and new movements in order to set them apart by a rigid theoretical contrast. To my knowledge, among the original European new social movement theorists, Melucci is the only one who has pointed out this problematical distinction, although in passing.[2] He does not, however, see the reification (of the object of inquiry) that would necessarily follow the binary opposition between the old and the new. Furthermore, the distinction subsumes a wide range of heterogeneous movements of our time under one totalizing concept, thereby treating these movements as a "unitary empirical object."[3] For yet another reason, it leads to the theoretical downplay of certain aspects of the "older" movements that may still be vitally pertinent to the study of the new movements.[4]

As is the case with any generic designation of such imprecision (like the "Third World," the "South," or "feminism"), attempting to distinguish a new phenomenon from an older one through the term *new social movements* indicates, among other things, the legitimate aspiration of theory to upgrade itself to the levels of contemporary modes of praxis. In the context of social movements, we may speak of the emergence of new phenomena when we encounter at least one of two conditions. Either some governing principles have lost their prevalence over the current modes of social and political practice (the question of praxis), or certain practices seem no longer adequately relatable to the concepts or propositions of "past" perspectives or theories (the question of theory). It should, then, be the task of new social movement theory to either identify such governing principles, or critically reflect on the various presuppositions of its own postulates. Once we attend to the point that *these two avenues of investigation are by no means mutually exclusive*, we will be able to see the necessity of narrowing down this inquiry in order to explore (as in the subsequent chapters) what implications for contemporary social or political thought the theory of new social movements entails.

The purpose of this chapter is to inquire into what constitutes the "new" in the new social movements according to the pioneer European theories of new social movements. Following a brief introduction to new social movements, I shall carry out this task by offering an interpretative and critical examination of three major new social movement theorists. I will show how these theories construct and deem *identity* to be the distinguishing feature of new social movements. This task requires a vigilant conceptual and theoretical gleaning of the related concepts and propositions of these theorists. It also necessitates a conceptual rearrangement of the relevant theories according to the trajectory of my inquiry into the "newness" of the new movements. As the epigraph to this chapter suggests, the question of how to perceive the logic of history, of continuity and change, is an age-old question, to which humankind returns at times when it experiences fissures in history. Accordingly, the experience of the present fissure, that is, the problem of "newness" in social movements in the context of heightened problematization of modernity, brings us to the radical phenomenology of Reiner Schürmann, which informs my textual strategy and criticisms in this chapter.

New Social Movements

On the other side, the reference to Third World national and
social movements was for other groups the way to discover or to create new
social movements in their own countries. This tendency was much more
visible in the United States and in France than in Japan, Germany, and
Italy during the late Sixties. It became predominant in most countries
during the late Seventies. Progressively, this new New Left became more
and more anti-revolutionary and libertarian. It opposed the identification of
social movements with state power.

Alain Touraine, "Social Movements, Revolution and Democracy"[5]

The term *new social movements* emerged to designate a wide range of contemporary movements: ecological and environmentalist movements, feminist and women's movements, AIDS, peace, gay and lesbian, indigenous or aboriginal rights movements, antipoverty campaigns, various solidarity groups, antinuclear protest networks, adequate housing pressure groups, mentally- or physically-challenged support networks, support action groups for illegal immigrants or refugee rights associations, self-help groups of mothers, villagers, farmers, and neighborhood residents. The emergence of the new movements is usually traced back to the 1960s. In Europe, the 1968 events, particularly the May student uprising in France, the rise and expansion of women's rights advocacy groups and organized antinuclear and anti-Cold War protests register the advent of new forms of social movements. In the United States, the civil rights and women's liberation movements, anti-Vietnam war campaigns, and the gay movement are frequently noted to have marked the inception of the new movements. As Touraine suggests in the epigraph to this section, by the late 1970s, in most Western countries, new social movements became forces to be seriously considered by the state, revolutionary movements, or political parties.

The gathering together of heterogeneous range of social movements and collective actions under the banner of new social movements calls for the enumeration of the common denominators of these movements. Touraine subscribes to a schematic binary between the old and the new movements in order to arrive at a preliminary definition of the new movements. By way of comparison, Touraine tends to investigate how the domination of revolutionary or liberation discourses weakened in the face of the practices of the new movements. He argues that unlike older movements, the new ones are not "representational." They seem, moreover, interested in awareness-raising rather than monopolizing the control of power. Furthermore, new movements are associated with the idea of democracy, while the older ones were preoccupied with the idea of revolution. Finally, the new movements fight for the rights of the individual instead of the rights of the citizen.[6]

There are probably as many outlines of the common characteristics of the new movements as there are social movement theorists. However, there are certain features that are nowadays widely accepted in the field of social movement study as the characteristics of the new movements. Let us summarize these characteristics. First, new social movements are cultural or social in their focus and action. Political action, in the strict sense of institutional and representative political intervention, is secondary to their cultural activities. Therefore, secondly, the new movements take place within the civil society, as opposed to the political society. This indicates that the new movements strive for social change by pointing out certain issues that often are not limited to the interests of a certain class in the strict sense. Third, due to the first two features, the new movements employ various strategies to alter individual or group identity and values as well as promulgate new or alternative lifestyles. Claims to group or individual *identity* as a particularity in contrast to other groups or the state in fact becomes the pivot around which the new movements are arranged. Identity claims are especially important if we remember that ever since the emergence of modern nation-states, the universal identity of citizenship has been conferred upon most individuals within the sovereign state's boundary, thereby channelling the citizens' practices and perceptions into their common identity. In this respect, the new movement's claims to identity have shown the inadequacy of the universality of national identity. Finally, the new movements mostly engage in direct action through different social networks or cultural institutions.[7] This latter aspect is widely referred to as "cultural politics."

These four intertwined features of new social movements capture the relationship between the new movements and the overall structural-institutional edifice of modern societies. However, the relationship itself contains certain crucial implications. First, the exorcizing of the class roots of contemporary issues (e.g., taking the issue of ecological crisis beyond capitalism to industrialism and nature-as-a-resource mentality) removes the burden of totalizing ideologies off the shoulders of these movements. Second, in the absence of formal political organizations, the organizational flexibility of the new movements largely renders the individual and the collective interchangeable (as during the inactive periods, a few advocates represent the entire network). Third, because of their lifestyle characteristic, many of new social movements not only involve personal or intimate relations, they also obtain membership primarily from networks of personal relations (many AIDS activists are related to people with AIDS.) Fourth, some of these movements are therefore highly decentralized, segmented, and nonhierarchical. In fact, the more marginal a movement, the more segmented it will be (such as various antipoverty groups). Only a few of these movements are organized, though partially, around the political party structure. This is the reason why Alan Scott has stressed the organizational distinctiveness of new social movements.[8] Fifth, these movements normally engage in nonviolent, intervention practices and offer resistance through civil disobedience (e.g., the human chain of peace and environmental activists). Sixth, the cultural aspect of these movements signifies the legitimation crisis of current political channels of intervention and of political leadership and representation and reflects the citizens' doubts about conventional political parties. Seventh, and herein lies my focus throughout this chapter, *new social movements stress individual or group identity such that identity becomes the key theme* around which grievances, actions, and strategies converge to cry the name of one defining being in the past, present, and future of an identity.[9]

If, as the pioneers of new social movement theory hold, resorting to individual or group identity stands as the prime characteristic of new social movements, then any theory of new social movements must acknowledge this transformation by adopting methods of analysis that can incorporate this cardinal feature. A theory of the new social movements must be equipped with the necessary means that enable it to seek, investigate, and analyze identity the way it is appealed to in the practice of the new movements. It should understand *identity as a particularity* that does not make claims about some ontological or essential universality of the identity to which all other particularities must conform. In other words, new social movement theory should be able to open new analytical spaces that would account for such claims to particularity. A theory that conceptualizes the centrality of identity as particularity in social movements I call a new social movement theory. Therefore, while excluding social movements theories such as relative deprivation and resource mobilization from this inquiry, I take the theories of Klaus Eder, Ernesto Laclau, Alberto Melucci, Chantal Mouffe, and Alain Touraine to fall in my definition of new social movements theories. A new social movement theory is a term that designates identity-oriented theories in distinction from other approaches to the study of social movements. Whether the methods, assumptions, and paradigms of these theories can adequately attend to the problem of identity is to be probed in this and the next chapter. Having acknowledged identity as the distinct characteristic of the new social movements, however, we will have to refine our inquiry into the new social movement by asking: Is identity-claim *expression* of some under-lying structural changes which are reflected in the practices of new social movements? Or, is identity *constitutive* of the new social movements? The way a theory responds to these questions will determine its approach to the new movements. Thus, within the new social movement theory we can distinguish between the "sociological" approach (Touraine, Melucci, Eder, and Claus Offe) and the deconstructive approach (Laclau and Mouffe). I call the first approach "sociological" (with the cautionary gesture of the quotation marks), because, as I will show below, this approach adheres to the classical sociological truism of seeking the raison d'être of the new movements by anchoring, one way or another, explanation in a "real" and ultimate domain called society wherefrom social action derives its meaning(s).[10] I call the second approach "deconstructive" simply because it is an application of the Derridean poststructuralist philosophy to the study of politics and social movements.

This distinction brings us to the critical examination of the postulates of the "sociological" new social movement theories of Touraine, Melucci, and Eder that designate "identity"(-claims) as what is "new" in new social movements. However, in order to be able to show the problematic extent of their assumptions, I need to introduce the radical phenomenological con-cept of "ultimate referentiality" that will guide us throughout our investiga-tion in this text.

Ultimate Referentiality

Only those to whom this or that representation is everything,
and therefore binds everything, also have an answer to everything.
The entire lineage of historical illusions is there to
supply examples of such fictitiously immediate relations.

Schürmann, "A Brutal Awakening to the Tragic Condition of Being"[11]

The elucidation of contemporary movements by new social movement theory reflects the transformation of certain practices of our time. But just as much, it also reflects challenges that have been posed against certain theoretical frameworks and assumptions. The practice of social movement theory has been, as it still largely is, ordered and secured by certain *assumptions* about the existence of transparent and readily meaningful relationships between different sociological concepts such as structure and agency. *Anterior* to theory and its components, these assumptions guide the theorist to arrive at certain truths about social phenomena. Postmodern theories nowadays call such vastly dominant assumptions "meta-narratives" (Jean-François Lyotard) to remind us that these assumptions stand beyond the happening of the narrative and are thus removed from inquiry. I will call *the metatheoretical positions that secure the fundaments of acting and thinking in a given epoch, á la* Reiner Schürmann, *ultimate referents*. The concept seeks to disclose an ultimate point of reference which operatively ordains the existing modes of understanding according to the hegemonically dominant principle(s) of intelligibility in an epoch. Schürmann uses the term to designate the metaphysical truth-bearing regimes that regulate action and thought in a given era: the Greek nature, the medieval God, and the modern subject are the clearest examples of ultimate referents. These ultimacies indicate "representations of a ground"—that is, representations of principles and codes that open a field of intelligibility and govern practices in an era. They reign over the present regime(s) of things according to the Truth of a fundament. Once articulated, truths of this kind assign specific locations and identities to different phenomena. Their success rests in the extent of their hegemonic internalization.[12]

I use the term *ultimate referentiality* in distinction from Schürmann's "ultimate referent." While Schürmann employs these terms interchangeably, I use the former term as a derivation of the latter in order to designate *certain articulations and formulations of the dominant, ultimate referent of an era within specific modes of thinking in the human and social sciences*. The modern era is governed by the principle of sufficient reason ("nothing is without reason"), which takes thinking as a quest "to render reason, *rationem reddere*, and to act [in order] to impose rationality upon nature."[13] In the social sciences, this modern principle of intelligibility finds expression in such ultimate referentialities as human nature, the rational-calculative individual, and structural determination, all of which have historically constituted the subtext of dominant "sociological" theories of social movements. Therefore, ultimate referentiality designates a point of moorage, a foundation or a ground that justifies an entire theoretical approach to social phenomena. As an *operative assumption*, ultimate referentiality simultaneously runs on two levels. First, it bestows upon a certain locus in the "real" a privileged status and unique power to define other phenomena by virtue of theoretical approach that corresponds (indeed: co-responds) to this locus. As such, this privileged, "real" locus reorganizes (within the theoretical framework) social phenomena and social life according to its own logic. Second, it constructs a specific set of concepts whose function is to secure the presumed, privileged locus in the "real" in the center of theory. Thus, theory produces an exact conceptual "match" of the "real" it posits. By rendering itself invisible through this double movement, ultimate referentiality directs theory towards reinforcing certain dominant but presumed conceptual grounds. From their meta-theoretical stance, ultimate grounds operatively ordain the components of theory according to certain logics and conceptual positionings such that the ground itself never becomes the subject of inquiry. I will show in this chapter that in their efforts to identify the raison d'être of social movements, the "sociological" new social movement theories impose certain theoretical constructs upon their objects of study. Once properly investigated, these constructs allude to the operation of ultimate referentiality. Although it has undeniable affinities with the popular poststructuralist term *essentialism*, ultimate referentiality does not seek to merely identify assumptions about an essence or a ground that elevate a phenomenon to the center. Rather, the term reflects how theory constructs and conceptualizes such centers, while at the same time, it constructs and legitimates itself through assumptions about ultimacy. It also links these operations to the dominant metaphysical principles of our epoch.

As mentioned, in examining the place of identity in the theories of new social movements, we will be guided by the question: Is identity *expressive* of some "deeper" social ground, or, is it *constitutive* of new social movements? It must be noted that despite significant overlaps, similar models of argumentation, and sociological approaches, there are important differences between the works of the three major figures of the "sociological" new social movement theory in Europe—namely, Touraine, Melucci, and Eder—that we are about to probe. Thus, the following provides a critical examination of the "sociological" new social movement theory around three major themes: the new social movements' historical place, their place in relation to class, and their characteristic of identity-claims.

New Social Movements as Movements of the Postindustrial Society

[A] society that achieves the highest level of historicity defines human agency only in terms of actions and relations.

Alain Touraine, *Return of the Actor*[14]

The thesis that the new movements are specific to the postindustrial, information society (as the workers' movement was the industrial type of movement) appears in the works of the three main figures of the "sociological" new social movement theory. From the early years in his career, Touraine advanced the idea that social action should be treated as the central concept of sociology. His studies of social movements are therefore at the same time studies of the centrality of action and conflict to the formation of modern societies, as well as advocacy for a sociology that adopts new methods of investigation and analysis accordingly. It is therefore not surprising that with the perceived advent of the new social movements in the 1970s Touraine was among the originators of the term *new social movements*. His study of the new movements is irreducibly multifaceted, but one can clearly observe the centrality of the postindustrial thesis to his social movement theory. The postindustrial thesis holds that from the early 1970s onwards a major historical shift has taken place in advanced Western countries from the industrial society based on the production of material goods to a postindustrial society or *programmed society* of informatics and symbolic objects. Programmed society is brought about by "the technological production of symbolic goods" that hinges on four components: research and development, information processing, biomedical science and technologies, and mass media. These components suggest that the "central investments are now made at the level of production management," and not, like the industrial society, at the level of organization of labor.[15] Programmed society is informed by three major shifts in the configuration of society: one from "mechanistic" tendencies to "human government" as well as political struggles; another from "reproduction" to "change"; and finally, the third shift towards "less unified" power.[16] These changes witness "the appearance of a *new* societal type."[17] Due to departure from work organization as a general principle of social governance (which weakens the idea that social change is the property of certain social milieu like the working class and the faculty of certain actors like the proletarians), programmed society reveals itself to be one of a "generalized 'mobilization' of population" in which institutions and avenues such as the current political implements tend to lose their intermediary role.[18] This society is no longer "a conveyer of history"[19] progressing as a unified whole toward a certain socio-historical configuration. The postindustrial society, therefore, "being freed from all recourse to essences, turns completely into a field of conflicts."[20] That is why Touraine calls for the omission of the concept of society from sociological analysis.[21] Unlike the conflicts of industrial society, postindustrial conflicts are not to be resolved somewhere along the path of historical progress or in a future society. In the postindustrial society, conflict is constitutive of action. Consequently, in the advanced Western societies, the liberal distinction between public (political) and private, which functions to organize conflict resolution and preserve societal unity, loses its prevalence. Conflicts now become matters of "private life."[22]

Hence, the *withered centrality of politics as the locus of conflicts* in favor of the field of culture as the domain where everlasting conflicts amongst a multiplicity of actors take place.

Thus, new social movements, or, "new societal movements,"[23] reflect the structural transformation that led to the postindustrial society. They are the movements of the particular social configuration that Touraine designates as the programmed society. Abandoning "the cultural orientations of industrial society"[24] (e.g., limitless growth and consumption, identification with *the* nation-state), these movements respond to and react against the postindustrial forms of crisis. With the withering of society as a unified totality as well as the dominant norms of progress, the cultural orientations of the programmed society become not only increasingly pluralistic but in most cases also divergent or even irreconcilable. Today, we witness a plurality of identifications, needs, and demands to the extent that we "no longer define ourselves primarily as citizens, and governments appear to be above all managers defending the interests of Japan or British Inc. on international markets."[25] To capture his notion of the postindustrial plurality of conflict, Touraine depicts "the image of two or more actors confronting each other in the name of their opposing interests, but sharing the same cultural model, such that each actor is defined negatively by their will to fight an adversary *and* positively by their will to be the agent of realization of cultural models."[26] This conflictual model of society has ramification for democracy today, for now "one can only turn to a conception of democratic action as the liberation of individuals and groups who are dominated by the logic of power, or, in other words, subject to control by the masters and managers of systems, who view them as mere resources."[27]

Despite his criticisms of Touraine's idea of postindustrial society and new social movements,[28] Melucci also draws on some fundamental "changes in historical circumstances" to explain the emergence of new social movements.[29] According to Melucci, certain processes in our societies reflect these changes. First, with the collapse of the distinction between public and private spheres, which resulted from the post-World War II societal changes, the individual's needs have become the expression of the individual's particularity vis-à-vis the society. Second, opposition to the sources of domination takes the form of deviance and marginality. Third, consequently, the struggles for group autonomy and freedom from political intervention prompt movements to deliver their actions in the cultural field rather than politics. Fourth, emphasis on group particularity and identity becomes a form of resistance against power within the cultural milieu. Fifth, with identity and the quest for autonomy gaining such importance, direct participation of action groups is stressed, and representational politics (as in conventional political parties) is largely abandoned.[30]

Consequently, Melucci announces the end of the industrial "cycle" characterized by industrial conflicts (between management and workers), the problem of nationhood, and the extension of political rights to the excluded. Such end, however, does not mean the end of struggles for citizenship or democratic expansion of rights.[31] In a way parallel to Touraine's "the end of society," the end of the industrial cycle means that contemporary social conflicts are increasingly divergent because the points of conflict are no longer irreducible to certain key issues. Melucci suggests that today "we can observe the formation of a new field of conflicts, which specifically belongs to postindustrial, complex or advanced capitalist societies."[32] These new conflicts are diverse because the information (postindustrial) society is based upon a complex system that presupposes individual receivers and producers of information. As such, it needs to improve the autonomy of individuals or groups that stand at the different terminals of the "high-density information" networks that are "dependent upon a degree of autonomy for their constituent elements."[33]

As a systemic component of the postindustrial society, group autonomy tends to radicalize the notion of democracy. The institutional conception of democracy, closely adhered to by liberalism, can hardly embody the diverse tendencies of different actors in complex societies. The eroding distinction between public and private spheres in these societies also means the blurring of the distinction between the state and civil society—a distinction that has been, and still is, one of the principles of liberalism. Here we face the paradox of the postindustrial democracy. On the one hand, the institutions push the actors for integration and political participation. On the other hand, standing at their myriad terminals in and around the information universe, actors strive for group autonomy and identity, and deliberately withdraw from such integration.[34] In Melucci's words, "the paradoxes of post-industrial democracy are linked to both the pressures for integration and the needs for identity building."[35] New social movements embody struggles for identity building vis-à-vis the political institutions. Thus, through their efforts to attain collective autonomy and freedom from state intervention, they uncover the issues that have been excluded by and from political decisions. The new movements, therefore, are movements for a new democracy. Their "self-limiting concept of emancipation"[36] allows them to offer the notion of "democracy of everyday life" and perceive democracy as the condition for recognition, autonomy, and self-affirmation.[37]

The postindustrial era, as mentioned, puts an end to the idea of society as a unified totality. According to Touraine, society has become a site of conflict where no presumably central actor can represent *the* rationality of society, not even the state.[38] Surprisingly, however, this assertion does not instigate Touraine to reject the idea that in every period there exists one central conflict. Stressing the notion that social movements are not agents of history, modernization, or liberation, Touraine does indeed acknowledge the existence of a plurality of movements. Nevertheless, he insists that due to the structural configurations in any given type of social organization and production only one conflict—to be precise, "*one* central couple of conflicting social movements"—is endowed with the potential to bring the status quo to a halt.[39] Stated differently, "there is only one social movement for each class in each type of society."[40] The reason for making this claim lies in the three components of any conflict. The field of conflict is determined by defining (1) the identity of the actor, (2) an opponent, and (3) the cultural totality that is to be won (which he calls "historicity"). Belonging to the same plane, these three constituents express the central conflict of a given type of society. The central conflict, therefore, is waged "by a Subject struggling against the triumph of the market and technologies, on the one hand, and communitarian authoritarian powers, on the other."[41]

Despite an acknowledged "critical distance" from Touraine in this regard,[42] Melucci seems to accept the argument that some movements will essentially play a pivotal role that can be consequential for the existing system. He writes: "Even though I am not in search of *the* central movement of complex society, I maintain that there are forms of antagonistic collective action capable of affecting the logic of complex systems."[43] As in Touraine's theory, Melucci does not find in the plurality of contemporary social movements any evidence to support the rejection of the idea of one central conflict for every societal type. The difference between Touraine and Melucci on the problem of the central conflict is rather subtle. Touraine grounds his assertion in the vigour of a system analysis in which the position (and one may safely say, "identity") of the actors within the social structure is pregiven: workers and management are actors who struggle to control the industry (field or stake of conflict). For Melucci, however, the field of conflict remains constant, but conflict is now a general stake open to the challenges of different actors regardless of their structural position.[44] In other words, Melucci does not accept the notion of structurally determined identities.[45] Actors cannot be constant because their identities will inescapably undergo changes in the process of conflict. It is the conflict that is pregiven, not the actors. The conflict, as in Touraine, may be structurally determined, but the identities of the actors are not.

Melucci not only views new social movements as the movements of the postindustrial era, he also perceives them, at the same time, as responses to the failure of modernization and the urge towards it. The new movements push toward a development that has been constantly impeded by the political system and the institutionalization of developmental requirements. Resistances against repression and struggles to open the institutions attest to this claim. The new movements are also, at least in Italy, responses to the "growing institutionalization of the left."[46]

As the postindustrial society has caused a shift from the older types of social movements to the new ones, so it has also prompted critical reflections on the methods of sociological inquiry. For Touraine in particular, neither postindustrial society nor the new movements can be adequately theorized, unless a new practice of sociology is implemented. Touraine calls this new practice "the sociological intervention" and conceives its task to preserve the relevance of the sociological project of modernity of which new social movements are but new expressions. Not surprisingly, the aim of Touraine's sociological intervention is to find the postindustrial counterpart of the workers' movement. The sociological intervention identifies the specific directions of the different new movements in order to register their diverse areas of conflict "which tomorrow will take over the central role that the workers' movement held in industrial society."[47] This task renders the sociologist an actor who engages with social movements in order to make social relations the principal object of sociological study and offer the movement actors self-analysis and reflexivity (by reflecting upon their action).[48] Touraine's purpose is clear. If, due to postindustrial structural shifts, any social system is organized around one central conflict, and if, at the same time, there are in programmed societies plurality of actors and conflicts, then the task of sociology will be to examine different social movements in order to determine which movement is capable of rising up to the central conflict. This explains why Touraine advocates the position that the object of study is social relations and conflicts rather than social actors or systems. The central conflict originates in the existing social relations that are themselves products of a major structural shift in Western societies. The sociological intervention, therefore, studies social movements in order to reveal the potentialities of the actors' social relations to them and to ascertain whether their social relations contain the capacity for historical action.[49] This being the task of Touraine's intervention, the sociologist researcher enters the study of social movements as an *agent* of social change (to consummate the postindustrial society?). As regards the method, Melucci takes a slightly different position. Criticizing the assumption that the action of a movement will necessarily contain a higher meaning, Melucci comes to view the relationship between the actor and the researcher as *"contractual."*[50] However, he draws on his own definition of the postindustrial society that emphasizes differentiation and variability in order to suggest that knowledge in such a social system becomes an indispensable resource for the actors. As a "particular type of actor" (a notion which echoes Touraine), the researcher can provide the movement's actors with valuable knowledge about their social relations. The researcher and the movement actors are brought to their "contractual" relationship by "the recognition of a demand for cognitive resources." Maintaining a cautious distance from Touraine's ambitious intervention, Melucci specifies that there "is nothing missionary about it [i.e., the relationship between the researcher and the actor], and it does not imply expectations about the destiny of the actors on the part of the researchers."[51]

One final note about the relationship between new social movements and modernity is in order. Touraine has devoted efforts to study the relationship between modernity and new social movements—a relationship which echoes his postindustrial thesis. In his book, *Critique of Modernity*, he presents the project of *new modernity* that revolves around the concept of the *Subject* and its ongoing and ceaseless struggle against various sources of power in society. According to Touraine, modernity refers to the violent invasion of all spheres of social life by *instrumental rationality*, resulting in the colonization of local reasons. It is chiefly characterized by the duality (Christian or Cartesian) between subject and object—a duality that nonetheless has monistic tendency. To achieve unity, modernity appealed to Reason, natural order, and progress: these three intermingled elements render modernity a *transparent ideology*—an ideology to be traced in the intellectual texture of any modern system of ideas. Although he collapses any totalizing view of modernity and tries to acknowledge that cultural differences have influenced principles of modernity, Touraine agrees that the expanding domination of instrumental rationality inevitably tends to minimize cultural differences. The passionate craving of Enlightenment thinkers for a unified world founded upon Reason rendered them blind to the fact that they mistook their own particular, historically- and culturally-bound, theories as universal projects.[52]

Since an incessant conflict between *rationalization* and *subjectivation* without the prospect of final resolution is the intrinsic characteristic of modernity, the Subject plays an important role in Touraine's critique of modernity. Subjectivation is defined as the production of the "I," the appearance of the Subject. In the premodern world, desire and reason were one; it was modernity that brought about the divorce between the two, placing reason in the position of governing desire. The concept of *Cogito* in Descartes exemplifies one of the most influential of such attempts. This leads to the breakdown of subjective reason and the advent of *substantive or procedural reason*. Like Foucault, Touraine identifies subjectivation as an extension of "governmentality." Docile bodies represent an undeniable evidence of the violent technologies of the "soul" through which instrumental rationality produced fragmented subjects. It is precisely in this situation when "the orders of objectification and subjectivation merge" and when power allies itself and identifies with rationalization. In Touraine's view, the Subject challenges such regimes of subjectivation upon which modernity is built.[53]

Central to the idea of new modernity is the notion of the Subject as *social movement*. According to Touraine, it is through the struggles against the fusion of power with technical reason that the Subject is produced and formed. The Subject is a *social movement* because its very existence lies in its struggles against all forms of governmentality. Touraine rejects the notion of social class in favor of social movements. As a social movement, the Subject is "at once a social conflict and a cultural project."[54] "The subject is the labour through which an individual transforms him or herself in to an actor, or in other words an actor capable of transforming a situation rather than reproducing it through his mode of behaviour."[55] As an oppositional identity, the Subject comes to existence by resisting the apparatuses: "We can speak of the Subject only when power intervenes, as it is the appeal to the subject that constitutes actors who define themselves in opposition to the ascendancy of apparatuses."[56]

By now, it should be apparent that Touraine's "new modernity" represents the postindustrial society as placed in the context of the historical development in the West. The term *postindustrial society* automatically designates demarcation from the industrial society and highlights a socio-historical transformation in Western societies. But both terms, "industrial" and "postindustrial" refer to modes of social organization of labor and distribution of products. By expanding the postindustrial thesis into the theory of new modernity, Touraine can offer a model of historical development that takes conflict and new social movements to be indicative of a "new" shift in Western societies. New social movements incarnate the Subject in Touraine's new modernity. They challenge all kinds of authority without offering a totalizing new social blueprint. They are examples of the subjects that refute all kinds of constraints whether they are disguised as social roles or justified in the name of order.[57] Constructed upon the rejection of rational-instrumental foundations of our society, the new modernity would be the field of resistances to powers by the Subjects.

Given the postindustrial theses of Touraine and Melucci as outlined above, let us make the first critical observation. The trace of a modality of thinking bound by an adamant search for an ultimate referentiality that can secure theoretical postulates in the writings of Touraine and Melucci reduces the new movements to *expressions* of the postindustrial society (and the new modernity in the later Touraine). Whether the postindustrial society is a notion that can be posited without having recourse to the new movements to justify its ultimate presence remains highly debatable in both Touraine and Melucci. Despite his efforts to defend the thesis that the new movements are the movements of the programmed society, Touraine admits at one point: "Only the organization of new social movements and the development of different cultural values can justify the idea of a new society that I prefer to call a *programmed* more than just a postindustrial society."[58] As if the new movements are the quintessentially postindustrial society's movements, elsewhere, he outlines the seven "stages" of transition from industrial to postindustrial society completely in terms of the transformation of the older social movements into the new ones.[59] Clearly, Touraine conceives of a mysterious fundamental connection between new social movements and programmed society. For, in Touraine's view, the new conflicts, to which new social movements attest, have emerged out of the postindustrial transformation. It is a legitimate avenue of investigation to proceed to such a historical shift from the point of view of social movements, as he sporadically attempts, but so long as social movements are conceptually subsumed under some operative structural shift, this explanation turns superfluous. We can clearly see how an event attributed to the socio-historical domain (postindustrial shift) constructs the "real" (postindustrial society) that serves as the supposed external ground (i.e., external to the new movements) which harbors explanations about the advent of new social movements. By diverting its investigatory efforts into certain channels, these *imposed terms of a pregiven ground* prevents theory from adequately heeding under what conditions social movement practices can change. It would have constituted a truly novel and radical turn in social movements study, had Touraine theorized new social movements in a nonreferential way (i.e., primarily in terms of modes of action they carry out). Having not taken that road, however, Touraine's postindustrial thesis remains trapped in the explanatory impasse of the ultimate referentiality of society. Melucci's looser adherence to the postindustrial thesis suffers from the same problem, as his unawareness about the implication of referential explanation damages his assertion that identity is not structurally determined. Melucci's theory cannot accommodate a nondeterministic notion of identity.

A second observation is also in order: the postindustrial thesis runs into a series of factual problems. Both Touraine and Melucci almost completely disregard the presence of new social movements (for example, women's, gay/ lesbian, antipoverty, municipal democracy as discussed by Latin American social theorists[60]) in the so-called Third World societies. As for Touraine, his notions of democracy and social movements are clearly taken after European and American models.[61] Eurocentric as it seems, such views bar Touraine and Melucci from seeing the fact that despite endemic political repression, resolute or absolute poverty, and persistent "underdevelopment" that define many Third World societies, new social movements have emerged and expanded in these societies. The fact that the privileged conditions Western new social movement theorists associate with the postindustrial society do not exist in most Third World societies is blatantly self-evident. If the historical society offers "sociological" explanation, then it should also be able to explain the new movements in Third World societies. Put simply, how can the defenders of the postindustrial thesis explain the emergence of (more or less) the same types of movements in societies where, apparently, no great socio-historical shift has occurred?

The European theories fall short in offering a parallel explanation of new social movements in non-Western societies. Interestingly, when Touraine confronts this kind of criticism by his Latin American followers and colleagues, his response is nothing short of a disclaimer. Latin American social movement theorists report Touraine's warning "that the categories developed by him to analyze European social movements can hardly be applicable to Latin American social actors."[62] One would expect this to cause the European new social movement theories to reflect upon their approach. But what happens is quite the opposite: Arturo Escobar concludes that for the reason of nonapplicability of his theory to Latin America, Touraine takes the stance that "most forms of collective mobilization in Latin America are *not* social movements proper but rather struggles for the control of the process of historical change and development."[63] Stated plainly, if a social movement does not conform to the terms (one is inclined to say "laws") of theory, then it is not a social movement at all. This position implies Touraine's privileging the European-American new social movement (and democratic models) as the bearers of the universal model of social progress. Such a theoretical attitude, of course, is compatible with Touraine's advocacy for "new modernity"—a project intended to show, via sociological intervention, the genuine road to the global development of humanity.

These two critical observations show how ultimate referentiality subsumes modes of action in the practice of new social movements under its pregiven theoretical categories. New social movements can only be explained in reference to an unquestionable ultimacy, here a presumed "historical society" and its transformation. But such referential analyses collapse once their ultimacy faces challenges to their universal frames of explanation. In the context of "sociological" new social movement theory, the postindustrial thesis represents one of the dominant referential explanatory frames. Another such frame governs the theory of middle class radicalism of Klaus Eder, to which we now turn.

New Social Movements as Middle Class Radicalism

It is the petit bourgeoisie that expresses the collective protest of the new social movements. The new social movements are—historically speaking—a second wave of the protest of the 'honest man' and petit-bourgeois radical democrats. . . . A phenomenology of the new social movements

must start from the assumption that they are part of the history
of the petit-bourgeois protest which has from the outset accompanied
the modernization of society.

Klaus Eder, *The New Politics of Class*[64]

Eder's distinct contribution to the "sociological" new social movement theory is his class analysis of the new movements. The older social movements are often characterized as class movements or movements in the name of a class. Communist or socialist parties as well as national liberation movements appeal(-ed) to the master discourse of class politics, which overdetermined the political aspirations and programs of those movements that were not, due to their original emergence, movements of a class or for a class (e.g., early feminist movements or the peace movement). The presumption that politics is inevitably and ultimately about the conflicting interests of antagonistic classes that are constituted by their position in the process of production gave rise to a notion of agency that took certain actors to be endowed with the unique capacity to lead the entire society in the direction of a total emancipation. The domination of the master discourse of class politics over different social conflicts lasted until the 1960s. Later, the proliferation and recognition of new social movements as nonuniversalist (as they do not offer a universal emancipation or a direction that would guarantee the welfare of all) and nonclass (as the new movements do not attribute their demands and objectives to any clear-cut class agenda) disturbed the formerly dominant discourse of social change. Most significantly, the prevalence of new social movements removed the idea of universal transformation and the notion of a historic agent that would lead all to the posttransformation Promised Land.

Class analysis, however, did not disappear altogether from new social movement theory. For social movement theorists like Eder and Claus Offe, despite their general nonclass appearance, new social movements prompt questions about the class bases of the new actors. Therefore, they devoted efforts to the task of reconstructing an analytical framework that looks precisely at the relationship between the new actors and their class basis in order to shed light on the raison d'être of new social movements. In this regard, Eder's work by far provides the most comprehensive class analysis of the new movements. Before analyzing Eder's theory, however, we need to glance at the ideas of Offe and Melucci on the class basis of the new movements.

Offe's categories of the class basis of the new movements include (1) the new middle class, (2) the old middle class, and (3) people outside the labor market in peripheral positions.[65] According to Offe, the new movements may represent a new genus of class politics, which he calls the new middle-class politics. Nonetheless, he recognizes that in contrast to the older working- or middle-class politics, this new politics of class is "not *on behalf of a class.*"[66] It is, in other words, the politics of identity, and as such is not, strictly speaking, subsumable under the universal terms of a pregiven social category. According to Offe, the new middle classes encompass a paradox. They are relatively privileged, yet they have been often excluded from the decision-making process. Offe concludes that new social movements today comprise one of the three major forces in the political universe. He identifies the other two as the Left (the unions and sectors of the new middle class) and the Right (sectors of the new middle class, sectors of the old middle class, and nonunion workers). Offe's triangular model indicates that class belonging is no longer considered as the definitive factor in class positioning. Hence, he concludes that the success of the new movements depends on whether and how the cleavages between the new middle class, old middle class, and the marginal elements in the new social movements will be overcome.[67]

For about a decade, Melucci cautiously adopted Offe's schematic of middle class politics. Although Melucci recognized that class analysis essentially belonged to the industrial society, he warned that he used class "as an analytical tool to define a system of conflictual relationships within which social resources are produced and appropriated."[68] The social bases of new social movements, he established, included the "new middle class"; the marginal layers of the labor market; and finally, members of the "old middle class." Melucci further identified two subclasses of the new middle class: "new elites who are just emerging and are challenging the already established elites, and 'human capital' professionals, who experience both the surplus of potentialities offered by the system and its constraints."[69] Melucci's earlier interest in offering a class analysis of the new movements expresses his motivation for the sociological "locating" of new social movement actors. However, in a later essay, Melucci retreated from class analysis. "I have gradually abandoned the concept of class relationships to address the question of systemic conflicts," he announced. "The notion of class relationships has been for me a temporary tool with which to analyse systemic conflicts and forms of domination in complex societies. . . . But in contemporary systems . . . classes as real social groups are withering away."[70] His turning away from a class analysis of new social movements indicates that for Melucci the relationship between identity and the social base is more complex than a relationship based on mediating cultural practices.[71] The acknowledged conceptual problems of class analysis, however, do not instigate Melucci to take the crucial step further and question the pregivenness of social conflicts.

Targeting the question of the new middle class radicalism, Eder offers a new view of class politics which aspires for "a *sociology of collective action* beyond agency and system."[72] Calling it the "crisis of class politics," hc acknowledges an increasing separation between class and collective action. He argues, however, that, rather than implying the disappearance of classes, the separation between class and action indicated the relative independence of collective action and class structure. Eder's work is particularly important in this field because, instead of seeking to shed light on the relationship between the new movements and the (new) middle class by merely looking at the class bases of individual constituents of the movements, he seeks a middle ground between the new movements and the middle classes. Thus, in pursuing the hypothesis that there are certain relations between class and action, he identifies *culture* as the intervening variable. Although class cannot provide sufficient grounds for understanding the rise and fall of social movements in modern societies,[73] it *"has effects on collective action through cultural constructions which are generated in historically specific life-forms."*[74] Once we question the formerly dominant assumption that social movements are direct reflections of the existing class structure, we will be able to relinquish the perspective of agency that regards collective actors as deliberately carrying out the task of transforming the course of history. No class can derive a privileged status from its social location or claim to be capable of generating a privileged form of social movement for that matter. Stated simply, "[o]ne's class origin is no guarantee that one's action is class action."[75] What accounts for collective mobilization is the specific forms of cultural orientations that collective action broaches.

Eder draws on Pierre Bourdieu to operationalize the hypothesized conceptual link between class and new social movements. Abolishing the notion of "class consciousness," Bourdieu refers to the categories of collective experience and perception as modes of reproduction of "objective class positions."[76] In its stead, Bourdieu offers the concept of "class habitus" to refer to "collective class unconsciousness," rather than "collective class consciousness."[77] The concept of class habitus provides Eder with the necessary means to deal with the complex relations between the subjective and the objective. Class habitus allows the actor to improvise within the determinate, objective structure. "What is decisive is Bourdieu's idea that this habitus has also to reproduce the subjective conditions of the habitus if it is to make possible the reproduction of its underlying objective structures."[78] The domain of habitus enables a different view of class as the independent variable in his explanatory framework—that is, as external to the collective practices acted out by social movements. It therefore leads Eder to "define *social movements* as independent of class, and conceptualize them in terms of a theory of collective action."[79]

Eder retains an "objective" notion of class. Moreover, he incorporates a (revised) Marxian distinction between "class in itself" and "class for itself"—that is, between the "theoretically constructed and statistically identified classes" and the (would be) "real classes." Since class constitutes his independent variable, it must be locatable and identifiable prior to his investigation of social movements. But how does Eder identify the "real" classes? By following Bourdieu through "describing class cultures on a structural level as generated by *class-specific schemata of experiencing, perceiving and interpreting the world.* Such schemata do not emerge at random; they are rather logically derived from the culture dominating a society."[80] By virtue of Eder's theory, culture becomes the domain where a statistically verifiable class becomes a "real" class—that is, a class unified through occupying a certain social or political position in society.

Inasmuch as Eder's approach to social movements is reminiscent of empiricism, he calls for the abandonment of the idea of the "natural existence of class." Class is not a social fact, but a social construction. Therefore, class relations are partly constructed by social movements. Thus Eder's "constructivist" theory of class, as he identifies it, entails three elements: agency; the context within which agency is located; and finally, the structural outcome of the action that has taken place in the cultural field. Agency refers to the capacity of a group of actors to (re)define those norms, values, and interests that set them apart from other social groups regardless of their demographic similarities or differences. The production of class cultures is, however, "limited by the cultural resources that can be mobilized in collective action. Agency is thus intricately related to the cultural space that it creates and draws upon in order to constitute and reproduce itself as a collective capacity for action."[81] Consequently, any conflict in the cultural milieu alludes to a class conflict, but only in an indirect and diffused way. Eder perceives social movement as a "collective *ego*" struggling with a "collective *alter*" over the control of "the development of a socio-cultural life-world." As such, a social movement has an image of its way of life and a notion about its antagonist.[82] New social movements, however, are not limited to the movements disseminating a particular life-world or lifestyle. These post-Fordist, postmaterialist movements include cultural movements and political movements. They challenge the current forms of social life as well as the domination of the modern state.[83]

Given these theoretical components, Eder explains the significance of his new class theory of social movements. He argues that the new movements are not merely movements of marginal(-ized) collective actors seeking inclusion. Rather, they "reveal" the antagonistic norms, interests, and values. Furthermore, Eder wishes to retain the possibility that the new movements will be part of the arising new social conflicts of radical middle class.[84] The concept of middle class allows Eder to trace the "evolution" of collective action from the labor movement to the new ones and stress the continuity, instead of rupture, in the historical development of the practice of social movement. The new middle classes of Western societies not only are the bearers of a "petit bourgeois habitus," they reveal a new type of class antagonism that goes beyond such problems as exploitation and injustice that were the predominant problems of the modernization period. One of the components of the old as well as the new petit bourgeois habitus is moral struggle, which is manifest in the moral claims of the new movements. The moral challenges of the petit bourgeoisie signifies "a specific class-bound moral lifestyle" which stands in antagonistic relations with other moral lifestyles.[85]

Resounding Marx, Eder points out that the middle class has neither succeeded to become bourgeois, nor has it been recoiled into the proletariat. As such, it inherited the conflicts of the two antagonistic classes and that is why it is able to voice its own needs. As the locus of petit bourgeois actors, new social movements engage in three forms of collective action to launch three forms of social protest. First, as cultural movements, they embark on a struggle against dominant moral values and norms and on a "symbolic crusade" to achieve recognition of the legitimacy of their culture. Second, as political movements, they create political pressure groups to struggle against various prevalent practices that undermine or weaken their status in society. Finally, as social movements, they strive to radically democratize social relations.[86]

The chief problem of the theory of middle class radicalism lies in the uneasy and indeterminable yet insistently presumed relationship between contemporary middle classes and new social movements. In spite of his efforts to construct an approach that can account for the complex connection between the two, Eder's postulate is a theorization of a simple demographic observation of the class composition of the new movement actors in Western countries. The example would be his identifying the middle class as *the* career of the ecological movement.[87] More importantly, Eder's theory falls short in locating the real classes. Since he does not wish to rely on a (positivistic) notion of class that derives the boundaries of each class from demographically verifiable characteristics, he turns to an intervening variable using Bourdieu's theory which defines class cultures structurally. Stated simply, this theory tells us that there are certain cultural practices that belong to, and construct, certain classes. The culture of a certain class dominates over others' in society in the form of available structures of class culture. When observing the current practices, we should be able to trace the existing cultural practices back to their class roots. These cultural structures condition the issues and struggles of the new social movements. The opposition of the new movements to the dominant cultural practices, therefore, should be necessarily indicative of class conflict. One can observe Eder's diligent yet futile endeavor to seek out a concept of class that is not pregiven or objectively verifiable (in the positivist sense), while his theory remains handicapped without it.

The concept of class habitus serves to harbor social movements within a knowable and verifiable social locus. As we saw, this was the preoccupation of the postindustrial thesis as well. One can effortlessly see how new social movements have forced theory to face its uneasy situation. In Eder's case, the explanatory paradigms theory employed to analyze the older (supposedly class-based) movements is seriously revisited, but eventually retained. Eder is not willing to give up certain founding assumptions of the formerly dominant theories of social movements — that is, social movements cannot be understood without an anterior knowledge about their sources of meaning (class habitus in Eder's theory). In other words, social movements cannot by themselves be the bearers or producers of meaning in society. Eder understands the problem, but he is not willing to give up his search for the ultimate ground. He draws on Bourdieu to avoid an "objectivist" view of class and construct an intermediary cultural space that links the new middle class to the new movements. Preoccupied by securing his postulation through "real" solid grounds, Eder remains yet another victim of the referential trap.

New Social Movements As Identity-Claims

Every conflict which transgresses a system of shared rules concerning the distribution of material or symbolic resources is a conflict of identity. The central question is why has the theme of identity become such a central issue? The probable reason is that it reflects the capacity of contemporary action to go beyond modifying and transforming the natural environment.

Alberto Melucci, *Nomads of the Present*[88]

Regardless of their focus and concerns, new social movement theorists almost unanimously characterize these movements primarily as identity-claims. Both Touraine's postindustrial thesis and Eder's middle class radicalism are, among other things, postulates about explaining the underlying reasons for the heightened place of identity in new social movements. Touraine holds the idea that all legitimating principles or metasocial warrants of human action have lost their own legitimacy. The collapse of such principles releases action from assuming the involuntary and unenviable burden of agency of a sweeping History that is yet to reach its point of consummation. The death of the playwright leaves the actors with the unsought task of setting the stage and authoring their own performances. Social actors now fight to gain, maintain, and enhance control over cultural orientations like knowledge and morality that define what Touraine calls the field of "historicity." Historicity refers to "the set of cultural, cognitive, economic, and ethical models by means of which a collectivity sets up relations with its environment; in other words, . . . a culture."[89] This concept captures the idea that various forms of social strife attest to the struggles between social forces for the control of cultural orientations in society. Historicity (which may include knowledge, investment, and culture) is the common social ground which holds actors within the existing conflictual constellations. A "social actor" is situated in social relations and is normatively oriented by historicity. In the absence of the field of historicity, there can be no social actor. We find in this situation adversaries who are "foreign" to one another.[90] By definition, a social actor is "an individual or group capable of transforming the social environment."[91] This attribute of the social actor indicates Touraine's position that, as cultural orientations, historicity always involves social relations, including and particularly, relations of domination.[92] It entails and receives its efficacy from class relations. These relations produce a polarity between, on the one hand, "the ruling class, which identifies itself with historicity and in turn identifies historicity with its own domination interests," and on the other, the ruled, "popular class, who come by their own historicity only through the domination imposed by the 'master', yet who seek to regain this historicity by destroying the dominator."[93] One is inclined to say that historicity has all the characteristics of a hegemonic social formation (although Touraine consistently avoids the term hegemony)—set, imposed, and maintained by the ruling class(es). One must be aware that for Touraine the term "class" does not designate an economically analogous aggregate of people. Rather, it refers to a situation, to the social groups in the field of culture, trying to expand control over historicity or striving to reappropriate it (if they are subjected to the domination of other classes).[94]

   While Touraine understands class as a situation, he views social movement as the action of a subject. He calls the subject an actor who questions the current forms of historicity. "*A social movement is the action, both culturally oriented and socially conflictual, of a social class defined by its position of domination or dependency in the mode of appropriation of historicity, of the cultural models of investments, knowledge, and morality, toward which the social movement itself is oriented.*"[95] The emancipation of action from all metasocial principles (the idea of modernity being one of the last such principles[96]) has given a new meaning to social movements. No longer perceived as agents of history, modernization, or the liberation of humanity,[97] social movements now take place within the context of historicity. Historicity is at the same time the locus of class actors and the stake of their struggles. That is to say, social conflicts are inseparable from cultural orientations. Thus, according to Touraine, social life contains three central elements: "the *subject*, as distantiation of organized practices and as consciousness; *historicity*, as the set of cultural models (cognitive, economic, and ethical) and as the stake of the central social conflict; and *social movements*, as the groups that contend in order to give these cultural orientations a social form."[98]

As discussed above, Touraine advocates a sociological analysis that hinges on the pivotal role of social movements and focuses on social action. Social movements involve conflict and pose imminent breaks in the prevailing cultural values or institutional rules. As conflicts over the control of historicity, therefore, social movements are different from "historical movements," as movements striving to shift to a different social organization, and "cultural movements," as movements struggling to bring change to cultural values. The challenges of social movements penetrate various social or cultural milieus, especially the public space, *Öffentlichkeit*—where the actor's experience finds a field.[99]

Thus, we live in societies where social movements mean collective actors struggling against one another in relations of domination to control historicity and where actors refuse to succumb to the apparatuses that deny their self-affirmation in the name of the society or a common good.[100] That is why new social movements claim and advocate their own specific meanings—that is, *identity*. With the new movements, actors create situations and social conflicts by defining their cultural orientations. Touraine recognizes the appeal to identity as the first stage of the formation of a social movement. This is when (collective) action emerges. The middle stage is that of the actual formation of the social movement in which collective action is strictly directed against an external form or force of domination (the State rather than the ruling class). The final stage takes place when the appeal to identity creates a barrier to the formation of the social movement—that is, when identity destroys the capacity for action. Touraine, therefore, holds the idea that appeals to identity must be studied when they are in the first stage.[101] Put differently, identity is the true force of social struggle only when it is not opposed to social change and when it takes place within the field of historicity against other social actors. Accordingly, Touraine's concept of identity refers to "a discontinuous series of identifications with models produced by mass culture."[102] Rather than alluding to a mode of being, identity represents the capacity for action and change that is defined in terms of choice, which in turn enables a distinction between "defensive identity" (the one principle that guides collective action), on the one hand, and "offensive identity" (several complementary principles which interdependently steer collective action), on the other. Therefore, a social movement, as Touraine defines it, always and inevitably surpasses being simply an identity-claim: "one can never identify a social movement with a claim of identity. The labor movement is never the working class, fully aware and organized."[103] Together, the definition of the identity of the actor, the opponent, and the cultural totality that is the stake of their opposition constitute social conflict. Here rest the roots of Touraine's unmistakable delineation of social action (social movement) from political action. A social movement entails all the three elements mentioned above, while political action only includes any two of the three elements at any given conflict.[104] Hence, as in Melucci, Touraine's separation between society and politics.

As for other theorists, for Touraine new social movements' identity-claims can reinforce democracy only when these movements transcend their own particularity. The actors of the new movements should not only be motivated by their own values, they must also recognize the plurality of other actors and their values and ideas against whom the actor immerses in an "us." New social movements actors should also retain "the sense of citizenship and of responsibility towards the community as a whole, so that an individual or group does not defend only his or its private interests but has a sense of social utility."[105] With social conflict being the main concept of the postindustrial society in Touraine's sociological theory, democracy is no longer conceivable without and outside social conflicts. "Democratic action upsets the existing order."[106] Social conflicts, embodied by new social movements, enhance and deepen democracy. Thus, the more pluralist a society, the more democratic it will be.[107]

In contrast to Touraine, for whom the study of identity is always subsumed under a more comprehensive sociological project, Melucci treats the concept of identity in its own right. In his analysis of collective action, Melucci emphasizes the construction of a "we"—as a collective identity "achieved" through negation[108]—by a group of individuals through common orientations organized around three axes. The first orientation, the relations of actors to the *ends* of their action, gives the actors a sense of their action. The second, the relations of actors to the *means* through which action is carried out, shows them the possibilities as well as the limits of their action. The final orientation, the relationship of actors to their *environment*, identifies the field within which their action takes place. These three orientations produce collective action, not vice versa. This is what he calls a "multipolar action system." Collective action, therefore, is by no means "a unitary empirical phenomenon." In other words, the unity of a movement, if it exists at all, is the outcome of collective action, not its source; it is the personage of the movement.[109] Therefore, every conflict is always a conflict of identities.[110] Since identity alludes to the *process* of attaining individual or group identity in a cultural field, it "is not something that is permanently given. Instead, it is a process of identity-formation which constructs and reconstructs itself in the life-course of individuals and groups and through their different faces, roles, and circumstances."[111]

Moreover, Melucci understands identity, through the concept of expectation as the intermediary concept between structural determinants and individuals' motivations. Any "theory of action that introduces the concept of expectations implies an underlying theory of identity."[112] It is through expectation that actors perceive their continuity within the environment—that is, in relation to other actors, opportunities, and constraints. Identity embodies the actor's continuity. But as a social phenomenon, an identity comes from the existing "*identity resources*" (i.e., the available cultural elements), which are in turn obtained from the knowledges and information available in the society.[113] In other words, identity finds in society the conditions (resources) for its existence. Melucci defines collective identity as "*an interactive and shared definition produced by several interacting individuals who are concerned with the orientations of their action as well as the field of opportunities and constraints in which their action takes place.*"[114] Thus, collective identity is also essentially the *process* of "*constructing*" *an action system*—a process which entails two aspects: the actor's "plurality of orientations" (that is, the actor's internal complexity), and his or her relationship with the environment.[115] Identity is, therefore, a shared definition of the opportunities available to, as well as the constraints imposed upon, collective action. Social movements, then, are action systems because they have structures built by the present goals, opinions, resolutions, and exchanges which take place and operate within a systemic field.[116] It is a form of collective action based on solidarity that upholds a conflict to break the limits of the system in which collective action takes place.[117] Moreover, appeal to identity signifies the actor's seeking a direct response to personal needs through participation in collective action.[118]

Melucci's definition of social movements is based on his conception of collective action. As an analytic construct, social movement is an "*ensemble of the various types of conflict-based behaviour . . . for the appropriation and orientation of social values and resources, . . . which transgress the norms that have been institutionalized in social roles, which go beyond the rules of the political system.*"[119] The action that takes place within a movement establishes a concrete link between cultural orientations of the actors and the systemic opportunities and constraints.[120] In new social movements, identity becomes the emblem of group or individual particularity. "In a structure in which ownership of the means of production is becoming more and more socialized, while at the same time remaining under the control of particular groups, what individuals are claiming collectively is their right to realize their own identity," holds Melucci. "Personal identity . . . is the property which is now being claimed and defended; this is the ground in which individual and collective resistance is taking root."[121] In information society, therefore, identity emerges as a means of resistance against the forms of rationalization of life that do not incorporate differences.[122] It is explained by making references to the symbolic grounds, in which identity becomes meaningful and subversive of the dominant codes that are created in high-density information systems. As identity-claims, therefore, new social movements give rise to modernization, institutional change, cultural innovation, and the selection of the new elite. They translate action into symbolic challenges that defy and disturb the dominant codes, exposing their irrationality (especially that of the new forms of technocratic power). Indeed, the new movements emerge as signs—that is, as forms (of movement) that become the message. With challenges taking place within the fields of codes, knowledge, and language, the new movements take on the form of networks immersed in the everyday life.[123] Similar to Touraine, therefore, Melucci views the new movements as forces of democratization in which identity, an inadequate term as it is, stands as the emblem of the contemporary forms of collective action.[124] But unlike Touraine, Melucci rejects the idea that the new movements replace the older ones as the *subject* of social change. Social movements are not "subjects endowed with an essence and a purpose within a *pièce* whose finale is knowable."[125] The perceived place of identity in the contemporary social movements leads Melucci to stress a distinction between the social and the political, to subsequently criticize the idea of the primacy of the political (which he calls "political reductionism").[126] He argues that the present cultural models and symbolic challenges cannot fall within the existing political institutions.[127]

By comparison, Melucci's position with respect to identity is better worked out and thus more lucid than those of Touraine and Eder. However, Melucci is far from abandoning the search for the mysterious ultimate ground. For him, every identity originates in certain "identity resources" procured from the knowledges and information available in the society. While making identity possible, identity resources impose certain limits on identity. Moreover, Melucci argues that prior to its surfacing, identity "hibernates" somewhere within the social texture. Therefore, he proposes a distinction between the stages of "latency" and "visibility" of identity. The actors "become visible only where a field of public conflict arises; otherwise they remain in the state of latency. Latency does not mean inactivity. Rather, *the potential for resistance or opposition is sewn into the very fabric of daily life*. It is located in the molecular experience of the individuals or groups who practice the alternative meanings of everyday life."[128] In other words, the actor precedes conflict because the everyday life experiences of individuals and groups are structurally determined. Stated differently, conflict is not constitutive of the actor. Actors are perceived as the products of society (as a ground) which assigns them certain modes of action. Thus, certain actors are endowed with the capacity for resistance against other actors due to their specific pregiven social predispositions. Regardless of the possibility of ever entering conflictual situations, they nonetheless remain actors. It is, then, only due to the social predispositions of the actors that new social movements "have created meanings and definitions of identity which contrast with the increasing determination of individual and collective life by impersonal technocratic power."[129] They are *by nature* in conflict with the current institutional or technocratic power. The identity of actors, therefore, comes from a potential to carry out an assigned or perceived form of action, regardless of the fact that action, thereby identity, can arise solely in conflictual situation. Identity precedes conflictual situations because it is a product of a fundamental social constitution. Latency provides Melucci with a key conceptual link between the "objective" conditions and the possibility of resistance and action. If there is a potential for resistance, it has to be knowable prior to action, and society is *the* source of such knowledge.

Melucci's entire theory of identity is indeed symptomatic of a general tendency, in the social sciences, of seeking representations of some presupposed, concealed fundaments. If we remove the ultimate referentiality that is operational in Melucci's approach to identity, if we do not posit some kind of essence that supposedly gives the latent identity its potential for entering into conflict once its conditions of visibility arrive, then *we will arrive at the conclusion that identity does not precede conflict*, but, as I shall discuss in the next chapter, is born out of conflict. Likewise, if we renounce appeals to the ultimacy of "society" as *the* inexhaustible source of action and meaning, we come to oppose Melucci's self-limiting separation between social and political movements. In that case, with Laclau and Mouffe, we understand the constitutive character of the political.

One can clearly see how the *ingrained theoretical assumption that explanation means the moorage of action to some unshakable, universally- and objectively-knowable ground* restrains "sociological" new social movements theory within a referential framework. Thanks to preoccupation with ultimate referentiality, Touraine's radical departure from teleological history and rejection of agency, nevertheless, do not translate into the rejection of all normative social types (e.g., programmed society or new modernity) as grounds of identities. Touraine, Melucci, and Eder recognize the centrality of identity to the new movements, but they seek to posit identity within the pregiven field of social by linking it either to a world-historical social transformation, a class, or the mysteriously endowed social structure, thereby viewing *identity claims as mere expressions of the "deeper" fundament of society*. Let us return to this latter point and its implications in the remainder of this chapter.

Identity, Action, the Social

What is being opposed are claims of cognitive ultimacy.

Schürmann, "On Constituting Oneself an Anarchistic Subject"[130]

The "sociological" new social movement theories have made important contributions to contemporary social theory. Their most significant contribution is the assertion of centrality of social action and conflict to society and the rejection of the idea that social movements are anomalies that disrupt the norm of social stability. Thus, the authors whose works I reviewed in the preceding pages have all acknowledged the conceptual end of society as an enclosed totality in which structural determination and historical destination simply define the place, attributes, and contents of its parts in general and the actors in particular. This has allowed them to rethink the foundations of society and criticize ideas that hinge on notions of social structure, class, or agency. Furthermore, the question of continuity of actors at the times of social transformations (as from industrial to postindustrial society), which Melucci raises, is a persistent theoretical problem that every social theory needs to address. Social theory must account for what actors bring from their past actions to the present types of conflict. The "sociological" new social movement theories have also acknowledged, quite correctly, and made efforts to analyze, the centrality of appeals to identity within contemporary movements. Having pointed out the inadequacy of some of the conventional sociological notions in the study of identity (such as the rational, calculative individual of the resource mobilization theory), Melucci and Eder proposed further investigatory avenues to the question of identity such as cognitive (especially Gestalt theory) and phenomenological approaches.

The "sociological" new social movement theories show that they have been motivated by the captivating "newness" of the new movements. But in establishing what constitutes the "new" in the new movements, in spite of their departure from their preceding social movement theories, they generally failed to make a radical break with the assumptions that steered the older approaches. Touraine's "sociological intervention" as the means that paves the way to the "new modernity" clearly unveils his attempts at rehabilitating sociology by a theorist who stands at the juncture of the forces of a rapidly changing society and a sociological analysis of its social movements that nevertheless retains its connections with the universalistic and positivistic traditions within the social sciences. His uneasy endeavor to salvage whatever he can from an essentialist social theory is responsible for many of his assumptions of ultimacy. After all, Touraine himself does not miss the opportunity to voice his concern that without the concept of central conflict "*sociological analysis may disintegrate completely*, to be absorbed partly by economic analysis and partly by political philosophy."[131] Now, at the time when having recourse to ultimate Truth is increasingly treated with suspicion, the very practice of sociology is at stake. In wake of the new movements, Touraine's response to the crisis of sociology amounts to revising some of its cardinal tenets, but he fails to submit sociology's fundamental principle of transparency of society to devastating critique. This is best evident in his sociological intervention whose mission is to save "sociological analysis" (he never clarifies the term)—a motive that will elevate him to the position of modern agent of his perceived historical transformation. Here, we can clearly see that sociology is not the product of modernity; rather, it is modernity that is a product of sociology. Given the tremors that jolt the foundations of modernity (which Touraine acknowledges in his *Critique of Modernity*), "sociological analysis" turns out to be founded on a shaky ground. The task of sociological intervention is to preserve the relevance of the sociological project of modernity and to show the actors the appropriate path. The Subject, the ultimate referent of modernity, is in Touraine's hands "relocated" to the realm of social movements. By virtue of this move, the rational-instrumental modernity gives way to a new modernity, in which not apparatuses, but social movements constitute the directions of social development. Exactly what distinctive logics inform the differences between the two modernities remain unspecified. Touraine's theory is unable to answer this crucial question.

It is clear that despite their claims, none of the three "sociological" new social movement theorists was truly able or willing to give up the notion of society as the ontologically unique source of the "true motives," as Marx and Engels would call it. From Marx's critique of German idealism onwards, we can see that attempts at securing explanations in an ultimate point of reference have not died out. Such attempts become problematical at times when theory meets its own crisis. In our times, new social movements emerged not simply as difficult objects for theory, but as objects that forced theory to face its own difficult and problematical position. The most pivotal task of the immense and detailed project of the European architects of new social movement theory entails the theoretical grounding of new social movements within a certain conception of society. A presumed historical transformation in the latter provides theory with an explanatory ground that renders meaningful claims about the raison d'être of the new movements. Typically, such a view needs to make the fundamental assumption that society is the a priori, in the full sense of the term, of its constituent elements. Preoccupation with the social grounding of praxis does not allow the three theorists reviewed above to see the great implications of their claim about the end of society as a totality as well as what is "new" in new social movements. By seeking to ascertain the social positions from which identity emerges, these authors still reveal the rather classical sociological notion of the transparent society. For only in a transparent society can identity be connected to, and become the expression of, a social locus. We cannot view society as transparent, unless we have already perceived of it as a reconciled entity. Only a reconciled society can bestow upon its constituents an ascertainable social meaning (like an identity). Despite bold announcements that society (as the object of sociology) no longer represents an enclosed totality (and hence the centrality of conflict), the theories of Touraine, Melucci, and Eder still cling on to a notion of "society" which functions as an ultimate referentiality, at which point social inquiry—which is ironically about society—stops. We inquire into social phenomena by fastening our explanations to society, but never inquire into the very conception of society that makes social inquiry possible. If society has truly lost its principle of total representation, if society is no longer capable of coherently representing all its components, then its components are no longer fully understood or explained primarily in relation to the referentiality of such phantasmic realm. Thus, by holding onto the notion of society as fully knowable and the pregiven source of social movements, the "sociological" new social movement theories in fact problematize their own postulates.

The entire project of "sociological" new social movement theories hinge on showing the transference of a presumed mysterious essence from its exclusive social locus to the actor who will reveal this essence through his or her action. The transformation of social action is understood only in terms of an anterior transformation in the structures of society. Action is therefore not analyzed in its own terms. It is subsumed under the terms dictated by the ultimacy of society. This is precisely why from the outset I separated the "sociological" new social movement theory from the deconstructive one. The latter's point of departure is the critique of what Laclau and Mouffe call "the positivity of the social."[132] Methods that posit the positivity of the social cannot adequately explore the various facets of the emerging phenomena and their oblique and perplexing, often concealed, relations with other social phenomena. Consequently, *methods that assume ultimate referentiality systematically and violently reduce the existing phenomena in their entirety to those phenomenal aspects of theirs that referential theories can accommodate.* Their violence stems from the positivistic methods and reductive categories they use to theorize social phenomena such as the new social movements.

Bound by ultimate referentiality, the "sociological" new social movement theories, despite their claims and efforts, remain blind to the possibility of a genuine theoretical move toward a nontotalistic concept of society. In Chapter 3, we will continue to pursue the question of identity, by exploring what will happen to the concept of identity in the context of the new social movements, once we renounce all appeals to ultimate referentiality. We will return to the question of identity from the vantage point of a radical critique of "the positivity of the social."

CHAPTER 3

Identity, Experiential Hegemonies, *Urstiftung*

The question is whether one is willing to think of praxis otherwise than in terms of determinations affecting an actor, otherwise than referentially.

Schürmann, "Adventures of the Double Negation"[1]

Once we debunk the metaphysical assumption incarnated in the idea of the ultimate referentiality of society that is prevalent in the "sociological" new social movement theory, we will find the questions that inform our inquiry dislocated. We shall attend to the problem of metaphysical thinking in extenso later, but suffice it here to mention that ultimate referentiality is metaphysical because it is operative based on the representation of some ultimate and pregiven point beyond our inquiry. Specifically in relation to the context of our investigation in the previous chapter, its metaphysical character reveals itself once we heed how ultimate referentiality operates by matching identity with the ultimacy of social loci. But ultimate referentiality, notwithstanding its wide authoritative exercise in the social sciences, is basically just an *assumption*. Once the positivity of the social, as an example of such ultimacy, loses its sway in the study of contemporary social movements, *identity can no longer be strictly an expression of some (presumably) empirically verifiable social locus*. Neither can it simply be a social construction, for that matter, nor a strategy containing goals, ends, and adversaries. The challenge that social movement theory now faces is to provide a theory of social movements that does not assume the metaphysical stance of seeking and asserting an ultimate point of reference whose preset standards would identify, explain, and secure social movements' practices.

The deconstructive approach of Laclau and Mouffe to new social movements takes up precisely that challenge and engages in the endeavour of theorizing the formation of the new movements without having recourse to various forms of ultimate referentiality. In the past three decades, poststructuralist thought has dynamically offered the possibility of *nonessentialist* approach in the social and human sciences. As is well known, the poststructuralist critique of "essentialism" calls for a decentering that would allow the play of the suppressed internal differences in a system.[2] Having affinities with the radical phenomenological concept of ultimate referentiality, the poststructuralist concept of essentialism designates an assumed presence of an operative center as the prime organizer of the practices which take place within the system. In the realm of social and political thought, poststructuralism has found one of its most significant formulations in the "postmarxist" theory of Laclau and Mouffe, whose work hinges on the pivotal role of antagonism despite, or because of, the evident waning of a unique, historical agent (proletariat). A poststructuralist political theory that enjoys Derrida's endorsement,[3] the theory of Laclau and Mouffe theorizes *identity* in a nonessentialist way, and most importantly, in the context of their theory of *hegemony*.

Turning to Laclau and Mouffe at this specific point prepares us to get one step closer to the key questions of this study about the relationship between the "newness" of new social movements and the possibility of arriving at a postmodern era. Having recourse to ultimate referentiality prevents one from pursuing the inquiry in that direction, because it quickly limits the scope as well as the extent of one's inquiry to the assumed boundaries of a ground. It does not, in other words, allow one to think, properly and in a nonreferential way, about the ontological institution of society. Laclau's and Mouffe's deconstructive turn in the study of contemporary movements provides us precisely with a radical point of departure from referential appeals. Therefore, the logical course of our analysis in this chapter requires an appraisal of the contribution of Laclau and Mouffe to the study of new social movements. Next, I will inquire about a key problem their theory produces for the study of the new movements—namely, a conceptual "missing link" between identity and social movements. This missing link is "experience." Since the postmarxist theory of Laclau and Mouffe is primarily a theory of hegemony, I will then turn to Antonio Gramsci to illustrate that Laclav and Mouffe have overlooked the experiential aspect of hegemony as Gramsci formulated it. The final step would be to introduce Claude Lefort's concept of *regime* as a phenomenologically informed concept that has affinity with the concept of *hegemony*, but, at the same time, sets the stage for a radical phenomenological theory of experience in the next chapter.

The Postmarxist Approach to Identity

The symbolic—i.e., overdetermined—character of social relations . . . implies
that they lack any ultimate literality which would reduce them to necessary
moments of an immanent law. . . . Society and social agents lack any
essence, and their regularities merely consist of the relative and precarious
forms of fixation which accompany the establishment of a certain order.

Laclau and Mouffe, *Hegemony and Socialist Strategy*[4]

Laclau and Mouffe trace the emergence of new social movements back to
the post-World War II hegemonic formation and antagonisms. Viewing these
movements primarily in the context of Western societies, they argue that by
the beginnings of the 1970s in Europe, the political panorama dramatically
changed and the new movements became widespread.[5] While calling "new
social movements" an "unsatisfactory term,"[6] they argue that the new movements, comprising a wide range of contemporary social movements, pose
serious questions for social and political theory because these movements
indicate the extension of social conflictuality onto various terrains of social
life which have no necessary socialist (or class) character.[7] The new antagonisms indicate "forms of resistance to the commodification, bureaucratiza-
tion and increasing homogenization of social life" against which new social
movements "manifest themselves through a proliferation of particularisms,
and crystallize into a demand for autonomy itself."[8]

   What is unique about the complex theory of Laclau and Mouffe is
their view of identity as conceptually interconnected with *hegemony* and
articulation. For Laclau and Mouffe every identity—far from signifying an
essence, a designation of an "*ontologically* privileged agent,"[9] or a historically
determined position within society, in other words, far from being *positiv-*
ity—is the effect of a "constitutive outside," that is, an external threat that
consolidates the elements within a structure. Therefore, every identity is
meaningful only within a structure or a discourse—that is, within a decentered
system of differences. In such a system, the identity of each element is
defined only when the system is able to define its own boundaries. Thus, the
identity of an element or an actor is never pregiven. Rather, it is the effect
of an element or an actor that stands outside the system—that is, an outside
threat against which the system comes to a closure, thereby positioning the
elements contained within the system in a relational way. A final closure of
the system—that is, the permanent fixity of differences between elements as
well as the boundaries of the system—from the within would only be possible by appealing to foundationalism—an approach which Laclau and Mouffe

refuse.[10] It is, then, only through an external element that the limits of a structure are defined, and the elements within it—identities—become meaningful. Consequently, every identity is inescapably a *dislocated* identity because the center that an identity at first glance appears to bear within itself is in fact a dislocated center that stands in external relations to the identity. Thus, the lack of an internal center (which has been conventionally perceived to be internal to elements) appears as a "constitutive lack" that penetrates every identity. Hence, identity as *negativity*—a concept which is incompatible with rational objectivity. Negativity, as Laclau argues, bears a *"constitutive* and *primordial* character."[11] The identity "woman" is a result of exclusion and subordination of women by patriarchal institutions and practices. A gay asserts his or her identity against the systematic practices of the dominant heterosexual culture that suppresses and excludes homosexuality. These identity-claims cannot precede exclusion and threat; they do not, as Touraine, Eder, and Melucci would respectively assert, result from a major structural transformation, dwell in the new middle class radicalism, or become visible, putting end to the latency (of a social locus).

Now, if what is beyond the structure is just another difference, then, defining the limits of the structure in which various identities stand in differential relations with one another would become impossible, and we would encounter a theoretical impasse. Laclau, however, differentiates between the elements within the structure (i.e., relational identities), and what stands beyond the structural borders should be understood as one of threat, indeed one of exclusion, and thus, one of *antagonism.* To summarize: (1) exclusionary relations are constitutive of all identities; (2) a system (a structure or a discourse) is required for differential identities, but the condition of constitution of identities is the exclusion by an outside threat; (3) in opposition to a constitutive outside, the relations among the identities within the discourse undergo a transformation. *Relations of difference* (e.g., a "woman" as different from an "ethnic" minority) among them become *relations of equivalence* (e.g., "women" and "ethnic" minorities join forces in an alliance against conservative government that is to slash affirmative action programs), but neither relation is pure or absolute. Identities, therefore, are never immediately given. They are the products of complex discursive practices. The *undecidability* between difference and equivalence renders each identity a symbolic representation of the entire system—and this is the moment of a *hegemonic formation.*[12] An identity is a "symbolic representation" because to be representative, it must not only stand for itself (relations of difference) but also for all other identities on its side (relations of equivalence). Furthermore, since the constitutive outside becomes a part of condition of existence of an identity, *the full constitution of identity is permanently deferred.*

The theoretical construct based on the poststructuralist notion of "constitutive outside" leads (in addition to a devastating critique of the positivity of the social) to the idea of the primacy of the political. Let us recall the reductive binarism of society and politics in "sociological" new social movements theories which allowed them to (unsuccessfully) avoid the aporia of politics and rendered society as the privileged stance of bestowal of identity. Beyond identifying the sources of conflict in the overall structure of society, the "sociological" new social movement theories fall short, to a great extent, of seeing conflict as constitutive of society. As we saw, Touraine and Melucci do acknowledge the constitutive character of conflict in the postindustrial society, but the ultimacy that reigns over their theories does not allow them to explore sufficiently the consequent radical outcomes of conflict as constitutive of society. This, unfortunately, perpetuates the double illusion that, on the one hand, full group or individual autonomy is possible, and on the other, increasing autonomy necessarily translates into greater freedom from conflict. The constitutive character of the political in Laclau and Mouffe allows them to offer a theory of new social movements beyond the historical conditions of Europe: where there are hegemonic exclusionary practices, there are identity-claims.

The political, Laclau argues, has two dimensions. First, *the political is the instituting moment of society*. But this does not designate the modernist notion of instituting in which the instituting moment was subsumed to the laws of society. For, given the subversion of a presumed internal and underlying logic governing society, *contingency* is the main characteristic of any political institution. This means that there is no sovereign locus from which the governing law can a priori arise. Second, all acts of political institution are essentially *incomplete*, for if this were not the case, there would no longer exist any social conflict. In that case, we would live in a fully reconciled society in which all identities would be completely equal to one another. Because all differences in a fully reconciled society are eradicated, there would be no freedom whatsoever in such a society. The inevitable incompletion of acts of political institution produces a *double movement*. On the one hand, there is the *expansion of the political at the expense of the social*. On the other, politicization involves the contingent production of the social, or put differently, *politicization decenters the social*.[13]

This perspective leads us to view any identity as *contingent*, because the condition of existence of any identity is exterior to it. Thus, "dislocation is the trace of contingency within the structure."[14] It means that there is a set of external relations between identities in a structure—relations whose permanent fixity, as mentioned, is ultimately impossible. Consequently, in a system of differences whose permanent closure (fixity) will never arrive, an *identity and the conditions of its existence are inseparable.* That is, the condition of existence of an identity is contingent (i.e., dependent upon an external agent), but the relationship between the identity and its condition of existence is necessary.[15] Identity is the product of "the crossing of contradictory logics of contextualisation and decontextualisation."[16] Insofar as it is perceived as contextual and relational, an identity acquires content and becomes meaningful. The deconstructive approach of Laclau and Mouffe to identity politics subverts the classical objectivist notion in the human and social sciences which holds knowledge to be true independent of its context and identity to preexist its context, as we saw particularly in Melucci's concepts of latency and visibility.

With respect to the limits of the structure, deconstruction allows one to illustrate the undecidability of the structure by disclosing the distance between the possible arrangements of the structure, on the one hand, and its actual, prevalent arrangement, on the other. Laclau calls this disclosure a *decision* insofar as: "(a) it is not predetermined by the 'original' terms of the structure; and (b) it requires its passage through the experience of undecidability. The moment of the decision . . . [therefore] is this jump from the experience of undecidability to a creative act, a fiat which requires its passage through the experience of undecidability."[17] Undecidability refers to the permanent unfixity of the boundaries of structure. It is through the decision of the subject that these frontiers can be defined. The subject is then the distance between the undecidability of the structure and the actual decision.[18] Since the valid decision made by the subject sets the limits of the structure (though in a partial way), it is not the expression of an identity. Rather, the decision is an act of *identification.* The *need for identification comes from the lack of identity,* as any identity is always already the signifier of an absent fullness. As shown in Chapter 2, ultimate referentiality presumes that the actor's being receives its essence from his or her specific place in society. As such, it forecloses identification (which implies lack of a pregiven identity) in favor of identity (as the matching of one's being with an anterior and operative essence). Identification, specifies Laclau, refers to the "unbridged distance between my lack of being (which is the source of the decision) and that which provides the being that I need in order to act in a world that has failed to construct me as a 'Modification' (*modus*) of itself."[19]

Laclau and Mouffe problematize the term *new social movements* because it arbitrarily groups together a number of diverse movements in opposition to the formerly dominant concept of class struggle,[20] thus implicitly conferring upon them agency (as in Touraine). Mouffe acknowledges the significance of such movements by alluding to the fact that they signify an end to the notion of the unitary subject, upon which Marxist and liberal politics are founded. The "unitary subject" refers to the subject that bears a universal and complete identity such as, purportedly, the "citizen" or the "proletariat." The position of the unitary subject in society is always clear beforehand, and he or she is not perceived to embody a multiplicity of identities. The theory of Laclau and Mouffe helps us understand a number of problems that exist in various strategies sought in and theorized by contemporary social movements activists. For example, some feminist and gay activists seek to postulate identity as the ground of their struggles—the view of movements that I called *expressive*. Mouffe specifically criticizes those feminists who believe that without a coherent identity the women's movement will find no real ground.[21] If, as submitted, it is not the "inside" but the "outside" that forms an identity, then women's identity cannot be the ground of the women's movement. Rather, women's identity will emerge out of their movements. This does not mean that identity proceeds from movement. Rather, since we are in a system of differences, the identity of the movement gives it a differential designation. Thus, identity plays a *constitutive* role in new social movements, in spite of the fact that, as will be discussed later, Laclau and Mouffe have not theorized this process. Furthermore, no identity can be claimed without reference to a context. An omnipresent or objective identity is a foundationalist mirage. This line of argument has serious implications for understanding social movements, namely, it rejects the notion that claims to identity are appeals to the pure particularism of a group. Here particularism refers to the claim that the identity of an individual or a group is so unique and specific that it can be definitively distinguished from the rest of identities, or from the dominant identity—that is, the "universal." Pure particularism is impossible because if one asserts his or her particularism as such, then, logically speaking, one must either accept the particularisms of others, including those particularisms against which one is resisting in the form of a social movement, or have recourse to an ultimacy to justify the superiority of one's own particularism over those of others. Resorting to pure particularism has led to the pitfall of one of the most painful forms of postmodern relativism that continues to entrap social movements, reducing them to lifestyle networks. In its most extreme case, this view amounts to saying that a pluralist society should recognize the identities of, for example, both gays and gay-bashers. The postmarxist theory of Laclau and Mouffe indeed not only tackles such a relativistic view of identity, it seeks a universal principle, against objectivist or foundationalist attitudes, out of the hegemonic formation of subordinate subjects. Politics is about exclusion, and racial, sexual, cultural, and other minorities in our contemporary societies all bear the scars of such exclusions. Precisely for this reason the subject of politics is the subject of a lack whose identity is constituted through acts of identification.[22] Cultural identity is not only the terrain, but also the object of the group's political struggle. The conflictual character of identity renders it the cardinal area in which "hegemony is exercised, because the definition of cultural identity of a group, by reference to a specific system of contingent and particular social relations, plays a major role in the creation of 'hegemonic nodal points'."[23] As the points of convergence vis-à-vis a common threat, these *nodal points* in effect produce a signifying chain which temporarily controls the discursive field by controlling the entrance of identities into the hegemonic terrain.

In a nonessentialist way, Laclau and Mouffe show how identity plays a *constitutive* and pivotal role in understanding the new movements. They also show the relationship between identity claims of actors and the forces that subordinate actors. Identity is defined in terms of conflict, as opposed to some pregiven social locus. With the collapse of the public-private distinction, conflict has now become pervasive, as various external forces (e.g., economy, media, bureaucracy) pose threats to the autonomy of the individual. It is in regard to conflict that the concept of *articulation* and its twin concept, *antagonism*, enjoy a central place in Laclau and Mouffe. Antagonism designates the ontological constitution of society. As such, it establishes the limits of society and social objectivity. As we saw, the impossibility of structural closure implies that no identity is ever fully present or complete. In the overabundance of the signified, identity is subject to the *partial fixity* of meaning. The event, the signifier, always produces more than one concept or signified. In Laclau's words, "Each element has a surplus of meaning because it cannot be located in a closed system of difference. And at the same time, no identity is ever definitely and definitively acquired."[24] This surplus of meaning is the quality that takes any social action to the realm of *metaphor*. Thus, as mentioned, social action always entails a *symbolic* character: a strike can at one and the same time means economic dissatisfaction of workers as well as their resistance against the regime.[25] The symbolic character of action is the condition of possibility of articulation. "[W]e will call *articulation* any practice establishing a relation among elements such that their identity is modified as a result of the articulatory practice," write Laclau and Mouffe. "The structured totality resulting from the articulatory practice, we will call *discourse*. The differential positions, insofar as they appear articulated within a discourse, we will call *moments*. By contrast, we will call *element* any difference that is not discursively articulated."[26] The decision is an articulatory practice whose effect is the construction of a structured totality, a discourse, by turning elements into moments. Therefore, any articulation is an act of *identification* by the subject. If the relations between different positions in a structure were determined a priori, there would be neither need nor any space for articulation. It is the lack of fixity of meaning, the metaphoric character of the social, which renders articulation possible. Articulation, in fact, discloses a "constitutive lack." What is particularly significant about articulation is that it involves (external) contingency. That is to say, if there were pregiven and necessary relations between elements, if elements stood in literal, not metaphorical, relations with one another, there would be no articulation as such, only fixed identities within an enclosed, or "sutured," totality. A completely articulated totality never actually arrives. Because of the symbolic character that is present in any system, moments, immediately after being articulated, become elements.[27] For, the *general field of discursivity*, as a reservoir of surplus meanings, at once assigns a meaning to an element and subverts it. Once the ultimate fixity of meaning becomes impossible, only *partial fixities* remain. Society as an enclosed totality, then, turns out to be impossible, and it is theoretically replaced by "the social" as the milieu corresponding to "the political"—the terrain of the constitution of social practices.

Now, we step onto a terrain where, through articulatory practices, certain discursive points, called *nodal points*, define the central issues and themes in the field of discursivity. Every nodal point highlights the discursive overlap among a number of *subject positions* within the structure—positions that are the effects of structural determination. *"The practice of articulation, therefore, consists in the construction of nodal points which partially fix meaning; and the partial character of this fixation proceeds from the openness of the social, a result, in its turn, of the constant overflowing of every discourse by the infinitude of the field of discursivity."*[28] If there were a free overflow of signifieds under signifiers, identity fullness would become possible. But, as we saw, every discourse is threatened by a constitutive outside which imposes itself (as well as its terms) upon the discourse as a *limit*, and as such, *overdetermines* the identity of its elements.[29] It is exactly at this junction that antagonism occurs: when identity fullness becomes impossible. Antagonism is "the 'experience' of the limit of the social. Strictly speaking, antagonisms are not *internal* but *external* to society; or rather, they constitute the limits of society, the latter's impossibility of fully constituting itself."[30] In antagonism, the denial of identity (i.e., the limitation of the flow of signifieds under the signifier of an identity), does not come from the inside (of an identity), but from an outside which reveals itself as a constitutive lack within the identity. But as the experience of the limits of the social, *antagonism signifies the lack of fullness in the identity of both antagonistic sides* as the metaphor[31] signifying an absent fullness. Antagonistic relations are, therefore, *real oppositions* that are produced by articulatory practices, and we cannot speak of antagonisms in terms of *logical contradiction* (the two terms almost synonymously used in Marxist discourse).

New social movements highlight the inseparability of identity and antagonism. It is the negation of the subordinate subject's identity, by the dominant subject, to achieve fullness and completion that creates the conditions for antagonism. But the subject occupies a plurality of subject positions that have no necessary relationship with one another. As such, far from a unitary subject, the subject is penetrated by a multiplicity of relations of subordination (i.e., dominant in certain subject positions and subordinate in others). It is through articulation and antagonism that the identity of the subject is fixed through an "us-them" relationship against an antagonist.

Hegemonic practices are totalizing in that they are attempts at filling the hiatus between, on the one hand, the *openness of the social*, which manifests the symbolic character of every signifier, and on the other hand, a *determined field of political* operations. What is significant is that the internal-external dialectic finds its most vivid expression in hegemonic practices. Drawing on Gramsci, Laclau and Mouffe, conceive of hegemony as a conceptual move away from the "internal necessity" of class alliance to the "external contingency" of hegemonic formation. Gramsci understood hegemony in terms of a "certain *unstable equilibrium* between classes."[32] Hegemony is essentially an aggregate around a core. For Gramsci, *apparently*, this core was class. But hegemony does not necessarily have to form around a class core. Since it becomes possible through articulation, the identity of the subjects participating in a hegemonic formation undergoes transformation throughout the process. Laclau and Mouffe hold that hegemony becomes possible because unfixity is present, and because there is uncertainty about the frontiers of the structure. Any attempt at fixing such frontiers can only highlight the contingency of the decision. Hegemony, therefore, is the theory of decision in an undecidable situation.[33] It is tightly linked with undecidability, for it designates a situation where *the experience of undecidability indicates no necessary course of action*. The more the experience of undecidability (i.e., the more the prevalence of disorder), the greater the responsibility for making decision.[34] "The general field of the emergence of hegemony is that of articulatory practices, that is, a field where the 'elements' have not crystallized into 'moments.' In a closed system of relational identities, in which the meaning of each moment is absolutely fixed, there is no place for a hegemonic practice."[35] As elements within a system of differences, Saussurean linguistics teaches us, every identity presents itself qua identity because it stands in a differential relationship with other identities within that system. Put differently, identity means being different from others (or, in Laclau's equation: "difference = identity"[36]). Every identity, in other words, is and always remains a relational identity within a hegemonic formation.

The condition of possibility of hegemony as a totality is the prevalence of equivalence over difference. Hegemony, then, is a part representing the whole of the structure. But it is actualized when a particular content, due to its symbolic character, overflows its own particularity and becomes the incarnation of the absent fullness of the entire system. In a hegemonic formation, the particular content of a signifier is emptied of its particularity such that it becomes the signifier of an absent fullness in the form of nodal point with which other elements could equivalently identify.[37] This function is possible due to the asymmetrical forms of power that make some subjects articulate the demands of others.[38] So, the universal (content of hegemony) is understood as a dominant particular,[39] and therefore, without an underlying and stable ground. Thus conceived, any hegemony is ultimately precarious, for, due to the overabundance of signifieds, the task of representing the entirety of the social is never definitively possible. Therefore, a hegemonic decision is *self-grounded, exclusionary* (in that it represses other decisions), and *internally split* (in that the hegemonic subject is subject of a lack).[40]

In terms of current political enterprises, hegemony is built on the "us-them" distinction in politics. It addresses the antagonistic dimension of all human societies, as all human relations are relations of power. But at the same time, it finds in the uneven social the possibility for building a pluralistic and democratic politics. The deconstructive conception of hegemony challenges the narcissism of certain fragmentary politics of pure particularism(s) based on the exclusion of all others. In order to avoid the peril of the total elimination of the *other*, Mouffe proposes that we turn our enemy into an adversary who is challenged and excluded, but whose right to defend its views is respected.[41] Radical, democratic citizenship, built pragmatically through the participation of social movements, becomes the common milieu for the convergence of new social movements.

Today, we witness the multiplicity and diversity of identities in the new social movements' practices. Should this diversity, which translates into the exhaustion of the grand narratives that dominate the modern era, necessarily mean that unified politics is no longer possible? The answer is no. The perspective that defends fragmentary politics, as opposed to unitary/unified politics, suffers from a double mistake. First, it takes diverse identities and differences as pure particularism, indeed as absolute, nonrelational identities each treated in isolation from others (an essentialist view). Second, it holds a limited notion of unity (i.e., as that which is always imposed), ignoring the possibility of unification and solidarity. Diversity is nowadays frequently used to refer to pure and irreconcilable particularisms. However, as political theorist Rob Walker states, today the "diversity of movements depends on an exploration of what it means to act on the basis of acknowledged differences."[42] The theory of hegemony is built upon an insightful exploration in that realm. Hegemony is indeed the theory of radical democratic citizenship in the era of despotism, ethnic cleansing, totalitarianism, fundamentalism, bureaucratic rule, neoliberalism, enforced homogenization of cultures, and the globalized commodification of all realms of life. It intends to reconstruct politics in the pragmatics of radical democracy based on agonistic pluralism in contemporary societies. Mouffe draws on the term "the political" (*le politique*) that she adopts from Carl Schmitt to show that the hegemonic politics she refers to always involves an "us-them" antagonism. Thus, instead of trying to eliminate the relations of power, radical democratic politics acknowledges them. Democracy, from this perspective, is a floating signifier whose fixity depends on the hegemonic articulation of the democratic discourse and the discourse of the rights. Thus, it is possible to gather under the signifier of democracy those signifieds that challenge the relations of subordination.[43] Therefore, radical democracy aims at deepening the democratic revolution. As such, it requires a radicalization of liberal democracy by applying it to ever more areas of social conflict via the replacement of a liberal conception of pluralism with the agonistic conception built upon the theory of hegemony.

The first-time electoral victory of the Italian Left in 1996 provides an illuminating example of the theory of hegemony as formulated by Laclau and Mouffe. Unstable due to split electoral tallies since the defeat of fascism, Italian politics shows the precariousness of the hegemonic field. With the dissolution or transformation of former parties (Socialist, Communist and Christian Democratic), the Italian political landscape now consists of two or three parties with 15 to 25 percent plus several other parties with 5 to 10 percent of the popular vote. This situation renders hegemonic alliance as a necessity for governance, since issues (and not party or ideological loyalty) function to bring together different forces across the political landscape. The Italian Left owes its April 1996 resurrection to a number of political positionings made by the *Partito Democratica della Sinistra* (PDS)—the largest offshoot of the Italian Communist Party. The 1992 political crisis that followed the uncovering of astronomical embezzlements as well as Mafia connections in the ruling Socialist party, created a political void that was filled in May 1994 by the center-right coalition of *Forza Italia*, *Lega Nord*, and *Alleanza Nazionale*. The coalitional government, however, lasted only seven months due to the defection of *Lega Nord*.

As the hegemonic core, the PDS recognized the necessity of an alliance consisting of the PDS, *Rifondazione Comunista*, the *Verdi* (Greens), and the left-wing Christian Democrat *Popolari*. The cultural confrontation between Left and Right stemmed precisely from the way in which they articulated the pressing issues (economic crisis, the Mafia, the environment, the European Community, and so on) that had been persistently haunting them. The PDS, in particular, maintained firm links with trade unionists of the *Confederazione Generale Italiana Lavoratori* (CGIL) and continued its presence on the municipal and provincial levels. It was, therefore, the assembly of social movements, issues and concerns, and local roots that, in 1996, in the third election in four years brought the center-left alliance of *Ulivo* (the Olive Tree) plus *Rifondazione Comunista* (which did not participate in the alliance) a victory over the right-wing *Polo* (Pole of Liberty of *Forza Italia* and *Alleanza Nazionale*). In contrast to the *Polo*, the *Ulivo* was able to maximally utilize the surplus of meaning in the cultural practice of politics. The *Ulivo* became the signifier under which a number of signifieds aggregated (and thus fixed the boundaries of the system) in opposition to the exclusion of the center-right forces. The rearticulation of issues of many movements and localities as well as establishing relations of equivalence between the parties of center-left in the wake of the deep crisis of a right-wing alliance incapable of properly addressing social demands brought that victory for the Italian Left. The Italian case shows how the practice of articulation in the conditions of radical subversion of literality can actualize a victory—one that has become a symbolic point of reference for a new "socialist strategy" in the somber aftermath of the fall of the Berlin Wall.[11]

The theory of hegemony indicates, among other things, that identity politics, the politics of new social movements, is not only capable of shaping institutional/party politics, but also, it can be the basis of a united, albeit precarious, politics. In fact, as an Italian observer comments, "if the organizational cages of the old parties [are] shattered, there is now little in terms of ideology or common interests that justifies the creation of large new parties. The party as we know it, the basic structure of democratic policy in the last century, is no longer relevant to the times."[45] In its general features, the Italian case represents the points that Laclau and Mouffe theorize using the concepts of constitutive outside, the primacy of the political, hegemony, and above all, the expansion and increasing influence of identity politics, represented by the new movements that either affect the agendas of the already established parties or start their own.

Having established the *constitutive* character of identity in the formation of social movements in a political field that is always hegemonic, however, we arrive at a critical problem in Laclau and Mouffe. Despite its undeniable merits, *their theory of hegemony is unable to show exactly through what operations an identity-claim grows into a social movement.* In my view, their failure to account for the operations that transform identification into social movement stems from two interconnected theoretical problems. First, their theory overstresses the performative character of identification. Second, their interpretation of the Gramscian concept of hegemony overlooks the experiential aspect of hegemony that is an exceptionally pivotal aspect in Gramsci's theory. These problems are precisely what we should attend to now.

Problems of "Performativity"

The condition for the emergence of the subject (= the decision) is that it cannot be subsumed under any structural determination, not because he is a substance of his own, but because structural determination… has failed to be its own ground, and it has to be supplemented by contingent interventions.

Ernesto Laclau, "Deconstruction, Pragmatism, Hegemony"[46]

Let us proceed from the point that Laclau's and Mouffe's theory of identity formation, which is at the same time a theory of hegemony, does not sufficiently account for the formation of social movements. They show that the hegemonic formation of society becomes possible when antagonism, as the ontologico-political constitution of society, sets into play the emergence of equivalence out of differences between actors' identities. This moment of antagonism is the *original* moment constitutive of every hegemony. It is original because from now on this moment is a point of reference in the hegemony, for it defines the terms of hegemony and hegemonic practices. However, the operation that prompts identity, as identification, to produce action is a presumed operation in Laclau and Mouffe. In their commendable effort to explain the new social movements in terms other than "determinations affecting an actor" (Schürmann in the epigraph to this chapter), Laclau and Mouffe arrive at a differential and *performative* approach to identity. This performative approach makes social movement conceptually almost indistinguishable from identification. It indicates, firstly, that *their work suffers from the lack of a theory of (social) action.* Observing the contents of their writing can easily support this criticism: Laclau's work is almost entirely on the question of hegemony, Mouffe's on democratic practices and liberal institutions. Their performative approach, secondly, demonstrates that *identification cannot adequately, let alone unproblematically, be theorized in terms of dislocation.* The root of these problems can be traced back to Laclau's collapsing the distinction between the *synchronic* character of hegemonic identification (hence, its performativity) and the *diachronic* movement that any identification sets into motion. In other words, by accounting for identification alone, one cannot automatically account for *temporality* as an indispensable feature of any social movement. Temporality here means the distance that has to be traveled from the actor's hegemonic constitution, on the one hand, and the possible point of arrival his or her identity alludes to, on the other. Put in different terms, temporality signifies the movement between the original moment of one's constitution (a synchronic moment) and one's subsequent identificatory vicissitudes and political positionings (a diachronic movement). Hence, temporality accounts for the changing character of identity and hegemony. Laclau and Mouffe quite rightly point out that the actor's identity transforms because of hegemonic identification. The most important effect of performativity, which Laclau defines as the equation of subject with the decision[47]—or, in other words, the equation of subject with the event—is the elimination or marginalization of other kinds of inquiry—namely, nondiscursive, nondeconstructionist inquiries. Even Laclau himself remarks at one point that a theoretical approach that is attentive to performativity should not hinder us from launching transcendental or cognitive inquiries.[48] Although his opposition of the cognitive to the performative seems rather arbitrary, it nonetheless signifies a cautious way of acknowledging, although in passing, the limits of his performative approach.

In addition, if identity is the principal characteristic of the new movements, then one needs to make a distinction between the content of hegemony, the content of each identity that makes up the hegemony, and the hegemonic and metaphoric articulation between the two. If antagonism is ontologically constitutive of hegemony, then it should be theoretically possible to account for just how dislocation of a given identity takes place, what route(s) the identity has taken to its (partial) fixity under the current hegemony, and what effects the fixity of identity has brought to the hegemony of which it is a part. For Laclau and Mouffe this is not a problem at all, because the modality of exclusion assigns the identity, in a pragmatic way, a content (a particularity) that can be hegemonized (a universality). The relationship between the universalization of a particular content, on the one hand, and the constitutive outside, on the other, is formulated through the concept of "empty signifier" as the signifier of a lack. An empty signifier is a signifier whose meaning is totally determined by the context.[49] For example, in the Cold War period, "democracy" meant anti-Soviet propaganda when used by the United States in its international rhetoric and foreign policy, and signified civil rights and the uncertain extent of their practice when used in domestic politics. The concept of empty signifier allows Laclau to announce that it is not as much the content of identity that is important politically as is the meaning the hegemonic context bestows upon it. One cannot but question the way Laclau's approach cuts off an identity in a hegemonic formation from all the contextual specificities that make it different from other identities. A conclusion that derives from my line of argument is this: *hegemonic equivalence cannot totally override elemental differences, but inevitably retains difference within equivalence* (thus, I reject Laclau's formula: identity = difference). The contingency of the content of hegemony, however, should not prevent us from seeing the necessary relationship between the hegemonized identity and all other identities in a hegemonic formation. In order to understand the fixity of identity in a hegemonic relation, we need to explicate precisely how each identity acquires its content (which it carries over to the current hegemony from the broken hegemonies of the past). Stated simply, why, in the Italian example, did the Greens, leftists and democrats, popular southern peasant parties, workers of the industrial North, and so forth, form the hegemony led by the PDS against the rise of the Right? Why these certain movements and parties and not other ones? Why are there historical affinities, *however precarious*, between certain social and political forces (e.g., trade unionists and social democrats)? The simple answer is: because of the (counter)hegemonic articulations they brought from past contexts to the present context. The performative approach cannot adequately explain the conditions that make only certain actors in our Italian example come together under the hegemonic formation. In other words, performativity cannot account for the continuity of identities that predicts their likely exclusion by the Right.

The conclusion seems inevitable: one cannot explain the relationship between identification and social movements in purely differential and performative terms. Laclau's equation of the subject with the decision does not allow us to properly understand the various contents that come to be uttered in the decision. To show that antagonism allows an identity to overcome its absent fullness does not necessarily shed light on how exactly this moment of fullness is realized through articulatory practices. In order to understand the fixity of identity in a hegemonic formation, we need to explicate precisely the historical conditions of possibility of each participant identity. We undoubtedly need a new concept that will illuminate the processes through which identity-claims emerge as social movements.

In the following section, I will show that this problem largely stems from Laclau's and Mouffe's specific reading of the Gramscian concept of hegemony. Their interpretation is so rigidly informed by the poststructuralist emphasis on the performative that they seem to lose sight of one of Gramsci's most important contributions to the study of hegemony: that every hegemony is built upon everyday experiences, as well as the historical and communal development of the experience that is crystallized in common sense. As if any diachronic investigation would automatically amount to essentialism, Laclau and Mouffe reduce Gramsci's theory to a synchronic study of hegemonic formation. My investigation, therefore, now takes us back to Gramsci for the purpose of offering an alternative reading of his theory of hegemony. But this reading must be offered under the proviso that the concept of "experience" in Gramsci, while "organic" and thus pivotal to his theory, is not adequately developed on its own right. It is rather implicitly, but frequently, addressed via his concept of common sense (and the related concepts such as consciousness, knowledge, and especially "philosophy"). Nevertheless, a theoretical acknowledgement of the significance of common sense to hegemony, regrettably belated as it may seem, will help us develop a theory of experience that is needed for the study of new social movements.

Experiential Hegemonies

[T]he theoretico-practical principle of hegemony has also epistemological significance. . . . The realisation of a hegemonic apparatus, in so far as it creates a new ideological terrain, determines a reform of consciousness and of methods of knowledge: it is a fact of knowledge, a philosophical fact.

Antonio Gramsci, *Selections from the Prison Notebooks*[50]

By the term "hegemony," Gramsci refers to a political configuration of the social in which the element of consent that is given by the citizens to the leadership overrides the element of coercion. Hegemony, therefore, entails an important sociohistorical project—namely, that of "creating a new culture,"[51] "diffusion in a critical form of truths . . . [and] their 'socialisation'."[52] Indeed, it is a "philosophical" project, which necessitates modes of perceiving the world by the consciousness of the led masses and the leading intellectuals. If the leaders do not succeed in promulgating certain themes and worldviews, the masses will refuse their consent. Hegemony, then, is not reducible to politics in the strict sense of the word. It is about leadership and direction (as the Italian word *dirigente* means)—indeed about *governing*— not "ruling" (*dominante*). Although Gramsci makes several references to Lenin in a respectful tone as the originator of the concept, his own reworked concept of hegemony surpasses significantly the former's parochial formulation. Observing the fact that the Russian proletariat comprised only a small minority of the Russian working people, Lenin recognized that the proletarian dictatorship could be realized only if it gained the support of the vast majority of Russian peasants. Thus, he advocated the formation of a class alliance. Lenin's formulation appears in Gramsci's earlier conception of hegemony in his 1926 essay, "On the Southern Question."[53] In this essay, among other things, Gramsci makes a distinction between leadership and domination (a distinction that did not exist for Lenin). His theoretical concern in this essay is to formulate how the "hegemony of the proletariat" can create a "system of class alliances which allows it to mobilize the majority of the working population against capitalism and the bourgeois State. . . . In Italy the peasant question . . . has taken two typical and particular forms— the Southern question and that of the Vatican."[54] The task of the proletariat would be to make "these two questions *its own* from the social point of view; understanding the class demands which they represent; incorporating these demands into its revolutionary transitional programme; placing these demands among the objectives for which it struggles."[55] If for Lenin hegemony was a tactic in the "democratic revolution," for Gramsci it increasingly became an indivisible condition for modern politics. Nonetheless, the point of departure for Gramsci (like Lenin) was to formulate the way in which the working class could win the consent of the peasants (as well as other subaltern groups in Italy). Given the great cultural, social, and economic discrepancy separating the industrial North from the agricultural South, his concern was to pronounce a practice that could end the subaltern position of the working class concentrated in the North along with southern peasants. Gramsci uses the term *subaltern* to designate the situation in which some groups are inescapably "subject to the activity of ruling groups, even when they rebel and rise up."[56] Although Gramsci uses the term to refer specifically to the working class, peasants, and other groups dominated by the bourgeoisie and its cultural associates (e.g., the Church), the term does not necessarily connote a progressive character.[57] It alludes to the particular configuration of society through hegemony and is thus principally a statement about an "objective" fact of the political configuration of modes of social positionings. The Gramscian view produces certain problems due to his perceiving class belonging to determine the identity as well as the political thrust of the actor. In other words, he takes the identity of actors as an effect of their specific standing in the mode of production, thereby anchoring the politics of the subaltern in the ultimate referentiality of economy (and its social formation). As a cautionary note, I must add here that class alliance for Gramsci involves the openness of the working class to the contingent elements in the society (e.g., peasant's demands) that are external to it, but these elements have considerable impact on the working class strategy for the revolution. This implies that, at least in certain moments in Gramsci, the hegemonic class does not necessarily have a class belonging. In other words, Gramsci's notion of class is an expansive, and therefore non-deterministic, category. Against those condemning Gramsci at the outset for his alleged essentialism, I think with respect to the question of class belonging, a *constitutive ambivalence* informs his theory of hegemony. I call it *ambivalence* because his theory, in my view, is founded upon two simultaneously divergent tendencies: one assuming the pregivenness of class identity, the other asserting the hegemonic formation of identity. Given this ambivalence, Gramsci rightly recognizes that the hegemonic positioning of the subaltern deprives them from autonomy and leads to the dispersion of the subaltern classes, which "by definition, are not unified and cannot unite until they are able to become a 'State'."[58] Once the subaltern classes become the state, as Gramsci recognized, a (new) hegemony, a new mode of configuration of society, will emerge. Formulated differently, the coming together of intellectual consciousness and ethics is the moment of hegemony which transcends common sense as a prepolitical belief system.[59]

It is due to his conception of hegemony as an originative political configuration of society that Gramsci understands the history of subaltern classes, qua subaltern, as "intertwined with that of civil society, and thereby with the history of States and groups of States."[60] In other words, the relationship between the subaltern and the dominant classes is only indirectly political in the strict sense of the word. It is primarily cultural and social. Here lies a two-fold point that is extremely subtle and crucial for understanding the Gramscian conception of hegemony. First, politics (strictly speaking) is secondary to the relationship between the dominant and dominated because it comes into play at the moment of hegemonic formation. Once the moment of hegemonic institution of society has passed, what we have is a p/rearranged social and cultural field with dominant and dominated repositioned around different themes. But just as this social and cultural field *proceeds* from the moment of hegemonic institution, it also *precedes* it, albeit in the rearrangement as instituted by the previous hegemonic formation. In our contemporary terms, we may call these two aspects *synchronic* and *diachronic*. Secondly, what is important in this way of formulating the place of the subaltern in hegemony is precisely, to use contemporary terms, the (re-)institution of the social by a hegemonic decision. It remains conceptually unclear why at times Gramsci refers to the bourgeois hegemony as domination (although it is ideologically clear). However, it is clear that hegemony invigorates a new beginning, a radical constitution of modes of life. As an original constitution, it allows the ruling classes to achieve a "historical unity," realized in the state, while denying the subaltern groups this very mode of existence, thereby forcing them into domains of dispersion and fragmentation. My suggested conception of hegemony, of course, defies many interpretations that take the state and civil society as separate entities.[61] In fact, Gramsci himself is very lucid about this, although he seems not to have possessed the proper language to elaborate on this pivotal proposition of his political theory. "This historical unity of the ruling classes is realised in the State, and their history is essentially the history of States and of groups of States," notes Gramsci. "But it would be wrong to think that this unity is simply juridical and political (though such forms of unity do have their importance too, and not in a purely formal sense); the fundamental historical unity, concretely, results from *the organic relations* between State or political society and 'civil society'."[62] "Organic," a Gramscian term, designates necessity (or, to be precise, "operative causality" in the methodological sense) as opposed to "conjunctural" which signifies "occasional" (or, methodologically, noncausal or associational) relations. (It is important to note that the relationship between the two is not fixed.)[63] As a political theorist, Gramsci does not hesitate to offer an institutional contrast between the state and civil society, these two "superstructural" loci of the social, as "the one that can be called 'civil society,' that is the ensemble of organisms commonly called 'private', and that of 'political society' or 'the State.' These two levels correspond, on the one hand, to the function of 'hegemony' which the dominant group exercises through the civil society over subaltern groups, and on the other hand, to that of 'direct domination' or command exercised through the State and 'juridical' government."[64] The key in understanding Gramsci, in my view, is to understand that his texts are by necessity multi-layered, as he would frequently use a term to designate a phenomenon in different social loci and in different relations where the function and meaning of the designated phenomenon would undergo variations.

Once we conceive of the relationship between the state and civil society not within the rigid and discrete categories of "politics" and "society" and their respective spaces and institutions but as an organic relationship, we will be able to understand that every hegemonic formation primarily amounts to the (re-)assignment of individuals, as well as the social and political institutions, to certain spaces and actions. Thus, hegemony represents an institutive moment that would bring all aspects of life into a new arrangement. It is precisely due to the organic relationship between the state and civil society that the state is rendered the locus of unity, and not because of Gramsci's étatisme or the conceptual primacy of institutional politics. Thus, the subalternity of dominated classes is conclusively overcome only through their capturing the pivotal "trench"—the state—in their "war of movement." *Ending subalternity will inevitably lead to a new institution of the society*, or it will not be a "permanent victory." In this respect, one of Gramsci's most essentialist passages is most illuminating. Arguing that subalternity can be overcome through agency, he proclaims: "If yesterday the subaltern element was a thing, today it is no longer a thing but an historical person, a protagonist; if yesterday it was not responsible, because 'resisting' a will external to itself, now it feels itself to be responsible because it is no longer resisting but an agent, necessarily active and taking the initiative."[65] In other words, the ontological privilege has conferred upon the proletariat by the logic of an eschatological history the unique duty and responsibility of transforming the society and instituting it anew. Once this "protagonist" of history subverts the conditions of its (and others') subalternity and becomes autonomous and hegemonic, it will reordain the entire configuration of society from the political stance of the state according to the pregiven essence of its agency.

It is important to note that, for Gramsci, politics, of which *hegemony represents an institutive moment,* and the sociopolitical arrangement it founds, are reflections of the economic base, and therefore, ultimately superstructural and thus referential in a Marxist way. At first glance, this seems to undermine my earlier interpretation of the notion of politics in Gramsci as an institutive moment. However, in Gramsci, the relationship between the economic base and the superstructure is not linear or unidirectional, but as he asserts, a dialectical one. He holds: "Between the premise (economic structure) and the consequence (political organization), relations are by no means simple and direct; and it is not only by economic facts that the history of a people can be documented. It is a complex and intricate task to unravel its causes and in order to do so, a deep and widely ranging study of all spiritual and practical activities is needed."[66] Contrasting it to the moment of hegemony, he explicitly criticizes what he calls the "mechanistic and fatalistic conceptions of economism."[67] Therefore, it is possible for him to conclude that "it is not the economic structure which directly determines political action, but it is the interpretation of it and of the so-called laws which govern the course it takes."[68] While the state and civil society both belong to the superstructure, they are not secondary to the formation of society (in comparison to the economic base). The positional and regional arrangements between the state and civil society, established through the political institution of the social at the moment of hegemony, rearranges economy and redistributes economic activities, while, interestingly, having the economy as one of the components conditioning the specific way of the hegemonic configuration of society. Unlike Mouffe, who forecloses from the outset of her analysis the question of economy by separating it from the political (that is, between "liberal democracy" and "democratic capitalism"[69]), for Gramsci, hegemony, though itself categorically belonging to the superstructure, makes possible the "necessary reciprocity between structure and superstructure."[70]

Gramsci introduces his Hegelian interpretation of Marxism to defend this position. He draws on the concept of "ethico-political history"—a concept used by the Italian Hegelian philosopher Benedetto Croce to designate the moment of unity between intellectual and cultural activities and that of the state. Notwithstanding an acknowledged distance from the Crocean concept, Gramsci refers to it as a "hypothesis" about "the *moment* of hegemony, of political leadership, of consent in the life and activities of the state and civil society."[71] He asserts that the philosophy of praxis does not exclude the ethico-political history, for the hegemonic moment is a moment of catharsis—that is, a historic moment in which the new emerges out of the womb of the old. What is more, in the emergence of the new there occurs the unity between base and superstructure, between the economic-corporate interests and the ethico-political ones. In this historic moment, the base (or structure) "ceases to be an external force which crushes man, assimilates him to itself and makes him passive; and is transformed into a means of freedom, an instrument to create a new ethico-political form and a source of new

initiatives."[72] Note that Gramsci's usage of the term *catharsis* is not acciden-
tal. A hegemonic moment is precisely a moment of catharsis, for it purges
the detrimental principles of the ancien regime from the life of society,
allowing the latter's rebirth based on new principles.

With hegemony designating the institutive moment of the social—a
moment that cannot be decisive until its incarnation in the state—*a new
kind of subject is forged*. Hegemony inevitably involves an "epistemological
significance"; and as the epigraph to this section suggests, "a hegemonic
apparatus . . . determines a reform of consciousness and of methods of knowledge." It is therefore "a fact of knowledge, a philosophical fact." What follows
is that every hegemony by necessity involves an important intellectual and
ethical aspect, whose function is to produce legitimacy for the leadership in
the eyes of the masses that are to be hegemonized. Note that in my interpretation, the term *leadership* no longer designates any group or class that
controls the state. Rather, it signifies any governing body that is constituted
by the principles invigorated by the hegemonic institution of the social and
thereby perpetuates those principles. In this sense, the moral-intellectual
aspect of hegemony is the condition of possibility of consent. Gramsci frequently draws parallel categorical distinctions between leading and ruling,
consent and coercion (or force), and hegemony and dictatorship. This has
its theoretical foundation in the irreplaceable moral-intellectual attribute of
hegemony.[73] The moral-intellectual aspect of hegemony will make possible
the growing of hegemony into a body of knowledge to be adhered to by the
masses—*a body of knowledge not only responsive to the everyday experiences
and perceptions of the masses, but also constituting these experiences and
perceptions*. This point is crucial. Such knowledge, however, cannot be
hegemonic, unless it is consummated by the hegemonized mass—to be
accurate, by the *hegemonic and hegemonized subject, who is (endowed by
virtue of his or her constitution) to recognize the operative logic of the social
and its fundamental principles* and to act accordingly. How precisely hegemony constitutes its subjects and how the consciousness of these subjects
perceives hegemony take us through one of the most intriguing labyrinths of
Gramsci's complex thought.

The point of departure for understanding hegemony, as the event of
instituting new subjects and new consciousness, is Gramsci's dictum that "all
men are 'philosophers'." Every human being, in other words, holds a conception of the world and of his or her place in it. Such conception is tightly
related to his or her everyday life experiences. Therefore, every single human
being engages in a "spontaneous philosophy"—a philosophy to be distinct
from the formal and professional activity that is carried out by specialist
intellectuals in academe. The fact that "everyone is a philosopher" indicates
that everyone's everyday life necessitates a continuous intellectual and cog-

nitive activity, however episodic and sporadic, which allows the person to maintain a constant awareness of his or her external surroundings, his or her place in the world, and the world itself. Gramsci finds popular philosophy to be contained, first, in language as "a totality of determined notions and concepts and not just of words grammatically devoid of content"; second, in "common sense," whose successful pragmatic evaluation he calls "good sense"; and finally, in popular religion, belief systems, and folklore.[74] Let us set aside the question of language, as well as those of religion and folklore (since they go beyond the scope of our inquiry) and focus on the relationship between common sense and hegemony. Common sense never refers to a single and unitary conception of the world. It is inescapably penetrated by fragmentation, incoherence, and contradiction.[75] Common sense dwells in the world of everyday experiences. Such experiences, by definition, are contradictory because they come from contradictory contexts of life. This, of course, does not mean that common sense contains no truth. Nor does it suggest that the individual informed by the conception of the world that is constructed through common sense will necessarily feel or understand such fragmentations or contradictions *as* fragmentations and contradictions. On the contrary, while, from a critical point of view, the "spontaneous philosophy" of each social group is in itself always fragmentary, it is usually not fragmentary on the existential and experiential level. On this level, on the level of consciousness of one's life experiences, all inconsistencies lead to a more or less enveloping "philosophy" that creates a milieu in which the thinking and acting of a subject conforms with those of others. "In acquiring one's conception of the world one always belongs to a particular grouping which is that of all the social elements which share the same mode of thinking and acting. We are all conformists of some conformism or other, always man-in-the-mass or collective man."[76] In his discussion on common sense, Gramsci cleverly foreshadows the problem of multiple sources of comprehending the world— a problem which in our day hinges on the concept of multiple subject positions (Laclau and Mouffe). He recognizes that an individual's conception of the world may contain multiple fragmentations because due to the increasingly complex loci of social and economic activity in modern societies, an individual tends to belong to more than one group. "When one's conception of the world is not critical and coherent but disjointed and episodic, one belongs simultaneously to a multiplicity of mass human groups."[77] This means that fragmented consciousness stems from experiences specific (but not necessarily exclusive) to different modes of life activity in different contexts. Gramsci, of course, could not have possibly anticipated that at the turn of the century a critical everyday philosophy would no longer inevitably imply coherence. He could not have seen that he was making an assumption, derived from Marx, when he suggested that critical philosophy was unified and unifying. Many new social movements of our day have posed practical challenges to the validity of this assumption and have remained nonunifying critical philosophies, despite the fact that they all contain elements within their philosophies that overlap with other particularistic critical philosophies. In other words, the new movements show us that a radical or critical conception of the world must not be necessarily total.

Now, if the subaltern are condemned to a fragmentary and episodic worldview under the current, bourgeois (hegemonic) configuration of society, then the hegemony of the working class, armed with the unifying philosophy of praxis, should logically put an end to such a fragmentary philosophy of everyday experiences. The moment of hegemony, therefore, brings consciousness into critical levels. The "war of position"—a military term that Gramsci used metaphorically to conceptualize the capturing of such hegemonic "trenches" as issues, positions, or practices—in the civil society does indeed instigate a critical consciousness in the subjects about the current hegemonic operations. In fact, without the slipping of the common sense into critical awareness, best manifest in the polemic (and propaganda) of the new against the old, the hegemonic moment is not thinkable. For Gramsci, a fortiori, this new critical consciousness is nothing but Marxism. He is indubitably right when he implies that the very mode of critical awareness of the world compels the individual to accept a new philosophy. But in explaining this process, he makes the uncritical assumption about the pregivenness of Marxism as the historically privileged and hegemonic mode of culture that ultimately replaces common sense and itself becomes a mass philosophy and a popular culture. A major conceptual culprit in making this assumption is his notion of organic relations. The assumption Gramsci makes stems from the presupposition that the working class is endowed with a unique ability and an organic connection to create this new, critical, and total worldview in the realm of common sense. Falling prey to his own conceptualization, Gramsci loses sight of the contingency that penetrates every relation, especially the ones that we perceive, empirically or theoretically, as necessary.

Important to our inquiry here, however, is the recognition that "the starting point must always be that common sense which is the spontaneous philosophy of the multitude and which has to be made ideologically coherent."[78] According to Gramsci, to render the spontaneous philosophy coherent is the task of hegemony. Indeed, one is inseparable from the other. As mentioned, the moment of hegemony is the moment of the unification of base and superstructure and the moment of the autonomy of subaltern groups. *Hegemony is the moment of the true knowledge about one's place in society* and of "knowing thyself" as a historically constituted being.[79] "At those times in history when a homogeneous social group is brought into being, there comes into being also, in opposition to common sense, a homogeneous—in other words, coherent and systematic—philosophy."[80] Put differently, the hegemonic and hegemonized subject is forged through the foundation of a new holistic worldview. Through autonomy and hegemony, neither thinkable without having been embodied in the state, the need for the construction of a new moral and intellectual order is experienced.[81] I must note that *the relationship between hegemony and critical philosophy does not involve a temporal lag.* They are two dimensions of the same historic moment.

Now, it should be clear what Gramsci means when he writes, "Every relationship of 'hegemony' is necessarily an educational relationship."[82] If leaders (in the sense of *dirigenti*) are to be truly leading, then they must establish an organic relationship with the led. This means that the organic relationship as such can precede the hegemonic formation. This relationship is realized through the specific process, marked by the moment of hegemony, through which a particular social group, represented by its intellectuals embodied in the party, becomes "totalitarian." Gramsci uses the term *totalitari* to signify "all-embracing" or "global."[83] Once "globalized," thanks to the hegemonic moment, a social group comes to articulate the issues and concerns of other subaltern groups. Thus, at one and the same time, the subaltern identity acquires content and identifies with a political project. However, to articulate issues of the subaltern through political institutions (i.e., through the state) would only mean force and dictatorship. To remain hegemonic, the leading social group must exercise "moral and cultural influence." Put differently, in global parties "cultural functions predominate."[84] In contemporary terms, this universalization of a particular group has its consequence for the leading party. It affects the "autonomy" of the party. For, a subordinate group seeking hegemony must always account for the interests of other such groups. In fact, hegemony "presupposes" such an incorporation of subordinate interests as an integral component that warrants its "certain compromise equilibrium" or "a certain unstable equilibrium between the classes."[85] A "united bloc" puts an end to the "multiplicity which previously existed [as it] was purely 'reformist' in character, that is to say it was concerned with partial questions."[86] It is through this process that the leading party becomes aware of its global character.

The global character of hegemony necessitates the *reconstitution* of individual actors, whom hegemony should represent as the subjects of the new leadership as well as their "resettlement" in new cognitive grounds and experiential terrains. Hegemony involves consent, and consent can only be procured from a people who share certain consciousness with, and whose life experiences are articulated by, their intellectuals and leaders. Hegemonic education, therefore, necessitates that the led pass through their experiences of emotion, passion, and feelings (dispositions Gramsci associates with popular culture and common sense) to understanding and knowledge (the products of intellectual activity). Gramsci calls this great achievement *historical bloc*.[87] The historical bloc designates the convergence of individual and subjective elements, on the one hand, and material and objective elements, on the other. It is through hegemonic knowledges that humans will be able to conceive of possibilities and, of course, to recognize that in order to realize a possibility, they must will it. Hence, to *"transform the external world, the general system of relations, is to potentiate oneself and to develop oneself."*[88] The hegemonic "education," as these lines suggest, should carry out the instrumental task of shaping new subjects out of the current actors. Hegemony is about the institution of society anew; it is therefore at the same time also the institution of "educated" hegemonic subjects. It achieves this through the incorporation of the actor's everyday experiences and their worldviews into the hegemonic conception of the world which is, at the same time and in a paradoxical way, the utterance of hegemonic principles.

Therefore, *a historical bloc signifies a moment in which a shared modality of life becomes an enveloping social force.* There is a pertinent emphasis on the role of intellectuals (leaders) in Gramsci. The relationship between people and intellectuals, he acknowledges, is one of representation. As leaders, the intellectuals come to educate the masses by rearranging popular beliefs, such that the fragmentary spontaneous philosophy (of the common sense) would emerge as a unified, critical philosophy. Since the relationship between the intellectuals and the masses is one of representation, the articulation of intellectuals renders hegemonic what people (should) already "know" in poor and unsophisticated ways. By doing so, the intellectuals' articulation transpositions people's everyday knowledges into a coherent hegemonic worldview. Hegemony integrates and (re-)positions everyday experiences and conceptions into its hegemonic master discourse. As such, hegemony is at once both a continuity from the past and an institutive rupture in the present. As the unity between the subjective and the objective, as the moment of recognition of possibility and will, the historical bloc will be represented by the specific modality of articulation of the masses' experiences by the intellectuals/leaders. It is precisely at this juncture that what is "objective" (i.e., what is to be declared as the truth independent of context) turns out to have derived its objectivity from the "historically subjective"—that is to say, from a "universal[ly] subjective" worldview, a constellation of specific elements, knowledges, and experiences, which finds adequate expression in the leaders' practice of linking the articulated experiences to the ontological principles at the moment of hegemonic emergence.[89] This important characteristic of the historical bloc (i.e., the universalization of a mode of life which is perceived through experiential relatedness and which forms a social force) is missing in Laclau's formulation of hegemony as the universalization of a particular.

This brings us to the crux of a theory of constitution of the hegemonic subject. If, as Gramsci teaches us, hegemony represents the moment of termination of dominance and the establishment of a leadership that is by essence global and all-embracing, a leadership that primarily and heavily derives its legitimacy from the consent of its citizens, then it involves a transposition of consciousness of its citizens. Indeed, the forging of citizens out of the subaltern represents the constitution of the hegemonic subject. Since, as Gramsci recognized, humans are always concrete beings and cannot be perceived free from the pregiven worldviews (common sense and folklore) and their components, the hegemonic moment, with its inseparable educational characteristic, should involve the rearrangements of the masses' everyday, doxic beliefs in a new, universal, and (more or less) coherent aggregate. Such an aggregate of consciousness allows communication between the hegemonic state and its subjects (citizens) and is the condition of acquiring consent. As one of the main operations of the delicate and complex hegemonic unity between doxic and epistemic knowledges, such a transposition of common sense should entail constructing the image of the hegemonic worldview as "objectively" true. Though such objectivity cannot be confused with the notion that invigorates the natural and exact sciences, it shares with it a pivotal component. Everything that does not conform to its truth must be submitted to critical examination, and most important, *from the vantage point of the existing hegemonic worldview* (somewhat analogous to Thomas Kuhn's scientific paradigm). Any new, anomalous, or unknown phenomenon must first satisfy the system of hegemonic knowledge—whose laws it defies due to its "newness"—about the latter's systemic inadequacies in experiencing the former's manifestations (recall the "sociological" new social movement theory). An unenviably austere endeavour. Hegemony is built upon the construction of an epistemic master-discourse, on whose principle(s) hegemony rests to govern the terrain called civil society by the state. After the completion of the hegemonic moment, consent, which in itself attests to the constitution of the hegemonic subject, will function to bound experiences of hegemonic subjects, of citizens, within the established epistemic boundaries. *Consent is the "matching" nexus between doxic experience and epistemic truth.* Indeed, now we can arrive at the conclusion that *any true hegemony must primarily be an experiential hegemony*, or it will not achieve consent as such. Not possessing sufficient conceptual means (namely, the concept of experience), I submit, Gramsci arrives at the above conclusion, but in different terms. He makes numerous references, as we saw, to common sense, everyday philosophy of the layperson, worldview, episodic and fragmentary consciousness, as well as Henri Bergson's concept of *élan vital*. The common denominators of all these concepts are the everyday experiences and the related doxic knowledges. *Experience, we can prelimi-*

narily observe, is about bound situatedness of thought and action. It is insepa-
rable from praxis. A successful hegemony should manage to sweep most, if
not all, experiences into the master-discourse in which different experiences
of the subjects through certain operations, as we will see in the next chapters, are interpreted and internalized in conformity with its governing epistemic
system. Hegemony penetrates the field of everyday experiences and appropriates them as its "grass roots" conceptual constituents. *As hegemony becomes*
more global, hegemonic experiences gradually become universal and add up to
the smooth hegemonic operations in ordaining a new modality of life. Now,
ideally, hegemony is there, everywhere, in the experiences of hegemonic
subjects; and it grows stronger out of them. Hegemony constitutes its own
subject and always remains, after its institutive moment, a never-ending
cultural project. Once *experiential hegemony* (i.e., hegemony appropriating
doxic knowledges into its epistemic universe), becomes prevalent, hegemony
derives consent from the subject's *hegemonic (or hegemonized) experiences,*
that is, those experiences that manifest themselves, in every locus of action,
as conceivable, viable, and desirable under the current hegemony.

The concept of *experiential hegemony* has several lessons for a theory
of social movements. First, it tells us how hegemony (re-)constitutes identities (class belonging in Gramsci) by (re-)defining identities according to the
hegemonic principle. Secondly, it shows that without the appropriation of
the experiential terrain—communicated, reflected, and challenged through
common sense—into the hegemonic universe, hegemony cannot endure.
Thirdly, experiential hegemony allows us to think beyond the public-private
distinction. It allows us to see that public and private spheres are both products of hegemonic constitution of the social. Private and public are always
mutually implicatory. Fourthly, it illustrates that subalternity stems from the
failure of hegemony to incorporate certain regions of experiences into its
universe. Subaltern experiences, in other words, are not represented in the
hegemonic principle. Subaltern consciousness is episodic and fragmentary,
to use Gramsci's terms, because it is detached from the governing principles
of society. Finally, from *experiential hegemony* to *hegemonic experience,* the
popular consciousness experiences continuity across rupture.

One can clearly observe that the terms used by Laclau and Mouffe to
theorize hegemony, while having undeniable merits, fall short in explaining
how the hegemonic formation of the social appropriates experiences. Although Gramsci, too, suffers from inadequate terminology and underconcep-
tualization to address clearly and directly the place of experience in hegemony
(albeit in a different way), his theory stands conspicuously above that of
Laclau and Mouffe in regard to experience. Suffice it, by way of summariz-
ing, to remind ourselves that the Gramscian concepts of hegemony, historical bloc, and common sense, closely interconnected in his formulation,

attest to his concern for exploring how hegemony, as the institutive moment of the social, emerges out of the universalization of certain experiences. It is here that the introduction of the phenomenological concept of *Urstiftung* or "original institution" along with the phenomenologically inspired concept of *regime* will enable us to take the final step before heeding the question of experience.

The Original Institution of Regimes

We arrive at a very different idea of *the political* if we remain true to philosophy's oldest and most constant inspiration, if we use the term to refer to the principles that generate society or, or more accurately, different forms of society.... [W]hat distinguishes one society from another is its *regime* ... its *shaping [mise en forme] of human coexistence.*

Claude Lefort, *Democracy and Political Theory*[90]

If, as discussed above, by definition, hegemony *originally* institutes society anew and derives consent through specific ways of experiencing the world by the hegemonized subjects, then the moment of hegemony—through a decision (Laclau)—is political. The political, then, gives a meaningful world to the subject to dwell in and relate to—a world of everyday praxis and experiences. This world is the aggregate of the current social, political, cultural, and economic arrangements and organization. If the political, through its ontological-institutive principles of society, animates a delicate balance between the state and civil society, then the two will be only different corners of one world, aspects of the same principle, domains of related experiences. In their overall trajectories, the said arrangements are inescapably converging, and despite frequent anomalous ruptures, they stay in conformity with the constitution of society through the delicate balance between the state and civil society. Though it has emerged out of the moment of hegemony, this balance is never pregiven as such, and the two are never fully delineated. The unfixity of terms and borders that exists between the state and civil society allows the political to intervene with its ontologically constitutive property in the hegemonic practices of everyday life. Such that a certain flexibility will make possible compromises between various elements of the world given by hegemony, so long as these compromises do not seriously threaten the politically constituted principles and the consequent general order of things. From this point onwards, I shall call this order of things, following Claude Lefort, a *regime*. I use this term along with hegemony, but for the purpose of showing that hegemony involves principles, the institution of these principles, and the structures produced or transformed due to the rising principles. The concept of regime shows that hegemony is not reducible to one sphere of life.

Derived from the truism of categories so ingrained in our language, the widely held distinctions between political, social, cultural, and economic spheres of life (which I call the epistemology of banal divisionism), and particularly the division between the state and civil society so cherished by liberalism, in fact *hide the operation of the political as institutive and reinforces the illusion of an ultimate freedom from one sphere while supposedly keeping oneself within the borders of another.* This illusion is indeed one of the pillars of the contemporary hegemony of liberalism, which allows its subjects to indulge themselves in their celebrated self-contained lifestyles, supposedly cut off from global deforestation, exploitation of the Third World workers, or bombing a "defiant" nation half a world away. According to Lefort, "it is impossible to designate a particular sector of social life as 'politics'." All forms of society, therefore, imply that "the notion of the relations between human beings and the world are generated by a principle or body of principles."[91] Thus, the concept of *regime*, as in the term *ancien regime*, "combines the idea of a type of constitution with that of a style of existence or mode of life"—a hegemonic principle, political by definition, that places our being in certain social loci amidst a specific elemental terrain to stand as a priori to our lives. It is in this relation that " '[c]onstitution' is not to be understood in its juridical acceptance, but in the sense of 'form of government'."[92]

What the concept of regime trains our eyes to see the threefold formation of society. It involves, as stated in the epigraph to this section, the *shaping* [*mise en forme*] of human coexistence. Shaping a regime also *gives meaning* [*mise en sens*] and *stages* them [*mise on scène*].[93] Lefort's sophisticated characterization of regime renders it of greater conceptual flexibility than hegemony, while retaining a certain affinity with Gramsci's conception of hegemony as the political institution of society. The threefold characteristic of the concept of regime is precisely what Laclau and Mouffe have not effectively incorporated into their theory, in spite of the references they make to Lefort.

As the shaping of society, however, a regime emerges out of an original moment of the institution of the social. Edmund Husserl uses the term *Urstiftung* (from *Stiftung*, "instituting," or simply, "giving") which translates as *primal institution* (or, original establishment) to refer to the beginning of an act, the origin of a style, or the inception of a meaning. Any primal instituting, any *Urstiftung*, creates a new arrangement of phenomena, or, a certain phenomenal style, so to speak. It is, at the same time, the bearer of possibilities.[94] "Primal institutions [*Urstiftung*] are good examples of that originative trait, but so are drafting parliamentary legislation, founding of the

United Nations, sitting down to begin a book, or choosing a life partner."[95] *Urstiftung* always contains within it a perceivable *Endstiftung*, a "final institution," as the horizon of its historical achievement.[96] Within this historical horizon marked by a perceived end and laden with possibilities, the existents find the context for their ontic meaning. It is this style and the movement toward a possible future instigated by *Urstifitung* that Lefort's concept of regime (via shaping, giving meaning, and staging them) captures, with optimal precision, in reference to the ontologico-political institution of society. The instituting moment of hegemony leaves its *stamp* on different realms of the social and grows into a regime to be experienced by the subjects as a matter of course in virtually every activity of life. The principles that the hegemonic *Urstiftung* puts in operation are acted out. They dwell in and enliven praxis. Once instituted, the hegemonic principles become engrained in everyday praxis, live in praxis, and notably, alter, if so happens, in the process of praxis they generate. Indeed, hegemony can be perceived as a movement, induced by and in the institutive moment, with a certain horizonal openness that enables hegemony to incorporate new elements and transform itself through the praxis of its subjects. With the horizon thus opened, the subject finds him- or herself in a new world, in a different network of relations, and with these two, into a renewed mode of intelligibility in which, despite the hegemonic "newness," familiarity and continuity still persist. That is precisely why in my reading of Gramsci earlier I asserted that hegemony in fact constitutes its own subject—a subject that sees him- or herself as "internally" related to this new world.

Conceived as the moment of institution of society, hegemony inevitably involves the construction of an episteme as universal knowledge. In fact, my argument is that this universal, and universally accessible, knowledge is the condition of possibility of leadership—which is, by definition, partly derived from the acquisition of popular assent—and thereby the construction of the hegemonic subject. Without the foundation of such a universal body of knowledge, hegemony, delicate, even precarious as it is due to the balance it must maintain at any given moment between the leaders and the led, slips into domination. In other words, without *epistemic hegemony*, consent, having its roots in the doxic experiences of those who are now hegemonized subjects, will fade into sheer coercion. *Experiential hegemony is the condition in which the reign of episteme allows only certain modes of doxic knowledge and certain ways of articulation of experiences.*

Just how the articulation of experiences becomes possible, how articulation conceptually links identity with social movement, and finally, how such articulations challenge regimes and their epistemic hegemonies, remain the topic that I will address through a reworked concept of experience in the next chapter.

CHAPTER 4

Articulated Experiences:
The Epochal (Trans-)Formations
of Identities and Social Movement

[P]roximity will be thought as a stable presence, as long as that which makes it proximal, the other trait of the present, is not also experienced as distant.

Schürmann, "Symbolic Difference"[1]

The emphasis on the conceptual relationship between experience and hegemony that was introduced in the previous chapter does not merely stem from scholarly interests. The fact of new social movements, their emergence and increasing prevalence—as movements that have posed serious challenges against the hegemony of modern liberal regimes in western societies by redrawing and/or collapsing the widely held boundaries of the social through the "politicization" of the experiential knowledges of different actors—makes this a necessary turn. Indeed, by invigorating movements that are closely related to the actors' experiences of subordination, new social movements allude to the political nature of experience (and experiencing), allowing us to trace experience back to the moment of hegemonic institution of society. Having submitted this, I therefore ask: how is it possible that, surrounded by elements of practical, everyday knowledges and significations that are overdetermined by the hegemonic worldview, at certain moments, we are able to articulate experiences different from, even contrary to, those that enfold us as parts of the hegemonic constellation of truth? How is it possible that we are able to refuse notions and beliefs that are in the air we breathe? How does it become possible, in other words, that at certain points, certain

73

experiences suddenly appear in opposition to the epistemic configuration of the hegemonic principles that govern society and thereby us?

I begin to answer these questions by outlining three possible modalities of identification. This outline sets the stage for the introduction of a new concept of experience, which in turn explicates the relationship between identity and destiny in hegemonic and epochal contexts.

Three Modalities of Identification

Then that suffering that united us made us speak, and we recognised that in our words there was truth, we knew that not only pain and suffering lived in our tongue, we recognized that there is hope still in our hearts. . . . [A]nd we were new again, and the dead, our dead, saw that we were new again and they called us again, to dignity, to struggle.

Zapatista Army of National Liberalism (EZLN)[2]

Let us begin by offering three different readings of such identificatory statements as "I am gay," "I am a woman," or the like. The first reading of these statements is: "I *am* gay" or "I *am* a woman." This reading indicates the positive conformity of an actor to the truth of a pregiven category of *being* called "gay" or "woman." It is a statement of truth about one's actual existence that intends to "match" the truth of a specific mode of being (it is called "adequation" in philosophy). In other words, "I *am* gay" or "I *am* a woman" are statements about the truth of the categories "gay" or "women." These statements tend to establish identity as a positivity of which we have a prior knowledge. Because of the "*am*," my being a gay or a woman now "matches" with the category *gay* or *woman*. Thus, the "I," my individuality, is already subsumed under the "am," my *categorial* being. The category "gay" or "woman" is prior and external to an "I" that has incorporated a category of being into his or her own being (the "am") and has thereby attained the truth of a certain category of being. This is mainly the way in which the "sociological" new social movement theories perceive identity. Since they regard identity-claims as positive statements ("I *am* gay"), they tend to locate it within a causal and positivistic analytical framework that seeks precisely to pinpoint the source of the category of being as prior and external to the self. The postindustrial society and middle class radicalism, for instance, are named as the founding sources of such categories of being. In "sociological" terms, by saying "I *am* gay" or "I *am* a woman," the identifying actor reports a pregiven social locus that is the objective basis of the category "gay" or "woman." Here, ultimate referentiality serves as the bond

between action and identification, because if one's being can be fully identified with the preconstituted category of being, as defined by one's belonging to an ascertainable social locus, then action comes to its end. Thus,
identification as such is never possible. Social movement, in this case, is
mediated, and not *acted*, literally speaking, by the actor: the actor carries out
the identity deposited in him or her to the point of carrying out the structurally assigned conflict. Since social loci have already defined the actor's
identities as well as the identities of other actors, they have always already
defined the type(s) of conflict actors should partake. That is why *action is
reduced to the agency—that is, an exercise of structurally determined fulfilment.*

The second reading is: "I am *gay*" or "I am a *woman*." In this reading,
to be a "gay" or a "woman" amounts to an identificatory movement toward
a category of being which has already made possible the thought of, and has
allowed the practice(s) proper to, the category "gay" or "woman." Here, the
"am" is no longer a verb indicating positivity, fulfilment, or "matching" the
truth of an entity (actor) with that of a pregiven category of being. Rather,
it now indicates a "not-yet" and a "would-be," for the "am" loses its centrality.
This represents the deconstructive approach to identity by Laclau and Mouffe.
The *social imaginary* that "gay" or "woman" represent puts into motion an
identificatory practice. A widely used poststructuralist term, *social imaginary*
is used rather in passing and rhetorically in Laclau and Mouffe. Discussing
the relationship between identification and social imaginary, Laclau remarks,
"the imaginary signifiers forming a community's horizon are tendentially
empty and essentially ambiguous."[3] While agreeing with his remark, I must
mention that the concept does not play an operative role in his theory. The
postmarxist approach does not bring to fruition the possibilities that the
concept of social imaginary releases for a theory of identity and action. This
is mainly because action is a presumed concept in the theory of Laclau and
Mouffe. However, as I will show below, *social imaginary* is a central concept
in understanding action, especially in the age of identity politics. I define a
social imaginary as the perceived point of actor's identificatory fulfilment,
that is, a nonnormative horizon that lies ahead. Being "gay" or a "woman,"
in our second reading, stands as a social imaginary because *it does not describe what one is, but the possibility or a perceived point of arrival representing what one can become.* As a perceived point of the actor's identificatory
fulfillment, a social imaginary always points at a certain direction and seeks
certain possibilities. Hence, identity as *identification*. We saw that, according
to Laclau and Mouffe, every identity is a dislocated identity. Since the presence of an outside threatens the identity of the actor and becomes constitutive of it, then antagonism, as the ontologico-political constitution of society,
sets into play the prevalence of equivalence over difference. This is the hegemonic formation of society. The original moment of foundation of society

enables an actor's identification with a social imaginary. This implies that the actor's identification with a social imaginary is not possible upon the actor's wish. Rather, it takes place in a specific way, because by virtue of his or her hegemonic constitution, the actor is a *hegemonic subject*. The terms of his or her social imaginary are mainly decided by the original terms of the hegemonic-epistemic formation. This kind of identification, therefore, always connotes the hegemony under which it has become possible. But at the same time, because of the very act of identification, which attests to the openness of the social, it indicates the possible or imminent failure of hegemony in giving its subjects adequate terms for identification.

I argued in Chapter 3 that we cannot adequately explain the relationship between identification and social movement in purely differential terms. A third reading of our identificatory statement shows just that: "*I am gay,*" or "*I am a woman.*" The "I" here links the actor's present stance as captured by the "am" with her or his social imaginary (i.e., "gay" or "woman"). Now, with the "I" connecting the two together, the "am" is no longer a positively ascertainable social locus. It has already surpassed its own present being (the "am")—that is, a stance which, by virtue of being connected to the "gay" or the "woman" has already moved toward a social imaginary (i.e., an "am" of an upcoming modality of being). The "I" that makes this link between the "am" as a pregiven being, on the one hand, and the "gay" or "woman" as a social imaginary, on the other, is nothing but an incarnation of the actor's *experiences*. Here, contrary to Laclau's usage of it, the term *experience* is not used rhetorically or, at best, as an auxiliary concept. Emancipated from the positivity of the social and moved away from the purely differential terms of identification, the "I" displaces the above schemes. The "am" becomes a point of departure as "gay" or "woman" become points of arrival. As the incarnation of actor's experiences, the "I" (i.e., the historical individual), is the pivotal concept in understanding the relationship between identity claims and the new movements. Suffice it here to mention that experience links a past to a possible future; it connects being to becoming. The "I," therefore, is at every glance a passing moment in a *temporal* movement. As such, the experience the "I" represents is always *context specific*. Experience enlivens a movement by allowing identification with a social imaginary. It is through the dynamics of experience that an identity-claim can grow into a social movement. Stated with precision, *articulation of experiences allows social movements to arise out of identification*.

The first modality of identification, as mentioned, prevails in the "sociological" new social movements. The second modality, also as discussed, belongs to the deconstructive new social movement theory of Laclau and Mouffe. The third modality of identification, finally, is informed by a radical phenomenological approach that is inspired by Schürmann's political theory.

Now, I must propose a reworked concept of experience and discuss its irreplaceable effects on the study of identity and its relationship with social movements. I will perform this task in two steps. First, I will study the conditions of emergence of experience by offering an interpretation of Samuel Beckett's play, *Waiting for Godot*. My rationale for turning to literature is simple: the play depicts a certain modality of human existence, not in disciplinary terms, but in everyday, experiential terms. Beckett's play allows us to develop a concept of experience that links human existence to the hegemonic conditions of experiencing. Next, we will turn to the documents of the Zapatista movement in Mexico to develop a theory that shows the relationship between identity, experience, and the formation of social movements.

Articulated Experiences

A starting point that neither abandons ordinary experience nor trans-substantiates it into the extraordinary will have to be looked for in something everyone is familiar with, however poorly; it will have to be a knowing that is not episodic, not contingent; a knowing whose seat is everydayness; from which other experiences and types of knowledge arise; and which does not in turn depend on some more primary knowing.

Schürmann, "Conditions of Evil"[4]

Along a country road, by a willow and a low mound, Estragon and Vladimir await the coming of Godot who would meet with them to inform them about his decision. The two ragged men had requested something from Godot, "nothing very definite," something rather of a "vague supplication," like a "kind of prayer."[5] Godot had told them that before reaching any decision, he would have had "to think it over," in "the quiet of his home," after consulting with his family, his friends, agents, correspondents, books, and bank account. *Waiting for Godot* in abject desperation, Estragon and Vladimir can conceive of no alternative. If Godot comes, they will be saved. But in a mysterious way, Godot's arrival seems already deferred, and this deferral is eternalized by the perpetual uncertainty of the two about the time and place of his arrival. In the nonoccurrence of an anticipative deferral, Estragon and Vladimir, though to different degrees, live in an *existential void*. In absolute senselessness, they meet Pozzo, a businessman, and Lucky, his quasi-slave servant and carrier. Despite their sheer positional contrariety—in fact, because of it—the lives of these two men are orderly and meaningful: Pozzo rules, steering Lucky by a rope around his neck, feeding him with his food scraps. Lucky is ruled, enduring absolute lowliness and furthest contempt in total docility and an amazing silence that is broken only once when he gives a long, brilliantly nonsensical lecture about everything and nothing. Later, a boy arrives to notify Estragon and Vladimir that Godot has delayed his coming until the next day. In their own peculiar indecisiveness, the two desperate men decide not to hang themselves until then: "We always find something . . . to give us the impression we exist."

Another day (the next?) of senselessness. Waiting for Godot, Estragon and Vladimir re-encounter Pozzo—now blind, anguished, and pathetic—and his servant Lucky. They still live in their own orderly world, as the ruler's incapacity has not affected the sway. The boy, not remembering Estragon and Vladimir, appears to notify them, once again, that Godot won't come until the next day.

The existential void of Estragon and Vladimir, which can only be filled fleetingly through petty decisions, indicates the *structure of anticipation*, of *awaiting* the *event*, in which they are *inserted*. This structure is penetrated by a radical undecidability. For under the conditions of the existential void, anticipation does not entail an action proper. In the absence of what we may call, to adopt a term from Edmund Husserl, *existence-sense [Seinssinn]*[6]— that is, in the absence of not only *meaning* (which the English word "sense" denotes), but also *direction* (as the French word *sens*, the Italian *sensa*, or the German *Sinn* imply), life is nothing but the contemptuous chain of momentary existences for these once "respectable" indigents, for whom, now "it's too late." To them, everything—places, roads, trees, and people—seem alike. In the absence of meaning and direction, Estragon and Vladimir are stranded in a nebula of homogeneous experiences. In this entirety, inarticulation reduces all experiences to a mass of colorless, trifling, hazy, and unrelated affairs of an equivocal past. These "past" experiences remain homogeneous precisely because of their en masse flow in the present. Existential void stems not from lack of experiences. Quite the contrary, it dwells in the amorphous nebula of homogeneous, pre-/inarticulated experiences—indeed in the indiscriminate flow of past experiences into the present. Without privileging some experiences over others, one cannot escape from existential void. Thus, the existential void of Estragon and Vladimir can only be overcome through the *decisive* (from the Latin *decidere*, "to cut off" or "to set apart"), yet still impending, act of Godot. Godot represents the act of decision. More precisely, Godot's decision represents the possible articulation of certain experiences—an articulation without which Estragon and Vladimir will be unable to act in a certain direction. The homogeneity of experiences (i.e., their inarticulatedness), practically amounts to the lack thereof. Hence, the existential void so grimly, but brilliantly, portrayed in Samuel Beckett's play.

If Godot is to bring hope to the inertia, then his act will be one of decision, and decision, as said, is always carried out through the articulation of specific experiences: an articulation that presupposes the "setting apart" of certain experiences, thereby shaping them out of the homogenous nebula of experiences. Godot's decision, if he ever arrives, would bring direction to the lives of Estragon and Vladimir by connecting together certain experiences of theirs. Far beyond temporally or historically locatable events, experience comes into being in the moment of articulation and through the act of decision. So Godot is also the name for the act of articulation—an articulation which adjoins existence with time in action as it gives direction; or, stated differently, an articulation which would register Estragon and Vladimir in their places in the world of sense, of direction. Although Laclau and Mouffe seem rather heedless of the existential aspect of decision, their concept of identification, in the context of our discussion, can be read to indicate the decision of *giving a certain direction to one's existence—that is, to act*. For through the *articulation of experiences*, decision, by definition, invokes a course of action and identification with a social imaginary that represents a projected future and a horizon of being. *Articulation, therefore, is Janus faced*: it looks backward, setting apart and shaping up certain experiences from the nebulous mass of experiences. But at the same time, it looks forward, intimating certain horizons and leading to certain imaginaries. As mentioned, the experience of undecidability is the experience of senselessness, lack of direction. The undecidability of structure means that by themselves, inarticulated experiences suggest no necessary course of action. Thus, decision is dependent on the (would-be) actor's act of overcoming undecidability through the articulation of certain experiences such that, in their overall matrix, these experiences open up a course of action before the (would-be) actor. Any act of identification is, using a Husserlian term, an act of *thematizing* the world, through which consciousness constitutes the context in which the nature of the decision is understood (but the decision is not necessarily made). We always *thematize* the world according to our ends. The thematization of the world indicates that we are conscious of the world as a *horizon*.[7] Godot's decision will thematize the world for the two men. It is through such a thematization and within the subsequent contextualization that their identities attain *content*. Let us not forget that, as the character of Godot implies, the contextualization itself is the effect of an outside. Under the conditions of existential void (i.e., inarticulation), experience as such always remains unthematic: the world appears to the subject as universal, but this universality is not a thematic ensemble of heterogeneous elements. In the play, Estragon's and Vladimir's conversations about the past is rather sporadic, haphazard, and most notably, uncertain. They are inserted in a nebula that lacks direction. Identification (and thereby decision) refers to a situation in which *certain thematized experiences set the content of an identity*. The decision is therefore the universalization of particular themes. Laclau's reference to the "acts of identification" (the effect of an outside) cannot take place without constant thematization of experiences (an operation of the inside, so to speak). And this conceptual link between identity and experience is precisely what a theory of identity and social movement requires.

The petty decisions of Estragon and Vladimir (e.g., postponing suicide until the next day) do not affect the structure in which they are stranded. Here the critical undecidability of the structure assigns them positions from which they cannot escape. Undecidability obviously does not suggest any course of action. It is in undecidability that Estragon and Vladimir succumb to their fate. A decision, an act of identification, must by definition be *decisive*—that is, it must alter the existing structural configuration of decision/ undecidability. Once decision brings the existing structure to pass through the aisle of decisiveness, identification will represent the moment of overcoming fate. *Identity now acquires a destining modality. In fact, identity and destiny are now one and the same.* This is what Godot's promise will present to the two awaiting men. But *what will make possible the opening of the specific destining path before identity is experience.* Indeed, identity stands before the sojourner as a grand façade to the marvellous chamber of experiences. Without a properly developed concept of experience, the notion of identity will never be adequately understood. Here, the reworked concept of experience leaves out all references to ultimacy such as the subject or the metaphysical matching of the past and present origins. Essentialism holds that the unity of experience and identity are made possible by some innermost essence that links them together across the linear time and such unity presumably predestines the future. At this theoretical junction, the concept of experience makes its discursive, anti-humanist theoretical debut.

The roots of the word "experience" go back to the ancient Greeks. Aristotle used the word *empeiria* (the Latin *experientia*) to refer to the observation of things themselves, their qualities and modifications under changing conditions and the knowledge of how things change.[8] The English word *experience* comes from the Latin *experientia*, meaning the knowledge acquired by repeated trials, which itself comes from *experientem*, the present participle of *experiri*, "to try" or "to test." The latter consists of the prefix *ex-*, "out of," and the obsolete verb *periri*, "to go through." In English, the word *peril* comes from the old verb *periri*. Peril designates "danger," but it literally means a "trial." Thus, experience has several connotations: to make trial or to put to test; to ascertain or prove by experiment or observation; to feel or to learn by experience; to give experience to or to gain experience from, but most importantly for this study, to suffer and undergo. It designates the knowledge gained by having undergone a trial (an examination process) and suffering and by having acted and ventured in a certain way. It is this meaning of the word *experience* that links the experiences of the English-speaking person in his or her own "house of being" (language) with the experiences of most other Western languages, in particular with those of Germans. The word *Er-fahrung* (experience) in the German language designates the same process—discovery and learning, but also suffering and undergoing. It is in this sense of the term that I take "experience" (*Erfahrung*) to include "lived experience" or *Erlebnis* (which earlier I referred to as "past experiences") that belongs to "life's urge."[9] In this sense, as Schürmann teaches us, any experience indicates the peregrine essence of being which uproots rational security as such. Thus, "the experience (*Erfahrung*) of such peregrination (*Fahren*) is full of peril (*Gefahr*)."[10]

Accordingly, the term *experience* does not necessarily signify a foundational realm of human action that finds expression in language and is therefore prior to it. Language is not representational of a "deeper" or pregiven world; rather, language is constitutive of human experience (and thereby identity and action). Emancipating thinking from the metaphysical and representational experience of language that has been and still is endemic to modernity, the reworked concept of experience will enable us to revisit language in a postmetaphysical, non-representational manner. Equally important, language will also open thinking to the possibility of transition toward a post-modern era.[11] Experience, therefore, takes place within the limits and the possibilities of language. Once this intimate relation between language and experience is properly understood, experience, this central concept of phenomenology, finds its place within the field of discursivity. *It is, therefore, my suggestion that experience is a certain mode of discursive closure brought about through articulation.* As any decision always passes through articulatory practices, so it is through the articulation of experience(s) that particular discursive elements—regardless of whether they are already actively present or lie dormant in relative oblivion in the field of discursivity (in fact in contemporary language)—converge under the signifier of a certain experience. As the signifieds of a particular signifier (experience), these elements will fill concurrently the discursive field and organize it under the banner of that particular experience. But it is not only the existing elements (active or dormant) in the discursive terrain that join the signifier of the articulated experience(s). Those elements that are currently absent in the discursive field, and their absences are marked by *traces* may also be rearticulated and reintegrated into the field of discursivity. I use the term *trace* in the Derridean sense, that is, put simply, as elements whose origins have disappeared.[12] As such, an experience could also involve the *summoning* of those traces which, in turn, "exhume" the elements that are buried under the layers of a collective amnesia. In short, an experience is the summoning of "past-perils" within the field of discursivity and arranging them under the signifier of the experience. Thus, any experience entails not only a contemporary character—as it summons elements—but also a historical character—as it must oftentimes care for certain absent elements in order to trace and reinstate them in the current field of discursivity. *The key to properly understanding experience is to note that while as a specific assembly of discursive elements and traces, every single experience has a unique history, the elements summoned up by the experience are not historically unique.*

But the historical character of experience encompasses a curious kind of pastness. This past does not normatively dictate a future. Neither is it a forcefully conscripted past that guards a predestined future wrapped in the glorious myth of a golden age, nor is it a past that is predestined to exalt or be exalted in a perfecting unification with a present that moves toward a monistic utopia. In terms of temporality, the "pastness" of the articulated (or rearticulated) experiences does not correspond to an objectified succession of affairs taken place in the past segments of the linear time. Nor is it a part of an eschatological time that will assuredly expire upon the will of God. Rather, this pastness comes close to what Heidegger calls the "historical"— *Geschichtlich* or "history-ish"—character of *Dasein*—that is to say, past as a property that is present-at-hand.[13] It connotes that these experiences once belonged to a world in which they were meaningful and projective, a world that may no longer be. But they belong to a past world by virtue of their present articulatedness. Articulation of experiences means that the past is not actually something gone by, but something that does and will manifest itself in the present and future decisions.

Once an experience is articulated and recognized as something that belongs to a "past," the pastness of experience (as a "past-peril") surfaces as having its roots not totally in any past event(s) that can be confidently and positively pinpointed, but also in the possible future discursive configuration of elements. This complex relationship between past and future, which disturbs the dominant, linear conception of time, is indeed the characteristic of the radical phenomenological concept of *destiny* (Geschick)—*that is, understood as a movement from one phenomenal site to another.* A phenomenal site refers to a certain mode of epochal and hegemonic arrangement of phenomena in which the actor/subject is inserted. Thus, a phenomenal site binds one to the events one needs to address, tasks one must perform, things one can use, the people one relates to and engages with, thoughts and ideas one may heed. *Since a phenomenal site, by virtue of its epochal origination, is always occupied by a community of persons and not a single individual, it is by definition political.* As such, destiny is not a movement toward the "matching" of an origin (*arché*) with an end (*telos*). It is radically different. To be "destined," Schürmann explains, means to be "bound for a particular place . . . [and] to have committed oneself to it . . . To speak of destiny is, then, to speak of places and of placing."[14] Destiny, therefore, designates the way new phenomenal arrangements may emerge. As mentioned, articulated experiences signify a certain discursive consolidation of elements, brought about via identification and decision. Through the discursive consolidation of elements we can distinguish a new phenomenal arrangement from an existing or ordinary such arrangement. So long as the "lived experiences" (*Erlebnis*) of Estragon and Vladimir remain unthematic (i.e., prior to articulation/decision), so long as the discursive elements pertaining to them remain in deep disarray, destiny will not manifest to them a course of action. The arrival of Godot and his expected decision will set their experiences as the content for their identity, for their place in the world. Here rests a subtle point. If, as submitted earlier, prearticulation experiences can only belong to an amorphous and homogeneous mass of "past" affairs, then no experience can precede articulation. To be, an experience must already be articulated. Here we need an important clarification. *Articulation is not primarily a human doing, but made possible by destinal placing and epochal shifts.* The actor does not articulate certain experiences by pure choice or in total freedom. An articulated experience gathers elemental signifieds under the signifier of a certain experience. Elements and traces, however, are not always present; rather, they reveal themselves in certain periods of history. That is why in the study of experience (*Erfahrung*), we should not limit ourselves to lived experiences (*Erlebnis*) as a sequence of past events that one "can capture . . . in reports."[15] Conceptually, the articulation of experience does not allow past events (as in lived experience) to become a foundational realm of present practices. For, as we shall see in detail, modes of articulation are ultimately given by epochs.

Articulation consolidates and positions certain elements and traces within the discourse. But if experience summons elements and traces, what calls upon experiences? The very act of articulation. The reason should be evident: experience cannot conceptually, temporally, or otherwise precede the elements and traces it summons, because experience is meaningful only in relation to a contemporary situation (i.e., to an existing or emerging phenomenal site). Psychology will tell us that we all have thousands and thousands of experiences stored in the infinite layers of our memories, but we never recall these experiences en masse and in a non-discriminatory manner. Rather than perceiving the existential plane as an *a priori* continuum (referential approach), we should think of it as surfacings penetrated by frequent ruptures. Such surfacings and ruptures are the manifestations of experience's own time-dimension: an "immanent-time."[16] Experience never has a character of continuity in the sense that it arrays a sequence of affairs. It can never be repeated; for each time, the world in which it is articulated is never quite the same. The repetition of an experience, then, always also incorporates transformations. Thus, experience is sylleptic. The utterance of every experience is always both literal and figurative (hence, the mimetic effect of every articulation of experience).[17] That is because articulation turns the experience (as the summoning and aggregation of elements and traces) into the content of the discourse within which the experience is articulated. Within this discourse, "[e]xperience can be the object of both a private *observation* and a public *description*."[18]

It is in this sense of the term *experience* that we can properly begin to think action in terms other than ultimate referentiality. Here, a clarification is in order. Essentialism and referentiality operate on the widespread, hegemonic (mis-)conception that it is the individual's experience that leads to identity. This assumption holds experience, as something emanated from the subject, to be the foundation of identity. In the context of the "sociological" new social movement theory, such notion led to an underlying assumption in Melucci's formulation of relations between everyday life experiences and identity-claims. Melucci writes: "Changes in everyday experience not only generate but also reflect new needs in the lives of individuals. Identity must be rooted in the present to deal with the fluctuations and metamorphoses."[19] This assumption exacerbates the erroneous view that identity and action somehow belong to separate domains. The reworked, nonreferential concept of experience and its relationship to that of identity abolish such referential assumptions in social movement theories. The suggested concept of experience eliminates the long presumed link between experience and the subject as the ultimate bearer and perceiver of experiences. It thereby releases experience from the subject, which is the ultimate referent of modernity. Experience indeed goes beyond all references to the subject because its articulation becomes possible, phenomenally and discursively, in certain eras. If we had conceived of experience as a primordial form or as the reservoir for identity, we would have been unable to find the proper theoretical sites of both identity and experience. Experience is subject to the same discursive laws, arranged by the political, as is identity. The difference between the two concepts lies in that identity attains its status due the particular content(s) it receives from experience, but experience cannot found identity. The context of emergence of both is nothing but the hegemonic formation that the decision gives rise to. We know that a phenomenon acquires different meanings in different worlds (as subsequently in different hegemonies). Hence, the organic union *identity/experience*—two modalities so intimately attached to one another in praxis that can only be conceptually distinguished. Contrary to many current day formulations, identity can no longer be perceived as the signifier of a category or a modality of being. Nor can it be understood as the signifier of a set of experiences. Since experience gives identity its content, it propels identity toward something beyond the "past-peril." Identity is now understood as the projective constituent of articulated experience. Identity/ experience, then, alludes to the congruity of pastness and futurity set in motion in the present—in the decision.[20]

The articulation of experience, as mentioned, is not a decision to be made primarily by the actor. Recall the argument that in order to be, an experience must already be articulated. Structural undecidability does not indicate that decision will completely be a human doing. For the sake of convenience and based on the conventional disciplinary languages, we may refer to the actor as the performer of acts (of decision) and locus of antagonism. However, in order to make a decision, the experiences to be articulated (i.e., the elements to be consolidated in the discourse), must already be knowable and available. The decision, in other words, must be intelligible. *This means that certain experiences are literally not possible or even conceivable at certain times.* They do not exist, so to speak, in certain ages. Therefore, the articulation of certain experiences becomes possible in certain eras. Only after an era has allowed for the articulation of a certain experience is the actor granted the language to articulate that experience. *Hence, articulation is only secondarily a human act because experiences are epochally given.* Let us consider the experience of "abused spouse": the experience was possible only *after* certain individual rights were socially recognized and became the law. It is only after a certain expansion of the notion of individual rights and the emergence of its proper language that the articulation of experience of the "abused spouse" became discursively possible. The possibility of (in)articulation of experiences lies in language itself.[21] Thus, languages are markers of eras. This indicates that experiences themselves, as the content(s) of identity, are dependent upon a context larger than the specific hegemonic formations. This larger context is that of the epochal, hegemonic principles. Schürmann captures this cogently in a most condensed statement: "*Epochal principles are ontic givens.*"[22] The elemental constituents of an experience are always epochally given. The way we think, act, and live are all manifestations of the epochal principles. In *Waiting for Godot*, interestingly, the decision of Estragon and Vladimir will be brought to them by Godot, for undecidability can only be overcome by a dislocated decision—a decision made by an outside (which is ultimately impossible). Godot, then, is the name for the dislocated decision. But more importantly, Godot may be the name for an epochal principle that is yet to appear—a principle that has not made itself intelligible in the era in which the two poverty-stricken men live.

In its ideal type, an epochal regime at its zenith can lead to the constitution of totalized subjects like Estragon and Vladimir in *Waiting for Godot* whose beings, including their experiences, were inserted in the pregiven, overwhelming mode of existence of a regime. Such totalized subjects are virtually impossible to depict in actual settings, for if the principles governing an era were so overwhelming, the researcher would as much be subject to them as would the layperson, and the question of the governing principle of the current era would not have been intelligible and therefore never raised. Only through a critical look into the past can one investigate total subjects. But such investigations are always subject of hermeneutic dilemmas. This must explain the privilege that fiction enjoys over actual case studies in depicting life in epochal regimes in their apogee. In Beckett's play, Estragon and Vladimir were totally taken over by the experiential hegemony under which they live. Even in their recognition of their inhumane plight, they could not conceived of any other alternative but to send an abject supplication to Godot (whom I interpreted as representing the principle itself). When hegemony is in such an efficacious state, all doxic experiences can only come to conform to the epistemic hegemony. Even the way out of one's plight cannot be uttered in terms other than those of the epistemic hegemony. The existential void that greatly affected Estragon and Vladimir signifies the specific world assigned to them under the very hegemonic principle, which Godot represents from his unreachable prominence. Phenomenologically, hegemony precisely refers to the moment of insertion and constitution, the emergence of a regime along with its inserted subjects, and as such, a moment of a constellation of a world that is always already political.

We shall explore the implications of this epochal theory of action and thought in the subsequent chapters. I will show how a radical awareness of epochal shifts will train our eyes to seek and our senses to be attuned to the emergence of the new. Now, we need to explore how the introduction of the concept of experience into the discourse of identity will explicate the connection between identity and social movement. Before proceeding in that direction, let us remember *while experience is the destining, identification is the movement toward that destiny. Without destiny, life is stranded in fate,* as we saw to be case with Estragon and Vladimir. Opening a horizon before life, Godot's decision could turn fate into destiny. Godot, of course, never arrived.

Identity As a "Receding Signified"

[A]n epochal constellation of unconcealedness and concealment always summons man to respond to the mode in which things present are present.

Schürmann, "Questioning the Foundation of Practical Philosophy"[23]

The discourse of justice and freedom that emerged since the 1 January 1994 uprising by the Zapatista Army of National Liberation (*Ejército Zapatista de*

Liberación Nacional, EZLN) in the state of Chiapas in southern Mexico brings us to the conceptual relationship between identity and social movement. In their effort to create a social movement, mostly composed of different groups of indigenous Mayan peasants of the intensely exploited and impoverished state of Chiapas, the Zapatistas, among other things, constructed a Zapatista identity with which Chiapanecan peasants could relate and identify. A Zapatista identity emerged as the signifier of the collectively and historically rooted experiences of injustice and oppression inflicted upon the indigenous *campesinos*. In the praxis of the Zapatista rebellion, this identity came to be embodied by Subcommandante Insurgente Marcos—as "all the minorities who are untolerated, oppressed, resisting, exploding, saying 'Enough'."[24] The Zapatista identity called for justice, freedom, and democracy and the Zapatista discourse—at times poetic, nostalgic, sarcastic, or militant (in the "old fashioned" way)—drew on a number of culturally bound elements that capture the experiences of injustice and oppression. Let us consider in more detail some of the most important of these elements.

The Zapatistas frequently identify their movement as a continuation of not only a tradition of peasant rebellion originated with General Emiliano Zapata in the 1910–1917 period when he led a peasant uprising, but also of the resistances that date back to the European conquest of the Americas five hundred years ago ("We are the product of five hundred years of struggle"[25]). In the roots of the culture of resistance, Zapata represents an immortal founder: "But Zapata is still there, alive and well. Go ahead, try to assassinate him again. Our blood falls as a pledge, let those with some pride left redeem it."[26] He represents as well an omnipresent overseer: "The severe gaze of General Emiliano Zapata will make sure that oppression, under some new name, will not be reborn."[27] In the collective memory of Mexican peasants, Zapata is still a glowing image. He represents the peak within a range of resistances against oppression and subordination of the Mayans. In the Zapatista discourse, Old Antonio, a mythical Mayan *campesino* figure and a close friend of Marcos, now dead, and his dreams, represents the collective experience of the five-hundred-year history of resistance. Old Antonio signifies the wisdom of a deworlded past—a wisdom that has been since the conquest of the New World under constant threat. Crushed, lost, and brutalized, this past nevertheless continues to illuminate the collective memory of Mayans with insights about the present. Standing for the congruent experiences of defeat and resistance, Old Antonio "dreams and . . . doesn't sleep" so that the Zapatistas remind people that in "this country everyone dreams. Now it is time to wake up."[28] He reminds Marcos that Indians simply cannot "give up" because that word does not exist in Mayan languages. If giving up is not spoken, then it cannot be real.[29] The word *resistance*, on the contrary, does exist in their languages. It is "real" and can therefore be articulated.

Resistance is not, and has never been, a chapter to be found in the history books authored by the victor. Therefore, resistance has paradoxically condemned to historical oblivion the existence of those who defy powers that be. Poor Mayan peasants have been repressed, ignored, and abandoned for a long time, so that the history of their resistance could have never found its way into the discourses surrounding power. But as Derrida tells us, "Repression doesn't destroy, it displaces something from one place to another within the system."[30] The Zapatistas have turned their ski masks, which protects Zapatista peasants from being identified and persecuted by the police and paramilitary, into the flag of the historically forgotten and forsaken. Zapatistas are without faces; they are anonymous just as indigenous people have been in the past five hundred years. But ironically, in anonymity they seek recognition, in facelessness, identity. Zapata (rebellion), Old Antonio (resistance), and masks (oblivion): these three major discursive elements, all centred around the (historical) experience(s) of oppression, now sit amidst such contemporary pressing elements as North American Free Trade Agreement (NAFTA) (with its malicious consequences for *campesinos*), military(-supported) suppression, neoliberalism, poverty, the ranch owners' abuses, migration, discrimination, and perhaps most importantly, the 1992 change to the Mexican Constitution that relieves the government from its institutional obligation toward land reform. These elements all dwell within the experience of injustice and oppression. So articulating such experiences in this specific context involves the summoning of all the said elements. As such, it gives the Zapatista identity its content. The Zapatista identity itself is the signifier of a *lack* (as Laclau would say), of what has been stolen from the oppressed Chiapanecans: *freedom, justice, democracy*. But this identity offers a unique possibility due to the specific constellation of the aforementioned elements under the experience(s) of injustice and oppression that give the Zapatista identity its specific content. "Zapatista" is, therefore, the name (identity) of insurgent indigenous peasant's being in late twentieth century Mexico.

Thus, the articulation of the experience(s) of injustice and oppression represents a decision in the context of contemporary Mexican politics. The Zapatista identity, therefore, cannot be perceived as preexisting identificatory practices. Identity/experience emerges in the configurative moment of identification/articulation—the moment of decision. This implies that the "original" modes of presence of the elements in the discursive terrain are of little significance to a current articulation. Zapata, for instance, has in effect been a present element in the Mexican social and political discourse since the beginning of the century. The Zapatistas, however, did not take Zapata as a received symbol. Rather, they rearticulated that element in such a monumental, almost prophetic, way that the entire movement came to be named after him. Rearticulation allows the Zapatistas to reconstitute the experiences Zapata could signify in a different world. But the world of Zapata had just recently passed (i.e., when the 1992 reform of Article 27 of the Mexican Constitution and of the Agrarian Code allowed government to withdraw support from those sectors that it regards as "antimodern"). This "reform" resulted in the government withdrawal of subsidies and intensified the impoverishment of peasants.[31] Thus, the reform eliminated the very part of the Mexican Constitution that crystallized the movement led by Zapata. More interesting is the case with Old Antonio who appears as the trace of the suppressed history of resistance of the indigenous people. Old Antonio's articulation of the past, conveyed to us through Marcos' surrealist, autobiographical narrative, discloses the traces of past experiences one cannot find in the histories of the dominant. Notwithstanding continued far-reaching suppression, resistance has been *repeatedly* attempted and continually practiced by Mayans, and the possibility of re-petition, as Derrida observes, is the constitution of a trace.[32] The collective memory of an experience becomes possible if in experiencing the actor summons the traces (through certain chains of signifiers) within the discourse. The signifiers in that chain might or might not be the "natural habitat" of the experience(s) of actors today. For, the experience may dwell, as it always does, in the metaphoric effect of every signifier (it is sylleptic, as already mentioned). It is in this complex process that the experience of oppression—articulated through the legend of Zapata, the myth of Old Antonio, historical oblivion, injustice, economic despair, and so forth—*destines*. The Zapatista identity (and the identification of Mayan peasants as well as a growing number of Mexicans throughout the country with it) is the movement on the path of destiny. At this moment, the structural undecidability, to use Laclau's term, is overcome by a decision. Showing forth a course of action, the existing discursive elements converge under the insignia of articulated experiences. Experience is not about lament; articulation of experiences never is. It is about the word, the cry that brings destiny, history, hope, dignity. It is about action:

> But *the truth that travelled on the paths of the word* of the oldest of the old of our peoples *was not just of pain and death. In the word* of the oldest of the old *came hope for our history.* And in their word appeared the image of one like us: Emiliano Zapata. *And in it we saw the place toward which our feet should walk* in order to be true, and *our history of struggle returned to our blood,* and *our hands were filled with the cries of our people,* and *dignity returned once again to our mouths,* and *in our eyes we saw a new world.*
>
> *And then we made ourselves soldiers...*[33]

Articulation of experiences always gives a meaningful content to identity whose profundity we can understand only when we inquire about identity beyond the terms imposed upon it by an outside threat. As is the case with virtually all modes of destining, in its regionality and particularity, the EZLN comes to imply that the hope and the social imaginary the EZLN struggle strive for—freedom, democracy, and justice—is and should be everyone's concern. In this sense, the Zapatista identity emerges as the signifier of a lack it intends to fill. It is important to understand the impact of the 1992 change to the Mexican Constitution because the suspension of land reform collapsed the hegemonic social imaginary and "deprived many peasants of their hopes,"[34] thereby giving way to the Zapatista social imaginary. But Zapatista identity must move in the direction opened by the destiny that has emerged through articulated experiences. Rather than signifying a specific mode of existence, the *Zapatista identity has the metonymic character of representing something larger than itself*: freedom, justice, and democracy—in short, "a new world." However, pacing on the path toward a destiny, identity as the signifier of a lack becomes a signified.[35] The salient characteristic of identity lies in that identity is a signified situated within a destinal movement. In the words of the Zapatistas: "We took a one-way path that permits no return, knowing that at the end, death and not triumph probably awaits us. And what would triumph be? Seizing Power? No, something even harder to win: a new world."[36] On the horizon(s) of any destinal path stands a social imaginary. Just as it is the case with experience, social imaginary alludes to modes of acting made possible by the epochal constellation of truth.

I argued earlier that the experience of "abused spouse" came into "existence" only *after* the recognition of individual rights which provided a proper language for the articulation of that experience. The actualization of the experience of being an "abused spouse" attests to the fact that the epoch has unconcealed the possibility of being something other than the "disciplined woman" or the like. Consider also the emergence of the identities "gay" or "lesbian" out of a social discourse surrounding sexuality that in the nineteenth century referred to homosexuality as perversion and thus the subject of clinical treatment. The discourse of sexuality in the past decades blocked a gay's connecting his sexual experiences and desires with an identity. For instance, the severance of a homosexual's identity from his or her experiences in the nineteenth century discourse of sexuality denied the homosexual the possibility of destinal movement by blocking the horizon(s) that the homosexual social imaginary opens before his or her eyes. Until the heterosexual hegemony over the discourse of sexuality slipped into self-exhaustion (which is indeed a long and complex process), the experience(s) of homosexuality could not be articulated in a destinal way. That is to say, the epochal unconcealment which allows for an experience to be discursively articulated also unveils a social imaginary as the horizon of possibility which the actor can identify with in the destinal movement emanating from experience. An epochal unconcealment can be initially defined as the intelligible and practical possibility of an arrangement of phenomena as well as the language, objects, and deeds they prompt, different from the existing one. (I will extensively discuss it in Chapter 6.) For the current discussion, suffice it to specify that the epochal concealment allows the condition of exhaustion of hegemonies. Thus, *although hegemony is the moment of original institution of the social, the epochal unconcealment is the truly originary moment which eventuates the existing hegemonic formations.* In other words, in comparison to the epochal unconcealment, hegemonies (in the strict sense of political institution of the social) of different kinds are only "original"—that is to say, *they are historically bound. Epochal unconcealment, on the contrary, is ahistorical,* and thus, humans are only secondary to it. It is because of epochal unconcealment that we could not have the hegemony of liberal democracy during the medieval times, nor could any medieval person have envisioned a liberal democratic society.

Awareness about the epochal unconcealment along with the aporetic constitution of identity allows us to conceptualize identity not from the "worm's eye" view of the actor, but from the "bird's eye" view of the social imaginary, which is itself "given" by the epochal unconcealment and only thus in companion or conflict with the existing hegemonic terms. A social imaginary refers to a possible, alternative phenomenal configuration that has unconcealed itself to the actor as a possibility. This possibility is born out of the particular modality of destining that articulated experiences have released. The view that takes identity as the actor's positionality in differential social terrains, and therefore limits identity to the category of signifier (of a lack or of an absent fullness, in Laclau and Mouffe, or else, of a certain mode of being always already present in the social, in Touraine) still seeks to constitute the subject of politics. The vantage point of social imaginary, which "sends" identity to the realm of the signified, allows us to think identity in *anti-humanist* terms—that is, in terms of possible phenomenal arrangements (social imaginary) unconcealed in the course of praxis. An elaboration is in order: a phenomenal arrangement emerges. For a while, it dominates the political terrain and constitutes its own subjects proper and then loses its grip, its apparent viability and perceived legitimacy, and finally fades into oblivion. When that happens, it also gradually fades out of life. In relation to unconcealment, therefore, the subject is only secondary. The subject's condition of possibility is nothing but the phenomenal arrangements whose unconcealment we may witness through articulated experiences—arrangements within which the subject is inserted. The subject of politics, therefore, does not primarily rise out of human aspiration. It emerges from the unconcealed phenomenal arrangements captured through hegemonic articulations of experiences. Any effort for the construction of a subject of politics is something extraneous to politics, as a phenomenal "intersection of things, action and speech,"[37] if not imposed upon it. The example of communism as a social imaginary that alludes to certain phenomenal arrangements constituting its own subject of history (the proletariat) clearly exemplifies this crucial point. If communism is conceived as a destinal movement, then articulation of experiences will render the construction of its privileged subject superfluous. If it is not so conceived, then all we have is a violent imposition of a predesigned course of historical action that cannot be carried out without a privileged agent.

From the vantage point of the social imaginary, which makes identification possible and gives the actor's identity its possible content—as its "opposite" pole, experience, gives the actual content—*identity as such is merely the name of a place, a position in the path opened toward the social imaginary*. These places, of course, are not fixed positions. They move along with every act of identification. That is to say, *identity recedes because with every identificatory move of the actor, the social imaginary also recedes in the horizon of possibilities*. Identification, in other words, does not reduce the distance between the actor's current place and his or her perceived place of arrival in the social imaginary. Therefore, receding is a principal characteristic of identity. In the words of Marcos: "We decided one good day to become soldiers so that a day would come when there would be no need for soldiers."[38] The Zapatista identity recedes in the face of the continuation of war, of the deepening and expansion of the struggle, of their achievements and their failures. In the earlier days of the uprising, the receding of the Zapatista identity became manifest when Mexico City demonstrators cried in support of the EZLN: "We are all Zapatistas!" and "We are all Marcos!"[39] Later in 1996, the Zapatista identity receded further as it came to embody a larger demand: the creation of a civil society, via FZLN (*Ferente Zapatista de Liberación Nacional*) whose purpose is the realization of the "original" Zapatista objectives (freedom, democracy, justice) in a nationwide campaign. Ironically, as the Zapatista social imaginary recedes in the expansion of Zapatista objectives, so did their identity.

Thus, what means to be a Zapatista today will not remain the same tomorrow. Identity is never fully realized. The social imaginary the actor identifies with will never be reached. As the identifying actor walks in the path of destiny toward the social imaginary, the latter recedes. But so does the actor's identity. The total realization of the social imaginary, the end of destiny, amounts to the total dissolution of the identity. But dissolution of an identity is at the same time its full constitution. This is a paradox. Total identification between me and what I identify with (my social imaginary) means that, first, I can no longer identify with anything else (full constitution), and second, there is no longer a social imaginary I can identify with (dissolution). As an actor, my full identification means the end of my being and acting. That is why in Marx's theory of the revolution the proletariat— for whom the communist revolution produces the conditions in which the proletariat can achieve the identity-fullness denied to it under capitalism— brings about the conditions of its own dissolution. *Thus, identity is defined as the perpetual presence of a receding signified.* The condition of the receding of the signified is at the same time its consequence: in receding, the signified does not just move back while still retaining its "origins" within itself. While receding, it incorporates "new" contexts, constituents, and complexities into the condition of its possibility. Indeed, the road of identification is built upon precariousness, as it is open to intrusions, inroads, detours, and blockades that are produced by different experiences or contexts and their corresponding imaginaries which crisscross within the field of discursivity. The Zapatistas, for example, began what they predicted to be long (Maoist style) guerrilla warfare against the Mexican state. But that changed within days after their uprising, as various domestic and international activists and nongovernmental organizations (NGOs) brought new contexts and turned the armed uprising into a nationwide movement. Guerrilla warfare became a "war of peace."[40] As a receding signified, identity reveals that its destining experience is not necessarily bound by the elements that exist in the current individual or collective memory. Identity is capable of incorporating other elements (and thereby experiences) that may not have been involved in its "original" destining experiences. The grounding of an identity in a past event, a "past-peril," is ultimately as impossible as is its full realization in the future. Identity is therefore the double-pull between the two dissolving poles of pastness and futurity. Between these two poles stretches the path of action. Now, action turns out to be the only modality of being. Indeed, acting becomes inseparable from being. As such, identity is now perceived as a signified, itself an imaginary whose depiction has been made possible through specific articulated experiences. And it will remain an ever receding signified. Thus, in the nonspace between the destining of experience—the glow on the path—and identification with an imaginary—the beacon in the dark—a movement is born. This movement, as all its contexts and contents are culturally bound, collectively practiced, and more importantly, epochally given, is always already endowed with a *social* character. It is a social movement. *A genuine destinal movement*, which always remains a *nonteleocratic* movement, *is carried out by the actor*, and not by the subject or an agent (I will return to this issue later).

Let us revisit the identificatory statements that I mentioned earlier for one final observation in light of the concept of articulated experiences. In the movement toward such social imaginaries (or as formulated earlier, categories of being) as "gay" or "woman," the category itself recedes, and thus, the actor's journey in a destined path toward the category becomes a never-ending peregrination. The movement renders the being of the "I" (in "I am a *woman*") as already inserted into a field which also includes the categories "gay" or "woman." In fact, the "I" and "gay" or the "I" and "woman" become inseparable, as no relations of priority or posteriority exist between them. Claims to identity ("I am X") indicates that the modality of being that such claims pretend, with gestures of originality, to hypostasize is already inserted into the present world: it is already made possible by epochal unconcealment. Now the actor (the "I") and his or her being ("gay" or "woman") both become parts of the same event of unconcealment. Knowledge of categories of being and of the event of unconcealment can never be attained before the event. Experience, as the summoning of discursive elements, replaces such beforehand, verifiable knowledges. Experience, identity, the summoning of discursive elements, destiny, social imaginary, action, and (categories of) being, all leap forth at one and the same time in one single event. Even thinking about that event is the part of the event that unfolds itself. Unlike the (positivist) first reading of identificatory statements (which posited the ultimacy of the social), here action does not terminate once an entity attains full identity with its categorial being. Now it is in action that I await the ever so deferring arrival of my identity as the truth of my being. *Acting and being become one.*

The Aporia(s) of Identity

Can one speak—and if so, in what sense—of an experience *of the aporia? An* experience *of the aporia as such? Or vice versa: Is an experience possible that would not be an experience of the aporia?*

Jacques Derrida, *Aporias*[41]

To assert that identity is a receding signified prompts a question. Wherefrom does the receding characteristic of identity stem? The answer is, from *the aporetic constitution of identity.* According to Derrida, the concept of *aporia* signifies a nonpassage, a refused or prohibited passage, "the event of a coming or of a future advent . . . which no longer has the form of the movement that consists in passing, traversing, or transiting."[42] In aporia, the context cannot totally determine the meaning. The concept allows Derrida to rethink not only such predicaments as duty, decision, and responsibility, but also and especially, death. As such, he identifies three types of aporia. The first type designates the nonpassage of an uncrossable border. The second type refers to the condition where there is no opposition as such between the two sides of the border—that is, there is no border. The third aporia, finally, signifies the state in which the milieu does not allow the existence of any path.[43] From these three types of aporia, it is the second type of aporia that allows us to rethink identity in a nonessentialist way. Identity has no be-yond—that is, no being proper across the border, in the distance (yonder) that identity may hypostasize. Recall that in Melucci's concepts of latency and visibility, action is set in motion by identity-claims. In other words, one's social position defines one's identity which in turn designates the conflict in which one has to engage in action. This means that action will logically come to an end once an identity-claim has been satisfied, that is, when conflict has been resolved (despite Melucci's insistence that conflict will *not* resolve). The concept of aporia challenges such misconceptions. It allows us to think action without having recourse to a terminal point at which action will stop. If there can be no *be*-yond in which the being of the actor will attain its full presence, then action proves to have no *telos*, no point of arrival or stoppage. In this case, all there is to our being, here and now, is acting. Once we come to terms with our contemporary *insertedness* into a field of action without borders, we all become strangers in an *unhomely* world. We, the identifying actors, become the souls who do not yet, or ever, inhabit.

The concept of aporia leads to a different mode of thinking action. Despite assurances that identity does not preexist action and is itself a social construction that is achieved through everyday life practices, an essentialist, referential notion of identity prevails in "sociological" new social movement theories. For them, the identity of the actor comes as the self-presence of the structure. That is, $A = A$. In spite of viewing identity as pregiven or a process, they all end up trying to substantiate identity by making references to certain social structural points of which identity is a derivative. What the "sociologi-cal" new social movement theories share with the older social movement theories is the idea that *agency* is the actor's highest potential. Agency means the carrying out of a structurally assigned mode of action in the predefined distance between one social locus to another. In fact, without agency, with-out identification with a realizable goal, the word *actor* means little and, in these cases, the term *actor* is only used by these theorists rhetorically. *The concept of receding signified shows that action will never turn into agency.* It is obvious that the aporetic character of identity radically challenges all versions of agency in favor of the *genuine* resuscitation of actor; "genuine" because it is nontelic action itself that now defines actor's being, and not any structurally designated mode of performance. In agency, identity is the ad-equation of the actor's action with the truth of his or her being granted to him or her by a structure of which the agent is assumed to have a predis-posed awareness. Laclau and Mouffe undo this essentialist idea by turning identity ($A = A$) into difference ($A \neq B$, or, in Laclau's formulation, "identity

= difference"). They unveil the essentialist camouflage and sever the link between a presumed metaposition and the regions it colonizes. But what we are left with now is only an outside threat and the possibility of relations of equivalence among discursive, differential identities (i.e., the possibility of hegemony) imposed upon them by the action of the outside. In other words, difference is operative in identification. The uniqueness of each actor (this includes his or her social imaginaries) is reduced to mere difference. With the radical difference governing the field of identity introduced into political theory, all actors are ultimately taken to be "isomorphically heterogeneous" (an oxymoron indeed) within the hegemonic totality of action, for it is only in reaction to an outside threat that different actions with different trajectories can converge. Identity stems from the actor's action in antagonism with the element that threatens the actor from the outside of the system. This means that the notion of agency in Laclau and Mouffe is radically dislocated, not subverted. Through equivalence, the actor becomes the agent of a hegemonic change determined by an antagonistic outside. Agency, therefore, is separated from the representation of being, as Laclau and Mouffe radically subvert the latter (antiessentialism).

Understanding the radicality that the concept of articulated experiences introduces to a theory of social movements shows why agency is no longer a sustainable concept. But the consequences of this assertion need closer attention. Let us turn to this task now.

Experiences That Disrupt Hegemonic Regimes

To the claim, voiced right and left, that we need norms in order to understand, judge and act, a phenomenologist's response has always been and should be: To learn what is to be done, no more is needed than insight into ultimate conditions of what shows itself to ordinary experience.

Schürmann, "Conditions of Evil"[44]

In this chapter, I explored the possibilities that the introduction of a reworked concept of experience inspired by radical phenomenology releases for (re-)thinking action. The radical phenomenological concept of experience puts action in its proper place in theory and enables a concept of identity that defies ultimate referentiality. The new concept of identity/experience also jolts identity out of purely differential terms. As such, the reworked concept of experience elucidates the relationship between identity and social movement as a destinal movement. Now, I must explain the relationship between destiny and hegemony.

By offering an interpretation of Gramsci in the previous chapter, I discussed that beyond being merely a type of institutional organization of the polity, hegemony refers to the moment of ontological institution of the social. A political moment indeed, every hegemony founds the principle(s) to govern, á la Lefort, the regime which shapes, gives meanings, and stages them, thereby regulating the relationship between various spheres of human activity. It is due to the phenomenological awareness of the hegemonic *Urstiftung* that I can problematize any presumed clear-cut distinction between such spheres as politics and society, or the state and civil society. But hegemonies have their life spans. Every hegemonic institution of society alludes at the same time to the moment of a hegemonic destitution. Destitution means the moment of exhaustion of the regime that has been politically shaping the social by implementing the hegemonic principle(s). It also means, as mentioned, that the hegemonic *original* institution is itself subject to a more *originary* moment, that is, the *epochal unconcealment*. In other words, the hegemonic *Urstiftung* which (re-)institutes the society anew and thus (re-)contextualizes the existing social elements, institutions, practices, and hegemonic subjects receives its own possibility and context from the epochal unconcealment. Hegemonic regimes constitute their subjects—the subjects that find the hegemonic principle(s) in accordance with their everyday experiences, expressed through common sense (which I called "experiential hegemonies") and thereby attest to, in the form of consent, the principles governing the current regime. *Therefore, the destitution and institution of hegemonies can only be experienced as disruption.* In fact, the experience of disruption always already is a disruption in hegemonized experiences. The two are indistinguishable. This modality of disruption is indeed Janus-faced: on the one hand, disruption occurs when the horizon depicted hegemonically turns bleak, and on the other, it happens when hegemony fails to emanate possibilities (i.e., when hegemony blocks destinal movements and turns them into fate). In *Waiting for Godot*, we witnessed how, in the apogee of its governing, the regime in which Estragon and Vladimir were inserted did not allow certain experiences to flourish, to become the contents that make identification with a social imaginary in a destinal march possible. They were stranded in the existential void instigated by the total hegemonization of experiences. On the other hand, disruption takes place when new horizons radiantly unveil themselves, emanating new possibilities, animating different destinal movements. For, the moment of destitution of hegemonic regimes is the moment of deliverance from hegemonized experiences. "'Inception' is first of all a matter of experience," states Schürmann.[45] *Inception is the moment and possibility of genuine articulation of experiences,* as experience has not yet been hegemonized by the imminent hegemonic institution, and as the actor, now delivered from the destituted hegemonic subject,

has not yet been hegemonized into the subject of the impending hegemonic regime. Under these conditions, any *genuine articulation of experience becomes transgressive*; and transgressive acting can, indeed does, collapse
hegemonies.

As the moment of *original* institution, we already know, hegemony also
constitutes the *hegemonic subject*, but it fails to do so in a totalistic way. The
hegemonic subject can only be totalized if hegemony is able to send into
complete *oblivion* its own moment of *Urstiftung*. The fact that no hegemony
is ever total, that we constantly witness resistance and defiance in different
regimes, tells us by implication that total oblivion is impossible. Thus, hegemony bears within it an element of precariousness. Consequently, hegemony constitutes its subjects as differentiated, not unitary, subjects. It is the
endless operation of hegemony to bring in the necessary equivalence and
thereby displace differences. The element of consent in hegemony will retain the differences between the subjects but now in a more or less unified
and regulated way. The plurality of liberal democratic subjects attests to this
fact. As such, the subject is precisely hegemonized but not totalized or
dominated. Such "openness" of hegemony, however, also means that all
hegemonies are radically penetrated by the different horizons that destinal
articulation of experiences release (as in the liberal principle of individual
pursuit of happiness). Hence the fact that the horizons unveiled through
articulated experiences could defy totalizing domination. This explains why
the social imaginaries of new social movements are not total. This does not
mean, as David Slater suggests, that the new movements directly politicize
the space in which they are constituted.[46] On the contrary, the spaces in
which these movements emerge are always already politicized ever since the
moment of the hegemonic institution of the social. Until a decade or two
ago, the grip of institutional politics was so powerful that it mostly contained
social movements within institutional channels and practices in Western
societies. Then we were dealing with hegemonies so expansive and totalizing
(but not total) that resistance was in many cases perceivable only through the
subaltern's total(-izing) break away (revolution). Today, we are able to say
that the social imaginaries of the new movements are not total, precisely
because the irreducibly multiple spaces of the political are no longer "successfully" institutionalized by the hegemonic state.

In Gramsci, hegemony qua hegemony ends once the hegemonic subjects become aware of their hegemonization and withdraw consent. In a
successful regime, consent becomes the articulation of hegemonic experiences. As was the case with the Zapatistas, the articulation of experiences
simultaneously rearranges the "past-perils" and intimates a future horizon,
which for the Zapatistas, involved breaking free with the elements of suppression and domination. Under hegemonic regimes, however, the articula-

tion of experiences is inescapably *stamped* by the hegemonic principle(s) and it can neither arrange "past-perils" that were not part of the hegemonic *Urstiftung*, nor can it unveil a future horizon that surpass the perceived hegemonic *Endstiftung*. In other words, articulation of experiences can only take place within the hegemonic ambit. Every hegemony constitutes its own consent-giving subject. Indeed, without this genus of subject the regime will remain irremediably incomplete. Once hegemony, as the epistemic frame of explanation that manifests itself within the world of common sense and everyday experiences, loses its grip over the subject, it becomes possible for the subject to break away from hegemony and his or her subjectivity. At that moment, in all likelihood, hegemony turns into domination, consent gives way to coercion, and the subject is rendered subaltern. In class politics (Gramsci) or what we might call "total politics," which divides society into two (seemingly) irreducible, conflictual poles, the experience of domination is the experience of all subaltern classes. In new social movements, however, the self-detotalization of the movements has complicated the picture. Now, the hegemony of liberal democracy in Western societies can still be maintained while only one sphere of life is conceived as domination. Analyzing this kind of intricate and compartmentalized relationship between hegemony and domination in western liberal democracies requires a complex endeavour which goes beyond the scope of this project. Suffice it here to mention that now hegemony is exercised in many spheres of social life, while a few other spheres of life are affected by the absence of hegemony and are thus seen as domination. Therefore, the subject of liberal democratic hegemony is, by hegemonic instituting, a fragmented subject who experiences recurring moments of subalternity and passes through different hegemonic or dominating spheres on the daily basis.

Consider the example of denying German citizenship to all non-German-born immigrants, especially those of Turkish descent.[47] So long as any hegemonic *Urstiftung* establishes a regime that tends to exert monopoly over *Endstiftung*, certain groups will be condemned to total or partial subalternity. As if the "Turkish" end-horizon, as something supposedly homogeneous and total, will allegedly distort the narrow German destiny put in motion by the hegemonic *Urstiftung* once it is allowed entry into German politics, the German identity of third generation immigrants of Turkish descent is rigorously denied. The identity and doxic experiences of these individuals cannot be negotiated under the sway of the epistemic violence that this notion of German-ness inflicts upon others. Ethnically, the Turks remain subaltern and marginalized. But other than that, they enjoy virtually all other institutionally recognized rights to which German citizens are entitled. This is precisely what I meant by the fragmentation of the subject in modern liberal democracies. Today, the fragmentation of sites of hegemony and domination is what many ideologies cannot see when they claim that, for instance, an environmentalist movement must automatically be against capitalism, consumerism, and the state, and for environmental taxes, progressive social programs and so forth.

My approach to hegemony through a *critique of ultimate referentiality leads to the subversion of the subject*. For, as is always the case, an ultimate referentiality cannot be fully operative without the constitution of the transcendent subject who, by virtue of its very constitution, will attest to and act according to the hegemonic-referential principles. In the case of the "sociological" new social movement theory, failing to observe the subtlety of the issue leads to rendering the actor invisible by veiling him or her under the cloak of the subject, despite their claim about the "return of the actor" (Touraine). The presence of the subject is best evident where "choice of identity" is described as the property of the individual. Any theorist who assumes ultimate referentiality is him- or herself a hegemonically constituted subject. The theorist who pays no critical heed to the operations through which ultimacy becomes hegemonic will never see the ongoing social practices that take place beyond the terms ordained upon them by such a regime.

Now, if hegemony constitutes actors as hegemonized subjects of an epistemic regime, how can the articulation of nonhegemonic experiences be possible? The answer is, through *transgressive* action. An action becomes transgressive initially by problematizing the existing epistemic hegemony and the regime thus founded. By virtue of such a problematization, one has already alluded to the possibility of breaking away with the existing hegemonic regime as well as to the possibility of the emancipation of the actor from the prison house of the subject. The possibility of nonhegemonic articulation of experiences indicates our *tragic insertedness* into the current hegemony of liberal democracy. It is tragic because it tears us apart between its actual hegemonic regime and its possible exhaustion, or, put differently, between the epistemic knowledge that attaches us to other subjects under the current regime and our common hegemonic destiny, on the one hand, and the nonhegemonized doxic knowledges (since hegemony is not total) that define our being and the corresponding transgressive destiny they put forward, on the other hand. Does this very knowledge and ability to critically articulate the governing principle(s) of the hegemonic regime not attest to our tragic existence, to our being riveted into this hegemony while recognizing in the most radical way its limitation and possible destitution in the "raggedness of today's existence"?[48] It does. In fact and most of all, this "tragic sobriety"[49] enables us to articulate the unique condition of our existence as we stand at the verge of a possible, radical shift of epochs and their corresponding hegemonic constellations and shows the primordially unbound character of articulated experiences. *Proximity*, as Schürmann states (in the

epigraph to this chapter), stems from our insertedness into the existing regimes and renders us blind to the mechanisms of acquiring hegemonic
consent. Under the hegemonic institution of society, and thereby with the
constitution of the subject, consent translates into the legitimacy of the existing regime. Hegemony, therefore, conceals an institutive difference between the "being" of hegemony and the entities it constitutes. It veils difference
with coherence. The radical phenomenologist is able to expose the operations of legitimation under the hegemonic regime and its moment of the
ontological constitution of the social through the *epoché* or "stepping back"
from what is. "Stepping back," the radical phenomenologist liberates him- or
herself from the blinding light of proximity. The experience of distance,
granted to us by the phenomenological "stepping back," allows us to experience our former proximity to the epistemic hegemony in a transgressive
way. This is the moment when the articulation of experiences disrupts the
hegemonic regime. It is a moment of disruption and change. The "stepping
back," therefore, enables a radical questioning that disrupts the stable presence of hegemony and allows thinking beyond the existing hegemonic presence and thereby perceiving new horizons.

Our study is an investigation about new social movements in the context of epochally given regimes. The next step, therefore, is to show what is
"new" in the new social movements and how this "newness" has something
important to tell about a possible transition to the post-modern era (which
I will embark on in Chapter 6). This task, however, cannot be adequately
dealt with, unless we first show precisely what principles of the liberal democratic hegemony do the new movements' articulated experiences, by way of
a practical distancing, disrupt.

Technological Liberalism and the Oppressive Categorization of "Transgressive" Actors

Institutionalized violence is visible to all today in the catatonic state that is the gift of generalized production and administration. Measured against these, much of contemporary violence amounts instead to counterviolence. If there is a regression in denouncing thoughtlessness, it is an analytical step backward from oppressions to the economies that make them possible. . . . What need to be analyzed are the principles born of epochs whose economy called for them. Genealogical analysis can show that these principles are not only deadly but also mortal.

Schürmann, *Heidegger on Being and Acting*[1]

The Zapatista discourse, as discussed, articulated experiences ("past-perils") of oppression and injustice which enabled a destinal, social movement toward the social imaginary that alluded to the possibility of freedom and justice. Any social movement goes through this process of formation. But, in the course of their struggles against the perceived sources of oppression, contemporary social movements must at one point or another deal with the state. That is not to suggest that two totally different regional laws (i.e., that of society vis-à-vis that of politics) each govern social movements and the state. Social movements and the state are different spheres within the same hegemonic regime, but they represent different or adverse horizons. The clash of horizons is what makes social movements confront and challenge the state and vice versa. In Western liberal democracies, the confrontations between social movements and the state are mediated through the discourse of rights and the entire institutional apparatus that is based on the corroboration, processing, and regulation of the rights of citizens.

As the first step toward the deconstruction of the concept of rights as an integral part of the hegemonic regimes of liberal democracy, the phenomenological "stepping-back" will allow us to refrain from the centrality of the anthropological notion of unitary subject on which the liberal concept of individual rights hinges. Laclau's and Mouffe's differentiation of three formerly equivalent terms—subordination, oppression, and domination—provides a perfect starting point.

Oppression: " . . . That Dangerous Supplement . . . "

The supplement is maddening because it is neither presence nor absence and because it consequently breaches both our pleasure and our virginity.

Jacques Derrida, *Of Grammatology*[2]

If, as Gramsci suggests, *consent* originally stems from and is a part of the built-in apparatuses operative in hegemony, and not simply from the citizen's "giving" of it as such (i.e., in total freedom, through choice and volition, and aware of the consequences of choice), then what are the mechanisms of the *systemic* construction of consent in liberal democratic regimes? Here, I shall provide an answer to this question by probing Laclau's and Mouffe's formulation of the "democratic revolution," seeking to unravel what their formulation has to offer beyond its authors' intent. The reason for this specific approach is twofold. First, the mere perpetuation of social movements, "old" or "new," primarily exposes and accentuates the problematic areas—problematic in terms of unveiling the unequal distribution of power among different actors—within the social. Second, as a result of the first premise, social movements name and define the unequal social relations that define power in every society. In practice, the *new* social movements name these relations *without assuming a unitary subject or a fully constituted agent*, and this is one of the reasons why these movements are "new." In their theory of the democratic revolution, Laclau and Mouffe show the relationship between power, antagonism, and democratic struggles. The differentiation between the three aforementioned terms provides a point of departure for the exploration of how oppression is operative in liberal regimes.

One of contributions of Laclau and Mouffe to contemporary social and political thought is to show that far from unitary, the subject occupies a plurality of subject positions that have no *necessary* relationship with one another. In other words, the subject is penetrated by a multiplicity of relations of subordination, possibly being dominant in some and subordinate in others. Thus, as Mouffe writes, the identity of the "subject is . . . always contingent and precarious, temporarily fixed at the intersection of those subject positions and dependent on specific forms of identification."[3] It is through articulation and antagonism at the intersection of subject positions that the identity of the subject is fixed in an "us-them" relationship between the subject and an adversary. But Laclau and Mouffe assert that the possibility of articulation, and thereby antagonism, rests on the availability and existence of the discourse of rights—a course of political development that they call the "democratic revolution." They borrow the term from Lefort who uses it to designate a situation in which "there is no power linked to a body. Power appears as an empty place. . . . There is no law that can be fixed, whose articles cannot be contested, whose foundations are not susceptible of being called into question. Lastly, there is no representation of a centre and of the contours of society: unity cannot now efface social division."[4]

In order to show the relationship between antagonism and the democratic revolution, Laclau and Mouffe differentiate between three formerly synonymous terms: relations of subordination, relations of oppression, and relations of domination. They identify the reason for the synonymity between the three terms to rest in "the anthropological assumption of a 'human nature' and of a unified subject: if we can determine a priori the essence of a subject, every relation of subordination which denies it automatically becomes a relation of oppression. But if we reject this essentialist perspective, we need to differentiate 'subordination' from 'oppression' and explain the precise conditions in which subordination become oppressive."[5] A "relation of subordination," in which an actor is subjected to the decisions made by another actor, is not antagonistic. It is merely a differential relation between the two. Since differentiality takes away from such a relation the positivity of the identity of actors, a relation of subordination does not automatically translate into antagonism. A "relation of oppression," by contrast, designates a relation of subordination that is transformed into a site of antagonism. With the expulsion of essentialist postulates, the challenge is to show how relations of oppression emerge out relations of subordination—that is, how antagonism emerges out of unequal social relations. According to Laclau and Mouffe, the existence of the democratic discourse makes the articulation of forms of resistance possible. This acknowledgement emphasizes the significance of a third category of relations, the "relation of domination." It designates those relations of subordination that are considered to be oppressive, unjust, or illegitimate from the perspective of a third (observing) subject. The third subject's perspective might or might not coincide with the opinions of those differentially involved in the relations of subordination. There is "no relation of oppression without the presence of a discursive 'exterior' from which the discourse of subordination can be interrupted. The logic of equivalence in this sense displaces the effects of some discourses towards others," write Laclau and Mouffe. "[I]t is only from the moment when the democratic discourse becomes available to articulate the different forms of resistance to subordination that conditions will exist to make possible the struggle against different types of inequality."[6]

This sophisticated observation of the democratic revolution and antagonism enables Laclau and Mouffe to not only offer a novel approach to contemporary politics, but also present new counterhegemonic strategies to activists. Nonetheless, the unproblematized presence of the third agent (relations of domination)—indeed, a theoretical incarnation of Laclau and Mouffe—renders them heedless of the significant theoretical discovery that the transformation of a subordinating relation into a site of antagonism discloses. By "stepping-back" from their focus on the third subject—this enlightened articulator of the democratic discourse—we gain new insights into the hegemonic processes of perpetuating the discourse of rights which eventually hides the *systemic* sources of oppression in the liberal democratic regimes.

If we abstain from and "bracket" the external subject, we will see that these three terms are not on par designations of three states of affairs between opposing subjects. The very term "relations of subordination" implies the speaking of a third subject. Because in the absence of the pregiven designation (made possible by the democratic discourse) of a relation as subordinating, that is, in the absence of a pregiven category that identifies a certain relation as subordinating, it is impossible for a subject to deem his or her present relations as subordinating. The reason for this impossibility is illuminating: the "matter-of-factness," to adopt a Husserlian term, of a relation of subordination renders it a part of the pregivenness of the subordinate subject's everyday life experiences. Since the subject is already inserted in a subordinating relation, since the subject inherits that relation, so to speak, as a pregiven part of his or her existence, he or she *cannot* critically reflect upon it. Subordination is a part of hegemonized experience of his or her life. Recall the example of "abused spouse." For the typical eighteenth century peasant woman (in many cultures) being battered was a part of women's life, despite the fact that it was totally resented. The notion of individual rights (and the language proper) that renounces certain behaviors as contrary to individual autonomy did not exist then to give women awareness about their subordination. My discussion about the relationship between articulation of experience and epochal unconcealment shows that *without the preexisting possibility of articulating a relation as subordinating, it cannot be thus perceived.* The actor's articulation always proceeds from the epochal articulation (unconcealment). So, whenever we designate a relation as subordinating, we imply that we have already been granted the possibility of such designation. In Laclau and Mouffe, the third subject (relations of domination) embodies this possibility in its self-actualization.

The conclusion seems inevitable: the very act of articulation of relations of subordination always means a *surpassing of it by the speaker*. One cannot know that one is subject to a relation of subordination, unless one has already transformed it into a relation of oppression (a site of antagonism). In other words, one cannot know that one is subject to a relation of subordination, unless one has already surmounted such relation—unless the experience of subordination has summoned certain elements into a destinal identification that moves toward a social imaginary (a receding signified) in the horizon of possibilities that disrupts the hegemonic subordinating relations. The condition of possibility of the transformation of a relation of subordination into that of oppression *by* the social actor, then, is the *experience of subordination* not as a presumed "natural" condition of the actor's life, but as one that is clearly imposed upon the actor by an adversary and is thus perceived and articulated. Two consequences follow: first, from a deconstructive point of view, a relation of subordination cannot exist prior to the advent of its specific relation of oppression, or in plain language, inequality cannot precede conflict, unless we either subscribe to an "objective" vantage point that is above and prior to this transformation, or resort, as do Laclau and Mouffe in a historical-pragmatic spirit, to a third subject who, from his or her "higher" standpoint, evaluates such relations. Secondly and with emphasis, if we disavow both of these positions, *the concept of relations of oppression turns out to function as a supplement*—in the Derridean sense of the term—of that of relations of subordination. As a supplement, the relation of oppression, the site of antagonism, first, *adds* itself to the relation of subordination, and second, is always *exterior* to it in the sense of "outside of the positivity to which it is super-added."[7] As the supplement, it is in fact antagonism, or the possibility thereof, that renders a relation of subordination perceivable as subordination.

Before exploring what the logic of supplement says about the relationship between oppression/antagonism and rights, let us place the argument in the theoretical framework of Laclau and Mouffe: they rightly acknowledge that in order for a relation of subordination to become a site of antagonism there must exist a discourse of rights. In other words, without the discursive possibility of articulation, the proper language, of the articulation of experiences of a certain relation as oppressive, it cannot be so conceived. The discourse of rights is the condition of possibility of the "chain of equivalence" that entails the potential to bring about the hegemony of the new movements vis-à-vis an enemy. The discursive possibility of articulation of oppression qua oppression is indeed the condition of possibility of *experiencing oppression as such.* This approach presents the anti-humanism that should inform every genuine post-structuralist theory (though, I think, it is not fully developed by Laclau and Mouffe and has, consequently, given way to a certain kind of pragmatism). Given the pregivenness of the democratic discourse, Laclau and Mouffe hope that through the articulation of the third subject (in the relation of domination) the democratic discourse will expand and encompass the rights of ever more marginal groups. They theoretically depend on the expansion of rights to warrant their chain of equivalence that is the precondition for the hegemony of subordinate groups. To address the problem "how relations of oppression are constituted out of relations of subordination," Laclau and Mouffe argue that the "logic of equivalence . . . displaces the effects of some discourses towards others."[8] In other words, an existing antagonism (i.e., an existing movement, and they exemplify feminism) can kindle antagonism in an existing relation of subordination. For, a subordinate subject can become aware of his or her subordination by way of analogizing his or her position with that of the actors who have already turned their own relations of subordination into a site of antagonism as manifested by an existing social movement. An existing right, which aims at rectifying a relation of subordination, introduces the possibility of its expansion onto other, existing such relations.

Since we have already established the threefold operations of constitution of regimes, we can clearly see that *for the construction of hegemony based on a chain of equivalences the democratic discourse is central and necessary.* The discourse of rights that dwells at the core of the democratic discourse allows a relation of subordination to transform into a relation of oppression. The recognition of a right, therefore, always intimates the termination of a source of subordination. Now, if we approach this problem in a Derridean way and look at oppression as the supplement of the recognition of rights—a recognition that is made possible by the discourse of rights— then we come to the conclusion that a right cannot overcome oppression: it can only displace it. For, now oppression as a supplement is an exterior that adds itself to rights (and to the forms of subordination addressed through the recognition of rights). In *Of Grammatology*, Derrida collapses the metaphysical binary that holds speech to be central to writing which is a supplement (Rousseau's postulate). Speech, Derrida argues, is only a grandiose pretence and it cannot exist as such without reference to writing. Writing is indeed "that dangerous supplement" which dislocates speech. By analogy, it is the discourse of rights which displaces oppression. Let me enumerate the radical implications of such a dislocation: (1) the discourse of rights has an undeniable *presence* in the liberal democratic regime. A right is a regulatory and rectifying termination of subordination. As such, it is a regulation that aims at conflict resolution. The supplementarity of antagonism and oppression appears "as destruction of presence and as disease of"[9] the hegemonic notion of rights. Therefore, (2) the discourse of rights produces "what it forbids, [and it] makes possible the very thing that it makes impossible"[10]—that is, oppression. However, (3) the presumed presence of the discourse of rights, which renders it the highest expression of liberal democracy, maintains its hegemony by making the hegemonic subject blind to the antagonism and oppression it conceals under the name of the rectification of a subordinating relation. Being blind to the supplement, Derrida teaches us, erases the trace of supplement to create the illusion of an originary. We are, therefore, hegemonically brought up to believe that it is the discourse of rights, as the "originary," that founds the liberal regime, and not its supplement, oppression (and thus antagonism). Thus, (4) as the supplement, oppression and antagonism are rendered (only) the "subaltern" implication.[11] Therefore, the logic of supplement allows us to rethink the liberal hegemonic discourse of rights and to unveil its two fundamental characteristics. The first characteristic is that oppression is inseparable from the rights and that the rights are not primary in relation to oppression. The second characteristic is that both rights and oppression are bound by the laws of what I call *"systemic oppression."*

Understanding oppression and antagonism as supplement, therefore, will place relations of domination and relations of subordination in the same class of concepts, designating the same relation from two different angles. Since the democratic discourse confers upon the third subject the privileged position of an epistemic knower, it renders the relations of subordination "subordinate" to the articulator of the democratic discourse. The articulator of the democratic discourse (the subject in the relation of domination) is granted the privileged place of suggesting certain relations as subordinating. As the supplement of rights, oppression shows us that beneath the *affirmative* character of the discourse of rights there lies the everlasting impulse of the *denial* that relations of oppression and antagonism perpetually bear. The third subject in a relation of domination (the articulator of rights) presents to us the relation of subordination as a universally knowable relation that has presence regardless of our opinion about it. The third subject derives this potentially universal knowledge from the universality of the discourse of rights, from the fact that rights are universally applicable. The concept of rights has, by definition, a universalizing tendency; but so do inequality and subordination. We must have pregiven models of inequality if we are to make judgments about certain relations. The democratic discourse provides such models, thereby enabling us to *affirm* a relation of subordination as unjust, oppressive, or illegitimate. But, if oppression is understood as the force that enlivens relations of subordination, the latter's lack, which is indeed the void intrinsic to the democratic discourse, is revealed. Therefore, no relation of subordination—in fact, no discourse of justice, equality, or democracy—can be conceived independent of a hegemonic regime.

Furthermore, the logic of supplement allows us to view the discourse of rights, as the essence of the democratic discourse, in a different light—that is, in relation to the original institution of modern liberal democratic regimes. As Lefort observes in a different context, "Discourse is indeed instituting: it governs the possibility of an articulation of the social."[12] Under the hegemonic liberal regimes, the discourse of rights defines our beings as modern *homo politicus*. The origins of any relation of subordination can be traced back to the moment of hegemonic *Urstiftung* of the social. *Urstiftung* is always political, but it does not merely found a political "entity." More importantly, *Urstiftung* has a presence that unravels its potential and its movement toward its *Endstiftung*. The fact that the formation of each particular relation of subordination cannot be determined once and for all and is dependent upon the discourse of rights indicates that primal institution of the political has its own logics. These logics come into play independent of our rational calculations—despite the interventions carried out by social and political institutions, even to a great extent, notwithstanding the perceived course of disclosure of these logics. *Once understood as the supplement of subordination and rights, oppression and antagonism can be perceived as a part of the original establishment of the Western regime of liberal democracy.* Indeed, oppression discloses all pretence to presence not only in relations of subordination, but also in relations of domination.

The radical character of oppression is properly understood if we view its position vis-à-vis the third, external subject in relations of domination. *The democratic discourse, which the external actor articulates, is itself a part of hegemonic constitution of liberal democracy. As such, the democratic discourse becomes a normative model for the liberal political life*—what Schürmann called an *arché*, a beginning "that starts and dominates a movement."[13] Just how and through what presuppositions (human nature, free will, choice, etc.) the discourse of rights came to dominate the western political constellations requires an independent and extensive historico-conceptual analysis of the works of Hobbes, Locke, Rousseau, Mill, and many other political philosophers. However, we can make this observation: the *arché* whose first, most concise expression emerged in the French Revolution dictum of *liberté, égalité, fraternité* (1789), later found its principles refined in Thomas Paine's *Rights of Man* (1791), and was subsequently critically engaged with in Mary Wollstonecraft's Critique of Rousseau in A *Vindication of the Rights of Woman* (1792). These precedents and documents were in fact the *ontic substitutes for the ontological*: they were responses to regional, particular conditions, voiced and formulated at specific stages of social development. Although they should not cloud other works through which the *arché* of modern democracy established its principles, these landmarks show how this *arché* has been dominating, in various ways, the democratic discourse to this day. "The *arché* as commanding is the *arché* as commencing, but *perverted into a referent*."[14] The notion that an individual is entitled to certain rights manifested the modality of epochal unconcealment and established a point of ultimacy that has been setting up and justifying all democratic practices in the West for two centuries. Virtually every practice, planning, and process is nowadays measured against the ultimacy of rights. So the democratic principles gradually transcended their regionality and historical specificity, became universal and grew into the normative principles that inform the democratic discourse in the West.

Thus, understanding the true place of oppression in the democratic discourse allows us to rethink modern liberal democracies. The democratic discourse, whose gist is the discourse of rights, has its presence in the assumed absence of oppression within its regime. It allows the democratic discourse to justify its perpetual authority as something "necessary" and "natural." Thus, under the hegemonic democratic discourse, oppression, as a supplement, "has no sense and is given to no intuition."[15] The hegemonic grip of modernity has rendered the democratic discourse to erase the traces of oppression and create the illusion of an inevitable presence. Historically, we have been constituted as the subjects of the modern liberal regimes and were influenced through the modern democratic discourse to see the concealing, the democratic concept of right, not what it conceals—that is, oppression. As such, despite our criticisms, we gave our allegiances to the democratic discourse. We became the *agents* who would carry forward, to its historical fulfillment, the democratic discourse.

The hegemony of the discourse of rights over us is immense and pervasive. The concept of relations of subordination, it seems, represents our subconscious attempt at compensating for the haunting nightmares about our recurring intellectual neglect in discerning how precisely modes of subordination and oppression emerge in society. After all, as articulated and propagated by the democratic subject in the relation of domination, *the democratic discourse manifests our conditions of being under the sway of modernity, and as we will see, bears an imposed modality of being and acting.* Neglecting this arch characteristic has grave consequences: once the democratic discourse is treated as the condition through which subordination can be overcome, those actors who identify with the democratic discourse as such and look into it to end their conditions of subordination are automatically transformed into the articulating agents of the liberal regimes. That is why the theory of hegemony of Laclau and Mouffe has no other way but to return to a politics of agency, except now there is no over-arching movement, no unitary, universal, historically endowed agent of change, nor any promised future to arrive at. There remains a pragmatic hegemonic formation when various agents congregate against an enemy.[16] But there is still the historical fulfillment of the democratic discourse that defines agency. Antagonism, as constitutive of the social, and the democratic discourse are now the only categories that pragmatically govern social action. The way out of this unwanted assignment, as we shall see soon, is to view the democratic discourse not as a given or a condition, but as a possibility.

What is the upshot of this radical phenomenological "stepping back" for the study of social movements? With the discourse of rights hegemonized, *modern liberal regimes provide a horizon for conflict resolution in society.* But through emphasis on rights, this mode of unconcealment veils the systemic oppression that inevitably supplements rights. Overcoming one mode of oppression, the *relational* one through the discourse of rights leads to an invisible but certainly no less dangerous mode of oppression: *the systemic oppression.* The logic of supplement shows us that *the centrality of the concept of individual and human rights is a hegemonic-epistemic idea.* The discourse of rights hides "that dangerous supplement" (oppression), thereby making proud gestures of centrality in the democratic discourse. Awareness about oppression as the supplement of rights should now subject the discourse of rights to a radical phenomenological investigation whose ramifications for political theory are nothing short of "maddening" (Derrida). This awareness grants the subjects of modernity an opportunity to articulate their experiences of oppression, setting into play the destinal movements that have become possible at the end of modernity. It is in breaking away with hegemonic inculcations that spring forth in a momentary emitting out of the democratic camouflage that experiences of oppression and the possibility of articulating them set in motion a destinal (social) movement toward a social imaginary. It turns out as one of the ironies of our lives that the peace and certainty of knowing and comprehending where we really stand in our time becomes possible only through the "maddening" experience of possible horizons, of possible thoughts and actions.

It is also ironic that systemic oppression emerges when relational oppression is supposedly terminated. It is true that the liberal discourse of rights intends to terminate or correct the relational modes of oppression, but in so doing, it conceals a systemic (i.e., a reductive and categorial), oppression that is part of the liberal regime's exercise of granting and protecting rights. As such, systemic oppression is not an essential part of the liberal discourse of rights; it is rather an inseparable (systemic) part of the regime founded upon this discourse. Let me emphasize that *while relational oppression and rights are binary concepts, systemic oppression and rights are not.* Disclosing systemic oppression is indeed a demanding task. For, the discourse of rights persistently displaces and conceals its supplement (oppression). An engagement with the regime that is in the air we breathe, radically subversive as it is, will require another "stepping back"—one that will eventually enable us to think in terms other than agency and to move beyond the democratic discourse and the discourse of rights. A radical phenomenology of the concept of rights in the liberal democratic regimes and its place in the sway of technological rationality will then be in order.

Tracing Oppression: The Supplement of the Liberal Concept of Rights

The double bind consists in the state's charge to unify its members into a whole while organizing their every dimension of private existence. Under these conditions—that is, if the organizational-totalitarian bind accompanies necessarily the liberal-atomistic bind—self-constitution cannot mean enhanced individualism.

Schürmann, "On Constituting Oneself an Anarchistic Subject"[17]

"Stepping-back" from the discourse of rights that emerged at the dawn of political modernity enables us to challenge our forgetfulness about the original institution of modern liberal democracy. It is through the subversive reminiscence of the modern political *Urstiftung*, as well as the principles and laws it founded, that today we can gain insight from exploring the possible connection between the emergence of new social movements and our present era of heightened discussions about modernity's end.

Despite its depletion into tyranny and coup d'état, the French Revolution set the *arché* (i.e., the marked beginning) of modern liberal democratic regimes. The discourse of rights is meaningful in connection to the liberal "principle of intelligibility,"[18] or *principium* which holds the principle of individuality to be inseparable from the concept of rights. Together, the democratic movement of rights and the principle of individuality have grown into systems of representative democracy, which in turn generated the *princeps* (i.e., the authority), via representative democracy, to command the society. Together, *arché, principium and princeps* construct a hegemonic movement towards perceived ends. As Schürmann observes in the epochal context, "The origin is the absolute opposed to all contingents. To be sure, from *arché* as the anticipation of *telos* to 'principle' as the anticipation of 'terminus', the form of thought remains the same."[19] This *telos*, this terminus whose arrival our society is to ensure, is nothing but the age-old telic principle of Happiness.[20] The *beginning*, the *principle*, and the *authority* have all been a part of the *original institution* of the modern society that has today

developed into the Western-type liberal democracies. The regime so constituted produces, in a variety of ways, the conditions for its own stable operations, such that the beginning, principle, and authority become part of one
"sedimented," forgotten package. The "reactivation" of the origins of the
democratic discourse enables us to rethink modern democracies *not* as a
unified, meaningful whole in which our activities and experiences as citizens
are almost always meaningful. Rather, such reactivation reminds us of the
fact that since the time when modern nation-state came to incorporate liberal democracy, the latter has been penetrated by a *systemic* paradox: modern liberal regimes agonally hold together the principle of governance and
the principle of (individual, expanded to the group) freedom.[21] The concept
of rights is best understood in this relation. A right, negative or affirmative,
guarantees the sovereign individual a space of activity free from state intervention or regulation. Liberal democracy posits as its defining characteristic
the centrality of the individual as the subject of rights. This is what has in
the past, as in the present, made liberal democracy a powerful source of
inspiration for people all over the world, as they are increasingly integrated
into the global interconnectedness of world societies and as they perceive the
threats of, or experience life under, totalitarian, authoritarian, or fundamen-
talist regimes.

In liberal democratic regimes, we witness a specific *phenomenal arrangement* within which the citizen, this subject and agent of democratic
principles, is *inserted*. The *arché*, *principium*, and *princeps* bring into being
a certain arrangement—indeed, an "economy of presence"—of the political.
The term *economy* in the sense of the Greek word *nomos*, "injunction,"
refers to the laws that govern a certain milieu (*eco-*). According to Schürmann,
each *ontic economy* is itself epochally given through unconcealment and is
therefore never primarily the product of human planning as such. Within
each economy of presence, *political regimes can be identified according to
the specific array of three constituents: words (language), things, and actions.*[22]
Politics is, then, "to join words and things in action."[23] As such, "when words,
actions, and things conjugate in an always provisionary network, an economy
of presence comes about."[24] Under the sway of the modern nation-state, the
paradox of democracy—that is to say, of governing and exerting its principles, on the one hand, and allowing freedom from such principles, on the
other—is translated into the distinction between the state and civil society.
Celebrated so enthusiastically by the thinkers and defenders of liberalism,
this distinction, however, conceals the political character of civil society. The
private, the civil society, is widely deemed as the realm of freedom from the
state intervention—that is, a realm free from "politics." This view sends to
oblivion the (ontic) *Urstiftung* of liberal democratic regimes and as such
conceals the political and politicizing moment that has given rise to the

Western democratic tradition. In the wake of discussions that commenced with Thomas Hobbes' *Leviathan*, this oblivion necessitated a binary between a universal (ontological), regulatory body, on the one hand, and what remains outside it, the sphere of not(-yet) regulated, on the other. Civil society is the realm of the sovereign individual so long as this sovereignty is exercised within the ambit of the sovereign, regulatory state. The state, which represents the political and thereby pertains to the public, paradoxically, is the guardian of the private sphere, of civil society, from which state itself is assumed to be excluded. Under the modern polity, only through the assured and enduring presence of the state (or its equivalent) can one have a totalizing (i.e., pertaining to all citizens) social imaginary (it is "total" by virtue of being the state, as Gramsci would say). As such, paradoxically, *the regulatory body of the state comes to represent freedom* and poses "freedom" as its totalizing social imaginary. The moment in which an individual identifies with this social imaginary is the moment of construction of the liberal hegemonic *subject*. As discussed, however, every social imaginary involves a movement. The state, therefore, ensures that the subjects of modern democratic regimes recognize the liberal democratic principles and take on the role of the *agents* that will take these principles to their point of consummation. Under liberal democratic regimes, the subjects are to identify with the discourse of rights and the agents are to perpetuate this discourse in the manner it is given by the regime. Awareness of rights, which constitutes the subject of liberal regimes, is the precondition which enables the state to appropriate its citizens into a specific genus of agency through representative channels and via negative or affirmative laws.

The implications of this line of argument are far-reaching for a social movement theory. Like many of his colleagues, Offe argues that new social movements "politicize themes which cannot easily be 'coded' within the binary code of the universe of social action that underlies liberal political theory."[25] Since the issues and themes that arise out of these movements belong to an "intermediate category," the new movements act in the space of "noninstitutional politics." Offe's observation about the locus of the new movements' action is, of course, quite correct if we presuppose the private-public binary. However, he does not see how new social movements go beyond any notion of the political based on delineated spheres of activity. In fact, by collapsing the public-private binary, the new movements undermine the very political-phenomenal arrangements out of which they emerge. As such, new social movements redefine politics by moving beyond the current political economy of liberal regimes based on institutional politics. Offe's observation tends to retain the binary as given and does not make any viable effort to radicalize it, let alone subvert it. His theory subjects new social movements' practices to the hegemonic conceptual framework of liberal regimes. The "reactivation" of the liberal original institution can unveil such internalized and operative assumptions. This is especially true with respect to the democratic discourse that is so central to the maintaining of the liberal paradox: that it has no other way but to constitute the citizens of the liberal democratic regime as the agents of the democratic discourse, or else, the liberal binary will inevitably fall apart. Put bluntly, the democratic discourse is ultimately unable to grant freedom to the free actors called citizens. By moving away from the *principial* private-public binary (as in the feminist slogan: "the personal is political"), the "identity politics" of new social movements rejects the hegemonic notion of the citizen. So long as the citizen is the agent of the democratic discourse, and as such, participates in the perpetuation of the institutional concept of rights, *systemic oppression*, which entails both rights and its supplement, relational oppression (antagonism), goes unveiled.

But what exactly does the term "systemic oppression" designate? Oppression comes the Medieval Latin *oppressare*, frequentative (i.e., expressive of frequent repetition) of *opprimere*, meaning "press against," "push down," "overwhelm." The English word "oppression," borrowed from Old French *oppresser*, consists of the prefix "*op-*," meaning, in Latin, "near," and the participle "*press*," which as a verb means "to squeeze," "to push," "to constrain." The transitive verb, to "oppress," then, means to "squeeze-near" or "press-near" (something or to each other). In our context, it would imply to push something near the center. Under the liberal, democratic regimes, the recognition and institutionalization of every right inescapably amounts to an act of "pressing-near." It amounts to oppression because every recognition of rights "presses-near" actors in a certain category of subjects called the citizen, the subjects that, having been inserted into this regime, must take on the role of the agents of the regime in order to guarantee the perpetuation of the democratic rights of the citizens. *This "pressing-near" is what I call systemic oppression.* The discourse of rights, in other words, can only recognize the rights of those actors it can, first, detach from their contexts of praxis, and second, "press-near" into categories and render the rights-bearing subjects. The discourse of rights is only meaningful within such oppressive institutional practice: a practice that displaces the actors from their worlds and inserts them into narrow, reductive categories in order to render them the subjects entitled to certain rights.

By defying or expanding the notion of the citizen, new social movements represent struggles for the opening of *new* political spaces. In the liberal democratic tradition, these political openings are to be ensured (and contained) through the recognition of rights of groups and communities not only to carry out certain practices in the civil society, but also to ensure the treatment they wish to receive from the state and its institutions through certain rights. In contemporary liberal democracies, every "successful" opening of the political space, therefore, will inevitably have to be regulated. Originally stemming from the "private" sphere, a social practice has to be "pressed-near" by the institutional concept and practice of right(s) in the political sphere (in the strict sense of the term). The strength of the liberal democratic system rests in its flexibility in opening new spaces which require new regulatory practices. Regulation enables the discourse of rights to conceal its "oppressive" operation with every recognition or expansion of rights. Regulation also allows the liberal democratic discourse to perpetuate the illusion that the private, the civil society, is independent of and thus not constituted by the political whose existing institutional configuration is the state.

Existentially, the systemic "pressing-near" of actors into institutional categories takes away the contexts of emergence of their struggle for recognition. But action is not meaningful without reference to such contexts. The truth is that the citizens of contemporary democracies have their constitution as the subjects and agents of the democratic principles in the original establishment of the democratic discourse. If these subjects were fully constituted subjects, we would not have reached the point of discussing them, for they would have foreclosed the possibility of emergence of (non- or antihegemonic) actors. But that is never the case because *the final establishment, the telos, is never definitively "final."* Radical phenomenology allows us to revisit the perceived entelechy that animated Husserl's concepts of *Urstiftung* and *Endstiftung* and arrive at the idea that *Endstiftung* is not unitary; rather it multiplies. As such, theoretically speaking, the original establishment of a regime loses its normative sway and its "naturalistic" pretence, despite its omnipotent, hegemonic gestures. Since the final establishment of the democratic discourse is not unitary, we witness, as the democratic discourse continues, a multiplication of the subject. The extent of this multiplication is not without limits. One great limit in this context is the subject's allegiance to the democratic principles. The extent of identification with the principles of democracy has always been the criterion of the polity for its distinction between "legitimate" struggles, on the one hand, and subversive ones, on the other. However, these limits are not completely dominating, and this explains why the multiplication of the subject beyond a unitary notion of the citizen gives way to actors who question the very principles of the hegemonic regime in which and against which they emerge.

Struggles for the recognition of a right always manifest the actors' resistances against the perceived injustice in the existing phenomenal arrangements within a regime. As such, every struggle for the recognition of a right is inseparable from certain phenomenal contexts and from the contents that the articulation of experiences of injustice signifies. Modern democracy allows, indeed channels, resistances in the regulated form of political agendas and demands. In order to be "heard" by the regime, then, the demand must be spoken in the language of the regime. Therefore, demands and struggles have to leave their contexts and alter their contents so that they could be "heard" by the existing political institutions. Thus, the demand is decontextualized in order to be appropriated by the democratic institutions. Systemic oppression occurs when the particular existential knowledges and modes of being and self-understanding (of a group of actors), manifested through demands and resistances, are "pressed-near" a certain universalistic and epistemic body of knowledge and its specific language called rights. The experiences of injustice that are articulated in the form of resistance and demand, essentially belong to unique and specific existential realms. That is why a subordinate group's self-knowledge is so unique and indispensable to its survival. *The discourse of rights binds these realms of experience (contexts and contents) by its parochial terms, reducing them to the only language it knows: that of categories of rights.* A right, therefore, signifies the "pressing-near" of those experiences that fall outside the language of rights. Via systemic oppression (as "pressing-near"), the discourse of rights privileges and imposes its own institutional world over the irreducibly proliferated worlds of actors. Systemic oppression tries to block the glow of those social imaginaries that are alien to the social imaginary of the liberal democratic regime. This makes clear why the master discourse of rights should have the citizens as its subjects and its agents. As the subjects, the citizens must not only "give" consent to the hegemony of this master discourse (and become subjects), they must, as agents, participate in the expansionist tendencies of this master discourse into all "private" worlds which still retain the transgressive elements that the present stage of political development has not yet regulated.

Systemic oppression reveals itself to the "abstaining" phenomenologist as a *trace* each and every time a right is recognized and upheld by liberal institutions. Despite liberal gestures and despite the undeniable existence of available avenues that make challenging liberal institutions possible from within, systemic oppression is operative in current liberal democracies. The discourse of rights, however, discloses itself as the end to (relational) oppression and antagonism, indeed as contrary to the subordination of one subject by another. Under the reign of the discourse of rights, systemic oppression can only be perceived as a trace, as *différance*: something of nonorigin, with no "*immediate* relationship with the divine logos"[26] of rights, a trace whose traces are constantly erased. As the trace of a supplement, systemic oppression disturbs the right's pretence of originality, centrality, and thereby, legitimacy. Therefore, awareness about systemic oppression demystifies the operations of the liberal democratic regimes and illustrates the fact that *the recognition of rights cannot escape its original decenteredness.*

Let us consider the example of the "single mother." Every informed citizen today knows that as a result of women's struggles, Western states have expanded their welfare programs to especially accommodate "single mothers." The hegemonic recognition of women's right to be the prime caregiver of children has resulted in the constitution of a new subject of the state protection called the "single mother." The category "single mother" "presses-near" a variety of experiences of parenting alone by different women in different situations and from different backgrounds. But once the category is implemented and the right of a lone female parent to be a "single mother" recognized, she faces inevitable loss of life opportunities as the never-ending task of childcare for a good number of years falls upon her shoulders. As such, she becomes subjected to certain institutionalized inequalities for a prolonged period. An enormous number of "single mothers" from heterogeneous backgrounds and situations are reductively homogenized, and thus "pressed-near" in this category of state protection. Thus, the doxic knowledges of these women about their needs and their hopes are violently discarded by the epistemic exercise of the necessities and rights of a "single mother" as defined by the state. The state has in its *arché* the discourse of rights and the principle of equality of opportunity both based on the principle of individualism. Now, as a subject of the state support and protection, she is transferred to the constitution of a new subject with certain rights: the "welfare mom." As one analyst observes, "When the normative applications of the notion of equality cannot be met, state intervention into women's lives is legitimated under the name of help and protection, and welfare policies are presented as bridging the gap among the states of unequal conditions. Under this hegemonic egalitarian ideology, the kind of equality that is offered by the state to women means the institutionalization of a state of inequality while espousing the objective of reaching a point of 'minimal equality'."[27] What is ironic is that the "welfare mom" is as much a product of the hegemonic state as it is the product of the women's liberation movements. This example allows us to observe that the right does not end subordination, nor does it terminate oppression and antagonism. Rather, the right *transpositions* oppression. The right is meant to regulate and administer conflict resolution. It takes the antagonism in relation of oppression (Laclau and Mouffe) and renders it invisible by granting the subject a certain right. *Rights cannot eradicate antagonisms; they can only regulate antagonisms by forcing actors into the subjects of state protection.* The oppression that is caused by one actor upon another (relational oppression) is now transpositioned into a systemic oppression in which the omnipresent, superordinate agent is veiled by the regulatory operations of the state. *What is more, every right presupposes, in fact designates, a homogenous category of like individuals.* The actor is rendered the rights-bearing subject so long as he or she remains in the boundaries of liberal democratic regime. "Pressing-near," the state displaces the subject from one regulatory category onto another, from one discourse to another. The state succeeds, nonetheless, to involve itself in this area as the agent with unique resources and powers and maintain the legitimacy of its practices by not only allowing women's representation in decision mak- ing, but more importantly, by transforming the discourse of women's oppres- sion and demands into the discourse of rights. Accordingly, institutional responses to women's issues by the state through the discourse of rights trap women in endless labyrinths of regulative categories that produce no less problems than they presumably solve.

The above example shows how a specific phenomenal arrangement gives a certain phenomenal position a specific identity. The state, the dis- course of rights and equality, the principle of individualism, various forms of representation, and the institutions of welfare state all enter into historically- specific relations that, today, eventually tend to "press-near" the actor we know as "woman" into a certain institutional category, a subject of state's protective intervention. This "woman" is now both a subject of hegemonic decisions of the liberal democratic regime and an agent of the discourse of rights who is to bring the discourse of rights to its historical fulfillment. Under the hegemony of liberal democratic regimes and via the discourse of rights, these specific phenomenal arrangements attest to the specific mode of concealment of oppression in Western societies. More importantly, they at- test to the certain economy of the political that regulates our societies, our identities, in fact, our beings and horizonal social imaginaries.

As mentioned, Schürmann observes that the political in every era is constituted through the historically specific matrix of words (language), things, and actions. Together, these three constituents indicate a specific phenomenal arrangement we know as a certain socio-political system. Let me illuminate Schürmann's point through an example. Under the socialist polity, the concept of rights stands in relation to the socialist society, its survival, function, and future. As such, the right of the individual is sub- sumed under that of the community, which derives its definition from the grandiose socialist developmental planning. Hence, the hierarchy of the soviets and the governance of the society through "democratic centralism" that would, ideally, convey "upwards" the demands and needs of the citi- zens in various communities and move "downwards" not only the rights, but also the extent of their application to each level of community. The state, in the socialist system, becomes the only agent capable of defining rights. It therefore functions according to the principle of, adopting a term from Max Weber, "absolute ends" which in turn defines the Happiness of and for all. Under liberalism, by contrast, the concept of rights is tied to the individual. The principle of individuality therefore allows myriad conceptions of happiness to emanate from individuals. It is not so much the community that defines the rights, as does the individual. Community, under liberalism, is the aggregate of the like conceptions of happiness emanating from sovereign individuals. The state is still the sole source of recognition of rights, but it is not approached in the centralized and hierarchical way as we saw in socialism. In the zenith of each of these two forms of polity, their specific phenomenal arrangements of speech, deed, and things maintain a grip over their citizens such that the polity is perceived as the only viable body of governance.

The traditional avenues of oppression, as the epigraph to this section suggests, seem to have exhausted their viability. But has modern democracy eliminated oppression as such? The answer is, no. The grip of political modernity in its democratic constellation had displaced and concealed oppression (as "pressing-near") through the discourse of rights. Thus perceived, oppression is the concealed trace of supplement that is operative in the liberal democratic regime. As such, oppression is not reducible to any term commonly placed in its rank. Subordination, domination, exclusion, subalternity, and marginality are all but different manifestations of the *self-originative* "oppression." Viewed systemically (as in "pressing-near"), oppression has little to do with human planning or intentions. Unlike any of the above terms, oppression does not designate specific relations between two subjects (one subordinate and the other superordinate). It cannot be overcome, like subalternity, through the (former) subaltern's hegemonic leadership. And it does not presuppose any discourse (that of rights, namely) as a springboard for democratic struggles of our day. Now, along with the increasing problematization of all different modes of oppression, it is time to heed specifically the transposition of oppression as "pressing-near" in the modern democratic regimes. If politics is a historically specific convergence of words, deeds, and things, and if the discourse of rights has an operative tendency to conceal oppression—now transpositioned and embodied in the modern institutional "pressing-near"—then the next radical phenomenological "stepping back" should be to locate, and thereby understand, the liberal democratic regimes of the West in relation to the epochal constellation of truth which put into operation and render intelligible the principles and practices that take place under the hegemony of the liberal regimes. Understanding the epochal context will enable a thorough investigation into the economic unconcealment that is enframed by technicity's domination over the political—a mode of governance that I call "technological liberalism."

Technological Liberalism and Democratic Struggles

If it is true that in the Western countries there is less oppression today than in past centuries (which I will not venture to assess), this may confirm the hypothesis that the traditional intellectual tools for oppression, the epochal principles, indeed "lose their constructive force and become nothing."

Schürmann, "On Self-Regulation and Transgression"[28]

The subversion of the long presumed distinction between the state and civil society exposes the role of the regulatory state in modern democratic societies. It brings us to the issue of rational governance so meticulously analysed by one of the greatest critical theorists of modernity, Max Weber. Weber's conceptual point of departure in his analysis of modern politics is, of course, the state and its built-in, inevitable bureaucratic apparatus. For Weber, the modern state's unique characteristic of the *"monopoly of the legitimate use of physical force"* is indicative of the fact that politics "means striving to share power or striving to influence the distribution of power" with this source of rights.[29] Characteristic of the modern state, the rational-legal legitimation of power necessitates a specialized body of the administrative, political officials. The development of modern states, then, came with the "development of politics into an organization which demanded training in the struggle for power, and in the methods of this struggle as developed by modern party policies."[30] The rational-legal legitimation of power stands in a reciprocal relation with the state's monopoly over the legitimate use of force. Legitimation creates the hegemonic consent (Gramsci) necessary for the state's functioning, while the monopoly of legitimate use of force tends to keep subversive threats at bay. One can observe that since Weber's time Western democracies have come a long way in terms of democratization of various aspects of social and political life. This observation, however, must not overshadow another: that in order for the state to rely increasingly on statutory and civil legitimation, instead of physical force, it has to develop a professional body of governance as the carrier and guarantor of democratic principles. This professional body of governance is nowadays developed to the extent that one can no longer agree with Weber on the decisiveness of force for governance, that is, on his premise that the "decisive means for politics is violence"[31] (violence in the sense of sheer force) under liberal democracy. Thus, the increasing legal and ethical legitimacy (successful hegemonization) of every liberal democratic state today pushes it to maintain its uncontested *monopoly over the legitimate distribution of rights*, while retaining the monopoly over the legitimate use of violence.

In this light, Weber's study of bureaucracy tells us something about the democratic discourse. Bureaucracy is (ideally) to level off "economic and social differences," and it is thus inseparable from the "modern *mass democracy* in contrast to the democratic self-government of small homogeneous units." According to Weber, "This results from the characteristic principle of bureaucracy: the abstract regularity of the execution of authority, which is a result of the demand for 'equality before the law' in the personal and functional sense—hence, of the horror of 'privilege,' and the principled rejection of doing business 'from case to case'."[32] Bureaucracy can achieve the objective of leveling off social and economic differences (and by implication, the resultant inequalities and antagonisms) only through a process that presupposes *abstracted, homogenized subjects*—a process Weber called "the *leveling of the governed*."[33] Through abstraction, bureaucracy turns living actors into homogeneous categories of subjects. Only thus can subjects be delivered into the rational-legal discourse and only so can the discourse of rights recognize its subjects. "In this," to recontextualize Weber's observation, "the bureaucracy is supported by the 'democratic' sentiment of the governed, which demands that domination be minimized."[34] The task of bureaucracy in democratic regimes is not simply to make and impose decisions upon the subjects, but to delegate authority from the citizens to the legal discourse and implement it back on the citizens. However, while democracy by definition inclines towards greater diversity, the guarantor of democracy shows a systemic tendency toward greater uniformity and homogenization in order to ensure regularity, rational administration, and calculated decisions.

As discussed, in the liberal democratic state the discourse of rights is realized through the historical constitution of the hegemonic subjects who are then transformed into the agents of the democratic discourse. We also saw that under the current democratic regimes, rights are not separable from the state-civil society distinction and the regulatory body that has bureaucracy as its highest form of organization. These key premises of liberal democracy attest to the *systemic inevitability of oppression as the trace of right to "press-near," in a rational, calculable, and reductive way, all existential diversity of the social constituents into the homogenized categories of the rights-bearing subjects.* It is paying heed to this systemic handicap in bringing rights to the actor qua the actor—and not to the subject nor to the agent of the existing regime—that opens new horizons before thought.

Given the fact of "pressing-near" (as in our example of the "welfare mother"), the state cannot "respond" to the actors that remain unbound to categorial abstractions. The liberal regime is only capable of intervening in the affairs of categories of subjects it has constituted and it can recognize according to the assigned categorial abstraction. The uncontested monopoly

over the legitimate distribution of rights indeed necessitates categorial abstraction. Thus, the state's interventions take place, as Jerry Weinberger
observes, "at such an abstract level that they serve only to mask manipulation
and control. Civil society is not a community of whole persons but is rather
formed from such reifications as 'consumer,' 'producer,' 'voter,' 'householder,'
'manager,' and so on. Liberal politics dismembers human beings into theoretical abstractions, which are then reassembled into manipulable constructions that impoverish the soul."[35] The necessity of the hegemonic subject
and the agent of democratic discourse—both instances of reductive, categorial
abstraction—for the liberal governance of society precisely rests on their
recognition and acknowledgement of the principles informing the liberal
polity. Of course, the systemic, reductive rationality of the liberal state should
not impede us from seeing the achievements realized under liberal democratic regimes. Nonetheless, the systemic features of liberal regimes (increasingly problematized through the practices of new social movements) must be
identified and opposed. Weinberger uses the term *technological liberalism* to
refer to the liberal regimes of our time. According to Weinberger, technological rationalism views every end not as something in itself, in its own place,
in relation to other things and ends, but merely the object for the autonomous individual: "Thus every end is the object of choice and *nothing* more,
and every end is commensurable with every other. . . . Technological liberalism obliterates the possibility of genuine human ends; it thus 'manages'
political life by denaturing the soul."[36]

It is through the administrative, regulative "management" of the social
that reductive rationalism links liberalism to technology. In fact, the technological metaphysics that informs contemporary liberalism is indicative of
what it has in common with other forms of the political state such as communism and fascism. Heidegger once wrote, "Russia and America, seen
metaphysically, are both the same: the same hopeless frenzy of unchained
technology and of the rootless organization of the average man."[37] As is well
known, Heidegger's nearly equivalential treatment of both liberalism and
communism, however sound it may be from a metaphysical standpoint was
probably among the factors that led him in 1933 to commit "the political
error . . . of seeing constructive strengths for [the German] people in Hitler
and his movement"[38] (an error which is not, in my view, separate from his
problematic identification of German as the language of Being[39]). Heidegger's
image never fully recovered the haunting prompted by this error and its
political and philosophical implications. Nonetheless, the abstraction of the
individual in the systems of political "managing" of human affairs and of the
institutionalized methods of governance, processes of which bureaucracy is
the supreme and most enduring configuration, indeed articulates the kinship
between the human tragedies portrayed in Franz Kafka's *The Trial* and *The*

Castle, on the one hand, and in George Orwell's *1984* and *The Animal Farm*, on the other. These narratives show the overwhelming extent of impersonal and alienating rule of abstract administration, with (as in Orwell) or without (as in Kafka) manifest ideological justifications. For Heidegger, *the abstract totalizing of technological rationality* is the common bond between communism and liberal democracy. The fact that communism—and I add fascism—have both collapsed and liberal democracy has experienced nothing but increasing global hegemony has nothing to do with the truth of this kind of kinship.

Now the question is what economic unconcealment has made technicity and technological rationalism possible? The answer lies in what Heidegger called "*Ge-stell*": the *technological Enframing*. Since we will discuss technological Enframing in extenso later, let us restrict our focus here to the elements that link liberalism to technology. Heidegger's attentiveness to the question of being, a question forgotten for almost two-and-a-half millennia, disclosed the metaphysical epoch which has been governing humankind through the domination of ultimate referents since the closure of presocratics' time. In his approach to the history of metaphysics in the West, Schürmann showed the relationship between the specific phenomenal constellation(s) of each era and the ultimate referent, as the "grounding ground" which such constellations were to represent. The "sensible substance [nature] for Aristotle [and the ancients], the Christian God for the medievals, the cogito [knowing subject] for the moderns"[40] constituted the ultimate referents of the different eras in the metaphysical epoch. In each era, the ultimate referent established a specific *arché* (i.e., a founding origin that establishes a modality of praxis); a *principium* (i.e., a first principle that governs that era); and a *princeps* (i.e., the legitimate authority to carry out the principle). As such, in each metaphysical era phenomena and modes of intelligibility were (re)arranged around certain principles. Each era is better understood by making careful observations about the particular configuration of things, acts, and discourses, and thereby, observations about how the humankind is *inserted* in society—how, in other words, individuals and communities live, act, perceive the world, and are related to society. In Schürmann's words, "Epochal principles are always ontic givens. Each of them opens modalities of possible interaction and forecloses on others."[41] A *phenomenological deconstruction* always seeks to identify what is present and what is absent in a given age to find out how man dwells and acts in each era because "*an epochal constellation of absence and presence calls upon man to exist in a certain way.*"[42] The economy in which we are inserted in this specific period of time corresponds to the epochal constellation of absence and presence.

Asking the question of being after such millennia-long oblivion will bring us the awareness about how we have been ruled for so long by metaphysical

referents. For, being remains veiled in the constellations of presence mentioned above. Every disclosing of phenomena, in today's terms, every actualized possibility, in fact, conceals other possible phenomenal arrangements.
Our contemporary age is no exception. Its essence can be grasped, as
Heidegger would say, "from out of the truth of Being holding sway."[43]
Heidegger identifies this age as the technological age, in which all phenomena "stand-reserve" or "stand-by" (Bestand). In the technological age, everything becomes supply and object for man. Technology, then, "is a means to
an end" and "a human activity." "The two definitions of technology belong
together. For to posit ends and procure and utilize the means to them is a
human activity."[44] The hegemony of scientific (i.e., mathematical-calculative),
rationality over virtually all spheres of life in our time is the indisputable
evidence for this assertion. But here technology cannot be merely seen as the
means to an end. It is in fact an age-specific constellation of phenomena, "a
way of revealing,"[45] indeed, which imposes a truth and sends back into oblivion
the question of being. Heidegger called this resolute domination of the essence of technology Ge-stell or "technological Enframing." The German
word Ge-stell (from Stellen, "to set" or "to place") translates into English as
"Enframing," "im-posing," or "posure." Heidegger uniquely hyphenates the
prefix "Ge-" to stress the active manner in which the placing or setting (like
imposition) occurs. Technological Enframing comes to impose upon us a
certain modality of being. This means that the "essence of modern technology shows itself in what we call Enframing [which is] . . . nothing on the
order of a machine. It is the way in which the real reveals itself as standing-
reserve."[46] The essence of technology, which I call "technicity," is to be
understood as a modality of unconcealment, which gives rise to a specific
phenomenal arrangement. A "metaphysico-scientific-techincal modality of
un-concealment," technicity im-poses upon phenomena, indeed frames them
up in, absolutization and reductive totalization.[47] Far from being a human
doing, technicity appropriates humans and takes them into its constellation.
"Modern technology as an ordering revealing is, then, no merely human
doing."[48] Heidegger emphasizes this point in an example. "The forester who,
in the wood, measures the felled timber and to all appearances walks the
same forest path in the same way as did his grandfather is today commanded
by profit-making in the lumber industry, whether he knows it or not. He is
made subordinate to the orderability of cellulose."[49] Man's taking part in this
reductive categorization and totalization of phenomena into supply does not
"elevate" man to the position of ordaining. We must not forget that technological Enframing is a mode of phenomenal unconcealment. "Since man
drives technology forward, he takes part in ordering as a way of revealing.
But the unconcealment itself, within which ordering unfolds, is never a
human handiwork."[50]

Now, the term "technological liberalism" should show its merit. It captures the imposition of a certain mode of political arrangement upon the democratic discourse. Technological liberalism alludes to the essence of modern politics as a mode of phenomenal unconcealment and reveals its intimate affinity with technicity: it is governed by the calculative categorization whose hallmark is nothing but the rationalized and reductive "pressing-near" that the recognition of rights constantly veils. The *"praxis* of calculative thinking thus seems to be technology"[51] and "pressing-near" exposes the connection between technological im-position and the hegemonic liberal governance.

The domination of technicity, which im-poses itself upon and frames our thoughts and actions, is obviously a *public* mode of presence: in the technological era all our actions and thoughts are stamped by *Ge-stell*. Schürmann is clear about the implication of the epochal approach to politics: "To the deconstructionist, then, the notion of the political covers more than the mere public character of an epochal stamp; but it covers less than the received notions of the political that denote the sphere of the city (opposed to that of the household), or civil society, or again a community based on the social contract."[52] Awareness of the epochal *stamp* dislocates all ultimacies in conceiving the political. Subjecting these ultimacies, reified binaries, and long-cherished ends to the nonreferential inquiry of radical phenomenology gives us an awareness that "liberates" acting and thinking from the impositions of epochally configured and hegemonized politics. "The epochal stampings in Western history have been political because, more evidently at each stage, they have forced the network of things, words, and actions of an age into the logic of domination."[53] There is no realm of life that can escape the technological "posure": its violent domination is *nearly* total. Technicity, Schürmann points out, "contextualizes things and humans under the most efficacious universal ever seen, yet it also singularizes them without world or context. Such is the conflictual condition by which it functions."[54] Predictably, as Weinberger remarks, this violent contextualization has a nihilistic consequence, for it denies the being of all that do not conform to its technological logic.[55] That is the reason why technological Enframing is unthinkable without seriously taking into account the violent, reductive contextualization of what is. The domination of technological Enframing necessitates what Schürmann called the "isomorphic contextualizing"[56] of the plurality of appearances of phenomena. Heidegger had already seen modern technology "dominating with a sameness of form the entire earth."[57] Isomorphic contextualization has been, Schürmann argues, the task of the philosophers as the functionaries of mankind.[58] The philosophers of modern democratic tradition are no exception.

Schürmann points out that there is always an "identity between the manifest order of an epoch and the political. . . . The political is the surface where the code that rules a historical field becomes visible."[59] Thus, the current constellation of liberalism, its institutions and principles, show themselves to the able eyes of the radical phenomenologist as bearing the stamp of epochal posure. This constellation finds its apogee in the principle, recognition, and implementation of rights, which, in the presence of the subject of the liberal regime, elevates its practices and institutions to the realm of the unquestionable. For the phenomenologist who "steps back" from the received, hegemonic notion of rights, the deconstruction of the current liberal democratic regime introduces great insights into the study of new social movements. It reveals the nihilistic character of all forms of institutional(-ized) politics by exposing the denial of the movements by institutional politics: originally appearing in rich, wide, and diverse modes, the new movements do not "fit" the oppressive isomorphic categories of liberal institutions. Liberal democratic regimes respond to the various modes of subordination against which these movements have emerged by "pressing-near" these movements and their actors into the categories of rights-bearing subjects. Thus, at least in principle, all movements are rendered "equal" under this regime. But this "equality" is achieved at the expense of diversity and difference. For, technological liberalism decontextualizes these movements, tearing them apart from their wholeness, their world, original institutions, and their diverse modes of life. It is indeed the case that the new movements are pushed, in subtle ways, toward homogenization so that they can be incorporated into the narrow categories of institutional politics. The word *category (katégorein)* means to "accuse"—that is, to "make explicit"). Under the powerful grip of *Ge-stell*, the voice of those who cannot speak the language of technicity is not heard. Tragically, then, institutional denial is transferred onto, and internalized by, the movements themselves. It is this kind of *self-denial*, a systemic feature of institutionalized democracy and of regulated, calculable conception of rights— rights that are "all equal (*iso*) in their forms (*morphé*)"[60]—that the Zapatista movement resists, *while many new movements, especially in Western democracies, seem to be succumbing to it.* What is striking is the extent of neglect of the systemic oppression under technological liberalism in most new social movement theories. Such neglect stems from assumption of ultimate referentiality and thereby uncritical subscription to analytical categories that in fact emulate the hegemonic practices (e.g., distinction between the state and civil society) imposed by the technological liberalism and the sway of technicity.

Characteristic of technicity and of its global domination, *isomorphic contextualizing* always comes in the same package with the consent of the *hegemonic subject.* The project of the original institution of modern liberal democratic regimes does not have isomorphism as a principle emanated from the subject. "Quite the reverse: only because every phenomenon has to be accessible to calculation—because its phenomenality is summed up in its calculability—does the subject have to occupy the place of central legislator. Establishing itself as the spontaneous source of the laws of being, the subject will be certain that these laws are the same everywhere."[61] The expanding global hegemony of universal isomorphism, the rule of norms defining our beings in all respects, is not the subject's doing, but it is not thinkable without the consent of the subject either.

The pervasive neglect of isomorphic contextualization which results in the reductive homogenization of social movements into categories of subjects entitled to certain rights is a common feature of those new social movement theories that do not radically question the liberal democratic discourse and its discourse of rights. The extent of such neglect is striking, but it mainly goes back to not having been able, conceptually, to heed the technological Enframing and its stamp on the modern liberal polity. Such neglect makes even a prominent political theorist like Chantal Mouffe take the position of defending liberal institutions, viewing them as necessary means toward radical democratic politics. It is a fact that Mouffe's agonistic pluralism presupposes representative democracy based on liberal institutions.[62] Mouffe does not attempt a radical democratic critique of the liberal institutions—these bureaucratically operative monuments of technological liberalism. She rejects the idea that principles of legitimacy can be subject to antagonism and that there can be plurality of positions at the level of "the basic institutions" in society. Her search for commonality among the new movements ends in accepting the im-posed (enframed) phenomenality of our technological era—an acceptance that obscures her sight to the possibilities the liberal democratic unconcealedness represses. She contends that "we should not have different legal systems according to the different communities. There must be something common, but a form of commonality which should make room for the recognition of differences in many cultural terms."[63] For Mouffe, the liberal institutions can cultivate shared values. "It is therefore through institutions that solidarity is created and maintained."[64] The problem with this line of argument must be apparent: it is *self-defeating*. If we retain the liberal institutions as what they are then the kind of antagonism that Mouffe advocates (in the form of agonistic pluralism) will turn out to be superficially reformist because it impedes genuine antagonisms over the legitimacy of basic institutions.

Not surprisingly, Mouffe's conception of radical democracy relinquishes the position of alternative to liberal democracy and becomes just a further stage in the evolution of the liberal democratic tradition. "Radical democracy is a way to reformulate the democratic project in another theoretical framework which makes room for the centrality of antagonism, of power relations, and therefore implies a different type of understanding of the principle of

legitimacy of liberal democracy," asserts Mouffe.[65] If the relationship between radical and liberal democracies is still ambiguous in Mouffe's remark,
consider this: "It is important that radical democracy not be seen as a radical
alternative to liberal democracy. . . . A radical democratic society will still be
a liberal democratic society, in the sense that we are not going to put into
question the basic institution of political liberalism."[66] Radical democracy, as
Mouffe views it, does (should?) not question the principles of liberal democratic society. "The purpose of the project is to radicalize it by extending the
sphere of equality and liberty to many more social relations. In a sense it
could be called radical liberal democracy. It is not an alternative to liberal
democracy."[67] Of course, it remains a mystery in what ways an agonistic
pluralism can be incorporated into the basic liberal institutions that she
intends to keep. In the face of ethno-nationalist frenzy that has since the fall
of the Berlin Wall ripped European nations apart and created grave human
tragedies of ethnic cleansing, systematic rape, and concentration camps,
Mouffe's worries about affirming commonality are understandably noble and
decent. But it is unfortunate that such concerns make her fall back into the
vicious binary of pluralism versus commonality. When this fictitious binary
ultimately forces her to choose one side over the other, she does not hesitate
to acknowledge "that the kind of pluralism which I am advocating is only
possible within the context of liberal democracy. Liberal democracy and its
institutions are the conditions of possibility of multiculturalism. So, in the
name of pluralism, you cannot put into question those very institutions,
because that would mean the end of pluralism. That is why pluralism must
have limits."[68] Interestingly, the limit comes down not to bind the basic
institutional practices of the liberal polity, but to impose limits upon pluralism, which is one of the central concepts of her postmarxist theory. Lacking
an epochal awareness, Mouffe practically takes pluralism as increased colonization of "many more social relations" by the liberal regimes' rights granting operations through isomorphic homogenization.

   The greatest surprise comes when she identifies her position to be
compatible with the hegemony of subordinate groups. We need to keep
institutions of liberalism, according to Mouffe, "to recognize the limits to
pluralism which are required by a democratic politics that aims at challenging a wide range of relations of subordination. It is therefore necessary to
distinguish the position I am defending here from the type of extreme pluralism that emphasizes heterogeneity and incommensurability and according
to which pluralism—understood as valorization of all differences—should
have no limits."[69] For Mouffe, it is not the extent of pluralism that should
decide the limits of institutional practices of liberalism. Quite the contrary,
the institutions should decide the extent of pluralism. The dualism that
Mouffe sketches between her position and "extreme pluralism" is rather

arbitrary. It rhetorically serves her to justify her problematical position. That one radically questions the institutional limits imposed upon pluralism does not automatically place one in the position of "extreme pluralism" (an inaccurate term that is supposed to taunt us). Mouffe further suggests that radical democracy "would be, precisely, an understanding of liberal democracy that would reintroduce the dimension of the political, that would recognize the centrality of power relations, and therefore uphold those struggles against the different forms of subordination, struggles which are needed for the democratic project to be pursued and developed."[70] How can such a limited understanding about the liberal regimes be compatible with the project of radical and plural democracy? Is not the idea of the preconstituted limits set for pluralism merely to channel and regulate conflicts essentially a liberal idea? Then what is "radical" about radical democracy? Simply acknowledging that antagonisms can never be done away with? If antagonism (and thus power) is the characteristic of the social, then *where does antagonism possibly lead, if it can/must not affect the basic liberal principles or institutions?* Mouffe obviously draws on the liberal discourse of rights to "radicalize" democracy. But under the epochal grip of Enframing, the rights, as granted by the reductive rationality of liberalism, only leads to the technological-systemic form of oppression of the violent homogenization of phenomenal plurality and particularity within the liberal political context (isomorphic contextualization).

Here, Lefort's concept of "democratic revolution," used by Laclau and Mouffe, shows that Mouffe's position suffers not only from her inattentiveness to the technological-reductive nature of liberal institutions, but also from the lack of a critical distinction between liberalism and democracy. In his reflections on the 1968 events, Lefort writes about democracy: "Democracy is a system that allows itself to be shaken and does not disarm the hope for change. It must not . . . be confused with capitalism, or with the rule of bureaucracy, or with the empire of technology, no matter how inextricably and tragically it may be linked to them."[71] Does the distinction between democracy and liberalism not allude to the possibility of being free from the technological-systemic "pressing-near"? What can we do after the rejection of technological liberalism? One thing is certain: "the demise of technological rationalism has important implications for our liberal order."[72] In the epigraph to this section, Schürmann suggests that awareness about the particularity of phenomenal arrangements leads us to learn about the economies in which we are inserted. Our very thinking about our epochal constitution is in fact preparation to exit it. By thinking being beyond the technological Enframing—which im-poses upon us only a certain access to being, thereby blocking our vision into possible ways of being—we have already *transgressed* its normative laws. The children of the technological age, we have come to experience challenging the hegemonic institutions that for long defined our beings in their own terms. In particular, we have gained the ability to see how *under technological liberalism "pressing-near" violently excludes our "past-perils" (experiences) from our identities* and rights. By virtue of *genuine* articulation of experiences—genuine in the sense of releasing before us destinal movements toward social imaginaries—we become *transgressive* actors: we defy the im-posed terms upon our beings by the regimes in which we are inserted; we undermine the hegemonies which try to reduce us to subjects and agents; we remember the original institution(s) of our hegemonic regime(s) as particular arrangements without universal justification; we offer, through our horizonal social imaginaries, possible economies of unconcealment. At the same time, technological liberalism, via systemic "pressing-near," forces us into the categories it can manage and derive consent from. Thus, we have come to experience the radical incompleteness of the ontological configuration of the social. Today, it is evident that no possible horizon is totally obscured. We learned that at its zenith, the epochal constellation (via its corresponding configuration in the polity) exerts the greatest extent of closure, but, as a movement of metaphysics, it eventually exhausts itself. Schürmann calls this self-exhaustion the *"hypothesis of metaphysical closure"*—a key concept on which the next chapter will hinge. Here, however, we should consider the possibility, and *merely the possibility*, of an era beyond the rule of technicity. We should consider what might lie beyond technological liberalism.

> "But where danger is, grows
> *The saving power also.*"[73]

These lines of Hölderlin allow Heidegger to think the saving power that rests in the danger of technology. Technology is in essence Janus-faced. It has within it both the violent reduction of phenomena (to mere supply) and the noncoerced "making" of phenomena. With the essence of technology, *Ge-stell*, "things are established in advance, reduced to objects of calculation by a thought that merely represents, or are produced by a posing and disposing interest."[74] But when it pushes itself to the extreme and exhausts itself, it negates itself. It allows for the nonreductive springing of phenomena.

The implications of this line of thinking will enable answers to the above questions. The true radicalization of liberal democracy comes not from in toto refutation of it, but from the decategorization and recontextualization concealed by its reductive categorization. This would be an "ensemble of things, words, and actions that thinking 'acts' and prepares a possible posttechnological economy not primarily stamped by institutionalized violence."[75]

Decategorization and recontextualization dwell at all times within the liberal concept of rights. And this brings us to Claude Lefort, one more time:

> The rights of man reduce right to a basis which, despite its name, is without shape, is given as interior to itself and, for this reason, eludes all power which would claim to take hold of it—whether religious or mythical, monarchical or popular. Consequently, these rights go beyond any particular formulation which has been given of them; and this means that their formulation contains the demand for their reformulation, or that acquired rights are not necessarily called upon to support new rights. Lastly, for the same reason, they cannot be assigned to a particular period, as if their meaning were exhausted by the historical function they were called upon to fulfil in the service of the rising bourgeoisie, and they cannot be circumscribed *within* society, as if their effects could be localized and controlled.[76]

If the formulation of right is by definition always already a reformulation, as Lefort observes, then all oppressive categories of liberal polity are essentially open to contention. There remains no sphere of life immune to the expansive reformulations of rights. Is it not by virtue of this essential lack, innate to the liberal concept of rights, that the new movements of our time challenge virtually all boundaries of institutional politics, collapse the distinction between the private and the political (public), and thus confuse the orders of our intelligibility as social scientists and social movement experts? Indeed. The Lefortian conception of rights collapses the distinction between the state and civil society, thereby contending the legitimacy of the modern state, its institutions, practices, and most importantly, its uncontested monopoly over the distribution of rights. What is more, Lefort's theory shows that the expansion of rights has nothing to do with the humanitarian gestures of liberal regimes: the expansion of multiplication of rights come from the being of rights and is, as we see today, reluctantly and slowly given in to by the liberal institutions only following decades of the new movements' struggles. Such a non-reductive, radical concept of rights opens the possibility of a modality of action free of institutional and reductive violence, and of a new mode of thinking, which allude to a possible (but not ultimate) phenomenal arrangement that allows democratic struggles to take various forms and arise from a plurality of loci, and as such, grants us the great challenge of redefining democracy through praxis. This last point invites us to revisit the strategies that new social movements have employed in practice to deal with the im-posed conditions of the technological liberalism.

Strategies: Translation, Appropriation, Metaphor

From the moment when the rights of man are posited as the ultimate reference, established right is open to question. It becomes still more so as the collective wills or, one might prefer to say, social agents bearing new demands mobilize a force in opposition to the one that tends to contain the effects of the recognized rights. Now, where right is in question, society—that is, the established order—is in question.

Claude Lefort, *The Political Forms of Modern Society*[77]

Were the *Urstiftung* of the liberal democratic regimes the founding of a beginning that ruled in absolute closure, we would encounter nothing but docile subjects and devoted agents of the already in-place norms and laws. We would not, moreover, be able to problematize its discourse of rights. But, fortunately, no *Urstiftung* can impose and rule toward one single *Endstiftung* because every original institution is subject to the eventuations of time as the horizon of all beings. *Urstiftung* for Heidegger, Schürmann states, "always results from a 'thrust of time' establishing a new focal sense of being."[78] Lefort's insightful assertion about the openness of rights in the epigraph to this section can be read to imply an epochal transition of the sense (meaning and direction) of *being* which we are living and experiencing while trying to comprehend its magnitude and radicality. We are living in the time of an imminent historical rupture between, on the one hand, the systemic, institutional closure of rights which "presses-near" the *transgressive* actors into its reductive categories, rendering them rights-bearing subjects, and on the other hand, the flourishing openness of rights, which seems to free the actor from such impositions. *Seeing, if we properly learn how to, the Janus face of rights, we find ourselves torn between two powerful pulls in opposite directions.* The aporia of rights becomes the domain of actors' exercise of freedom and dissent that identity embodies. New social movements are to be understood in this historical context, where actors, perceiving the opening and resisting the subject and the agent, "move" to free rights from systemic im-positions. Given the openness of rights, a *movement within social movements* is identifiable in three moments: a movement from *translation* (of what a right is and what is one's relation to it, the first moment) to *appropriation* (of the right for oneself by pushing for its expansion, the second moment) to *metaphor* (which means the essential openness of the right, the final moment). Let us in the remainder of this chapter investigate these three moments by refreshing our memories about articulation of experiences as put forward in Chapter 4.

The actor's identity is not, as argued, a positive referent in the structural foundation of the social. Identity is always already an act of identification which contains a curious mode of decision. The decision does not have its origin in the subjectivity of the actor but in the actor's specific modality of *insertedness* amidst the existing phenomenal arrangement of things, words, and deeds—in short, politics. A fully constituted "decision" stems from a condition of existence in a systemic closure in which the actor is rendered a fully constituted subject living his or her fate because the "decision" does not suggest any course of action other than what the subject has been systemically assigned to. This somber condition of existence was depicted in Beckett's *Waiting for Godot. Genuine—that is, non-systemic—*identification (with a social imaginary), therefore, is by definition decisive, for it introduces a rupture in the im-posed fate. Identity, therefore, will necessarily acquire a transgressive destining character. The view that looks at identity as merely differential misses the crucial place of destiny in understanding social movements. It also heeds not the fact that articulated experiences give each identity a particular content by summoning elements from the past and linking them to a horizon of possibility in the future. This destinal horizon is where a social imaginary reveals itself to the actor and sets up possible points toward which the actor moves. In other terms, social imaginary is what the actor identifies with. That is the moment of emergence of a *social* movement because the term *actor* can never refer to a private individual *stricto sensu*: by virtue of the actor's political constitution, she or he is always public and situated within a community. Thus, following Schürmann, destiny is a movement from one phenomenal confluence of acts, words, and things to another. Destiny is made possible by the epochal unconcealment; therefore, each era has intelligible destinies specific to it.

Under the liberal democratic regimes, the point of departure of any movement is the knowledge of the rights to which each citizen of the polity is entitled. Such knowledge secures the foundations of the liberal democratic polity. It is, to adopt a term from Hans-Georg Gadamer, the citizens' "prejudice," (i.e., their "deep common accord,"[79]) as they live in the political community. Thanks to the hegemonic constitution of the subject, this deep common accord preconditions, in congruity with institutional rationality and reductive categorization that inseparably accompany any recognition and legislation of rights, all movements from their very inception. The hegemonic constitution of the subject becomes in fact a component of the life-world of every actor. As such, it always has a certain presence in the way experiences are articulated and greatly influences the destiny thus set forth. A successful hegemony always sends its own *Urstiftung* into oblivion. This sending into oblivion we call, following Husserl, "sedimentation." Veiling the *contingency and particularity* of its conditions of emergence behind the cloak of a presumed historic necessity or superior, universal rationality of some kind or the other, sedimentation allows hegemony to pretend to be the only viable horizon. In fact, it is sedimentation that makes possible the deep common accord that distinguishes the subject from the actor. By definition, hegemony must institute the governing principle of everyday praxis and then send into oblivion the instituting event in order to perpetuate and expand its principle(s). Hegemony also includes its epistemic paradigm in the realm of experience and creates hegemonized experiences that lead to the constitution of the agent of the liberal democratic regime—the agent who will warrant the perpetuation of the democratic discourse. Liberalism, the epistemic hegemony of our time, generates hegemonic experiences derived from the prejudicial knowledges of the separation between private and public, freedom from arbitrary rule, and representative democracy. *Since the actor is always born into the hegemonic regime, we can only speak of the actor conceptually.* The concept of *actor*, as used in this text, always implies a nonhegemonic act of *transgression*. The actor can emerge out of the subject and the agent by refusing the hegemonic terms he or she has internalized. The genuinely articulating actor resists both the subject and the agent. She or he is aware of the particularity and contingency of the principles governing the existing regime by recalling the hegemonizing moment of primal institution. To the actor, all principles are in the end nonuniversal. This reveals something of utmost importance: that the "pressing-near" of the rights under the regulative operations of technological liberalism sets into play a specific mode of hegemonic destining. The domination of this modality of governance, therefore, not only influences the way articulated experiences connect to destinal movements toward a social imaginary, it also blocks certain destinal movements (identifications) by rendering inconceivable, literally, certain social imaginaries.

Every actor's struggle to overcome his or her relations of subordination necessarily entails seeking the institutional recognition of rights. As Lefort teaches us, the recognition of a right always entails the recognition of more specific rights, indeed the reformulation of rights ad infinitum. In seeking recognition, then, the first step will be an act of *translation*. The prospective actor, now engaging in antagonistic relations with the sources of his or her subordination, perceives in the dominant conception of rights the possibility of articulation of his or her own experiences. But the discourse of rights preexists these experiences and does not allow a free destinal movement to spring forth from the actor's genuine articulated experiences. Experience is translated into the terms that already exist in the discourse of rights. The women's suffragette movements in Europe and North America in the late nineteenth and early twentieth century translated the experiences of womanhood into the language of liberal humanism, equality, and freedom which the discourse of rights and the democratic principles of the time already contained. The recognition of the women's right to participate equally with men in representative democracy, of course, did not reflect the various forms of subordination that women experienced. *Translation* took the struggle of women against various relations of oppression into a different realm. While initially submitting itself to the "pressing-near" of institutional recognition of rights, the struggle of women progressively enforced on the liberal institutions the making of a new category of subjects: woman. By transporting women's experiences to the language of the then male-dominated discourse of rights, translation enabled the recognition of women's right to vote. At this point, a totally nonhegemonic destining of the articulation of women's experiences was not possible. Though still inescapably reductive, the suffragette movement freed women from being completely silenced in the presence of the category of men in the exercise of representative democracy. To have the power to vote, however, became the springboard for further recognitions of the rights of women—rights that, remarkably, no longer draw on such principles as equality (with men), but seek to challenge reductive categorizations in favour of those rights that are specific to women as a distinct social stratum with many shared experiences and similar social imaginaries. This represents the moment of moving toward the *appropriation* of the discourse of rights. Appropriation takes place when a movement attempts to undermine the (hegemonic) destiny imposed by the "pressing-near" of rights into the destiny opened by certain "transgressive" articulation of experiences. It is in the moment of appropriation that the enforced settlement of the subject in a category of rights comes to reveal its *innate fissure*. Appropriation, in other words, aims at radically altering current institutional practices involving the recognition of rights. Now, women claim rights in the terms derived by their common womanhood such as the right to be protected against domestic and other kinds of systematic violence or against discriminations based on their reproductive faculty. We must note that appropriation does not transcend translation. Women' struggle for pay equity, for example, still appeals to the principle of equality (with men). However, we can safely claim that a movement will pass a turning point once it arrives at the moment of appropriation. Translation allows an excluded group to include itself in the present, but now expanded, space provided by the hegemonic principle of rights. Appropriation allows the partially recognized group to seek and push the expansion of that space. It contains an inexhaustible possibility for the radicalization of the discourse of rights and shows that the discourse of rights is essentially open to rewriting and reformulation. Appropriation indicates that the basic principles and tenets of the political can be challenged and changed. Thus, appropriation always alludes to the next moment—namely, the moment in which right appears as a *metaphor* as when *the right emerges as "transferring" something into a different place.* The translatory and appropriatory moments make possible the moment of metaphorical emergence of rights. The transference that metaphor intimates is a manifold one. Metaphor transfers the right bound by bureaucratic codes and reductive categories to the right as the incessant call for its reformulation. It transforms the hegemonic subject into the counterhegemonic actor and the law into aporia. In short, *metaphor prepares for the implosion of the system of regulation, calculation, and categorization, alluding to the prospect of a self-exhausting domination.*

Still, there remains something significant untold about translation, appropriation, and metaphor. As is well known, the revolutionary movements had a tendency to reinstate the denied rights of the subordinate classes (which they presumably represented) by subverting the present regime and instituting the society anew. As such, the revolutionary discourse never allowed the rights to undergo the three transformative moments described above. To the revolutionary discourse, the rights of the citizens were exclusively carved on the stone of the hegemonic instituting of the regime (and the subject along with it). The prospect of transformation of rights depended on the level of societal development—a transformation that was predicted in the movement from the *arché* of instituting toward the *telos* of a historical fulfillment. The nonrevolutionary movements (e.g., European communist parties), however, had come to terms with the transformable characteristic of rights, but their totalistic view of society never removed from their approaches to politics the prospect of a full reinstitution of society. It is only with the practice of new social movements that, thanks to the self-exhaustion of the totalistic view of society, the concept of rights and its aporetic character came to play a pivotal role.

New social movements showed us that the aporetic characteristic of rights has been a part of the original institution of the modern liberal democratic principles—a characteristic that the fathers of liberalism could not have perceived. *The aporetic character of rights is precisely that which saves* in the face of the dominant danger of "pressing-near" so powerfully operative in current day liberal regimes. As reductive categorization loses its grip over the subject, the latter gradually acquires the ability of apprehending new phenomena. The moments of translation, appropriation, and metaphor represent the movement of consciousness away from the purely hegemonic terms. The transformation of consciousness undoubtedly transforms the subject to varying degrees. It shows how the intellectual constellations of truth shift along with the economies of presence of phenomena. A transformation of this kind, which is always a transference (metaphor) into a different realm, makes possible the introduction of a sense (direction and meaning) different than that of the existing economy of phenomenal arrangement, which, through systemtic oppression, is to force experience into its own directions. The Zapatista movement is indeed exemplary in this respect. Unlike many new social movements that seem from their inceptive moment to be prepared to embrace institutional categorizations to acquire the rights that include in the liberal package of rights (e.g., many gay movements), the Zapatistas' aim to radically democratize Mexico's dubious liberal polity—by emphasizing consultations, community involvement, local and global NGO participation, reinforcing municipal democracy, recognition of indigenous rights, and so on—indicates their creative response to the bringing of various kinds of subordination to an end without succumbing to the systemic "pressing-near." The Zapatistas' refusal to transform into an institutionalized party and to seek formal political power tends to deepen democratic processes by denying the state's uncontested monopoly over the legitimate distribution of rights. Such refusal challenges the democracy industry of technological liberalism that produces isomorphic products called citizens. But in cases of challenging institutional/constitutional rights, a citizen's acts of resistance always produce a double effect: that of affirming his or her citizenship (by having recourse to his specific space in polity [i.e., identity]) and that of denying the existing concept of rights that is constitutive of his or her citizenship.

The moments of translation, appropriation, and metaphor become in the hands of the actors strategies of their resistance against systemic oppression and reductive categorization—indeed, means of resistance against being transformed into hegemonized rights-bearing subjects. These strategies stem from openings in the system and only secondarily the product of actors. Any genuine articulation of experiences is indicative of a move toward multiplication of rights because it challenges the limited hegemonic destiny that the liberal *Urstiftung* sets for the subject. Articulated experiences set their own contexts and thereby challenge the isomorphic contextualization of technological liberalism. Therefore, articulated experiences mark the emergence of the actor out of the fettered subject and compelled agent. In our time, the genuinely plurivocal articulations of experiences show the destinies that tend to break away from the already weakened grip of the regimes of technological liberalism. These destinies have been blocked by the systemic oppression concealed by the liberal concept of rights for so long.

The radical subversion of the subject and the agent and the subsequent birth of the actor can become possible through *genuine* articulation of experiences. These articulations are genuine, as mentioned, in the sense of giving rise to a new destiny that would undermine the im-posed destiny of the existing economy that governs the arrangement of things, deeds, and words and constitutes a world within which the subject is inserted and for whose completion the agent strives. A genuine articulation of experiences, therefore, defies the existing epochal-hegemonic insertedness. Although the actualization of such articulation depends on the sober actors, the very possibility of genuine articulation of experiences is not a human doing. Insofar as a new phenomenal arrangement discloses itself as a possibility, the actor can respond to its call by moving toward its place (destiny). Under the conditions of full domination, as portrayed in *Waiting for Godot*, a genuine articulation is impossible, despite the intuitive experiencing of the anticipated exhaustion of the rule. Full domination is the greatest force in *Urstiftung* of the social. But the fact that no *Endstiftung* is ever total indicates that the ultimacy the original institution puts in operation loses its sway as the regime thus instituted exhausts itself. This is so because there are always more *originative pulls* than any *Urstiftung* which threatens the originally instituted ultimacy that sets into operations the principles and rules of a regime.[80]

One final note: the agent of the liberal democratic society seizes the subject such that the subject cannot *radically* question the democratic principles and their operations. Here the word *radical* is key. For if the economic unconcealment of modernity has rendered technological liberalism the dominant modality of regime in the West, then in order to pass to post-modernity we must be prepared to question this regime radically—that is, not as the truth, but as "half truths."[81] We cannot know whether liberal democracy can adapt to the post-Enframing, post-modern modes of political unconcealment. What is certain, however, is that in its present constellation, liberal democracy does not allow "a genuine confrontation with the technological world."[82] Once we properly understand the connection between technicity and liberalism (crystallized in "pressing-near"), we arrive at the possibility, given the Janus face of technology, of transition to a non-im-posing, nonprincipial society. Thanks to our awareness of ultimacies and their rules, we are witnessing today the waning of the quest for *arché* as a ground or foundation or for *telos* as a normative principle. For us, the children of this transitional era, the task is to deconstruct the principles that govern our time. So we ask, how will we live, act, and think in the possible nonprincipial, post-modern era? The next chapter will attend to this crucial task.

CHAPTER 6

An Epochal Theory of Action

The task consists . . . in thinking being as presencing and as differing from its economic modalities. This task for thinking will be completed successfully only through a deconstruction of the principles that administer an age. That is where phenomenology, now radicalized, encounters the problem of acting.

Schürmann, Heidegger on Being and Acting[1]

The radical phenomenological inquiry into the concept of identity brings us to the point where we need to view the epochal context in which identity-claims become possible. Now, it is time to link the question: "What is 'new' in new social movements?" to the question: "Are we postmodern yet?" Linking these two questions places new social movements in the context of time as the horizon of being and specifically in relation to a possible epochal shift. This task requires a specific attentiveness to the question of the post-modern which owes its epochal articulation to Heidegger's "hypothesis of metaphysical closure" as explicated by Schürmann.

The Hypothesis of Closure: Are We Post-Modern Yet?

According to the hypothesis of metaphysical closure, the principial economy
expires in our age, and the nonprincipial becomes a concrete possibility. To
realize that possibility, that potential contained in today's order of things,
it would be necessary to accept the absence of any meaning-bestowing
center and to step from the age of Janus to that of Proteus. We may, in
fact, have taken that step for quite some time already.

Schürmann, "On Self-Regulation and Transgression"[2]

In spite of the heightened discussions about postmodernity's presumed arrival and its seemingly increasing prevalence in arts, literature, music, body,
mind, culture, city, society, and politics, today we are still left with the question, "Are we post-modern yet?" If, *stricto senso*, modernity refers to an era
in which the principle of reason (in Leibniz's dictum, *"nihil est sine ra-*
tione")—a principle of which foundationalism, technological rationalization,
teleology, or metanarrative are just various critical, theoretical expressions—
comes to govern all aspects of life, then post-modernity should almost by
definition signify a transmutation of that principle and the possible surpassing of the modern era that is so instituted and governed. Specifically, we
need an epochal theory that would account for acting and thinking in the
possible destitution of the principle of reason. Therefore, now it is time to
present a synopsis of Schürmann's epochal theory.

In introduction to his *Heidegger on Being and Action*, Schürmann
declares his project to engage "in raising the inherited question of the relationship between theory and practice, but considered under *Heidegger's*
hypothesis that metaphysical rationality produces its own closure. That inherited question is to be raised anew, then, from a perspective that forbids
couching it in oppositions such as 'theory and practice'."[3] Here, the term
"metaphysics" is to be understood as the search for an ultimate foundation—
that is, "a *hupokeimenon*, a 'substrate'. Metaphysics is [therefore] a funda-
mentalist quest."[4] Metaphysical epochs emerge through founding Firsts, called
arché, which provide "legitimacy to the *principia*, the propositions held to be
self-evident in the order of intelligibility. They also provide legitimacy to the
princeps, the ruler or the institution retaining ultimate power in the order of
authority."[5] Together, *arché*, *principium*, and *princeps* establish a specific
constellation of truth of an era that renders certain modes of action and
thought intelligible, even required. That is to say, the configuration of *life*
itself is organized around the governing principles of an era. That is why,
even to the untrained eyes of layman, different eras can be distinguished
from one another according to certain common practices and belief systems.
We can all conveniently and understandably speak about the ancient times,

dark ages, or our own period, or the colonial era, the great depression, the sixties, and so on, and our designations will be widely comprehended. Strictly speaking, the history of the West has witnessed three succeeding metaphysical eras (or epochs), each governed by its own *principium*. The metaphysical principles and their founded epochs are: "the sensible substance for Aristotle [and the ancients], the Christian God for the medievals, [and] the cogito for the moderns."[6]

From institution to its zenith, the reign of the *principia* over epochs goes unnoticed, as these principles make no pretence toward their principiality or foundationality. Rather, they become hegemonically operative in the everyday life by establishing self-evident, self-legitimating norms of action and epistemic worldviews. They become parts of the pregivenness of the world for the community, indeed, matters-of-fact. Principial epochs always send their origin into oblivion. Forgetfulness about their origination veils the operative dominance of these principles and renders current norms neutral and natural, "just the way things are." An epoch is, therefore, "'reduced' to the way things, words, and actions are mutually present in it . . ."[7] The mode of arrangement of entities (ontic givens), the way they are plausible and intelligible in a given era is always an indication of the principles that govern that period. Moreover, this mode of arrangement reveals the mode of epochal unconcealment. But, as mentioned, the unconcealment (*alétheia*) of epochal principles always entails concealedness (*léthe*). Every actual and manifest arrangement cloaks possible arrangements. In short, *every actuality veils possibilities*. The hypothesis of closure holds the idea that each principle "has its ascent, its period of reign, and its ruin. We can trace the rise, the sway, and the decline of a mode of presence so instituted by a First, that is, we can trace the *arché*, the origin as the founding act of an era."[8] Epochal principles have their moments of institution, their period of uncontested apogee, and then a prolonged episode of destitution. Their "death takes disproportionately more time than [their] reign."[9] But the way epochs rise and fall is indeed most curious. As Michel Haar observes, "Epochs for [Heidegger] do not succeed each other smoothly, nor do they derive dialectically one from the other, but burst suddenly like buds on a branch, in a mixture of necessity and play."[10] We do things in this way now, and *suddenly* we do them in another way. There is the sixties and *suddenly* it is gone. Eventually, we can distinguish between eras and the things that have changed, but we cannot experience the "suddenly" itself. The "sudden" shifts, the very bursting of the existing practices in the place of the older ones, does not announce itself: *we suddenly enter new epochs without awareness of our entry*.

This point brings us to the point that the hypothesis of metaphysical closure cannot be properly understood without the introduction of the Heideggerian distinction between the *present* (entities), *presence*, and *presencing*. The Greek term *eon* (being)—which, it is said, was forged by the

presocratic thinker Parmenides—entails a radical *difference*. As a present
participle, it entails both a *verbal* and a *nominal* form. Thus, *being* means at
the same time "to-be" as well as "being" in the sense of "entity." In its verbal
form, *being* signifies an occurrence: "For something 'to-be', it must . . . enter
upon the stage of presence, linger, and then withdraw. The verbal form
emphasizes this entrance into presence and the possible exit."[11] But the
nominal form refers to the entity thus present. Thus, the term *eon* contains
an "intrinsic motility"; it "is the name of that twofold play, presencing on the
horizon of possible absencing, and the present entity standing fast in its
presence. It is the name for the duality (*Zwiefalt*), 'to be—entity'."[12] In
"ontological difference," neither of the two forms holds an ultimate reason
for *being*. This duality is revealed in unconcealment: what is concealed
remains in shadow and what is unconcealed imposes itself. *Unconcealment
manifests the absencing, the withdrawal, of a present arrangement when presencing
gives a new one.* It is indeed for *Being and Time*'s pathbreaking recovery of the
long hidden question of *being* that today we are able to understand "the
intrinsic motility and temporality of being"[13] through which a possible epochal
arrangement of phenomena (called post-modernity) manifests itself to us.

But presencing cannot be adequately understood without reference to
another presocratic, Heraclitus, and his concept of *phusis*, or *presencing*—
that is, *coming-to-presence as self-manifestation*. Here a distinction is in order.
Presencing is originary and ahistorical; presence is original and historical.
Once we view the duality between "to-be" and "*entity*" with respect to phusis,
we find that the "ontological difference" translates into a "temporal difference" between "the triad: present entity—mode of presence—event of
presencing (*das Anwesende, die Anwesenheit, das Anwesen*). This three-tiered
temporal difference is Heidegger's last word in his systemic, non-humanist,
inquiry into being as time."[14] If properly understood, the distinction between
presencing and *presence* abolishes the last possible residue of humanist metaphysics and calls for a systemic and anti-humanist approach. Rather than a
diachronic genealogy of origin, an endeavor we partake during the times of
epochal reversal (when one epoch leads to another), we must think of
presencing as a *synchronic "event"* (*Ereignis*) of the profusion of origin—an
event that takes place in the *self-establishing* of an *era*, which we call, *stricto
sensu*, an *epoch*. As is known, Heidegger borrows the term *epoché* "not from
Husserl, but from the Stoics. This word thus does not mean objectivation, or
the methodic exclusion by a thetical act of consciousness, but a 'stop,' and
interruption, an act of halting. The history of ontologies appears to Heidegger
as a multitude of ways in which things render themselves present, in which
presence lets them be."[15] *Presencing* is therefore to be understood in regard
to *truth as alétheia*, that is as myriad of constellations of unconcealment and
concealedness. Thus viewed, epochs of presence designate both presence as
it reserves itself in the entity and presence as stoppages that move away the

"fields of intelligibility" from fields of "possible life that make up our concrete history." In the history of presence, according to Heidegger, there have
been three great inaugural moments: "the pre-metaphysical dawn, the classical reversal that founds metaphysics, and the transition, which has become
possible today, toward a post-metaphysical age."[16] At these halting points, the
difference between presence and what is present manifests itself. Schürmann
summarizes this crucial point:

> Heidegger's notion of *epoché* thus temporalizes the difference
> between what is present (*das Anwesende*) and presence (*Anwesen*
> understood as a verb). The way things are present varies from
> epoch to epoch, and once a reversal (*Wendung*) has inaugurated
> a new mode of presence the previous modes are irretrievably lost.
> We can trace the rise, the sway and the decline of such a mode
> of presence; that is we can trace its origin in the sense of *arché*. We
> can also unearth the theoretical and practical foundations on which
> a past epoch rested; that is, we can trace its origin in the sense of
> *principium*. This word designates indeed both the theoretical "prin-
> ciples" of a time and its practical *princeps* ("prince" or authority).
> But what we shall never be able to trace is the origin as *Ursprung*:
> the mode in which, at a given age in history, things emerge into
> presence, linger, have us dream, suffer, pray, make war, trade, etc.,
> and then, a few decades later, lose that way of being with us.[17]

Presencing eventuates a new economy of presence which in turn
manifests a new phenomenal arrangement. But presencing as such founds
nothing. It comes to pass. It is literally and emphatically an event. It cannot
be understood in terms of foundation, ground, or reason. In the sites, however, where the (epochal) presencing occurs, an economy of presence enables new phenomenal confluences and thereby a new constellation of truth
that makes the phenomenal configuration intelligible. Certain practices
become no longer intelligible or plausible and slip into hiding and oblivion.
Bearing different significations, entities (re-)appear in this new economy of
presence in different fashions. Thus, the difference between the present
entities and their presence marks an era. That is, each era comes with a
constellation of truth that is specifically "its own." Consider Schürmann's
example of stars as they reappear in different economies of presence: "They
have one way of being present when Aristotle treats them as divinities endowed with reason, soul and causal efficacy—the only intelligibles we can
also see. They have another mode of presence when, to a medieval person,
they are creatures each propelled by its angel, and another mode still in the
early modern designs of celestial mechanics."[18] That is how "disciplining
one's woman" a century ago becomes "spousal abuse" in our day. Some

practices are totally unintelligible from one economy of presence to the next. Child labor, prevalent throughout the history of human civilization, is becoming unthinkable in our day. From ancient Greek, to the medieval, to modernity, to the technological Enframing: with every epochal shift, presencing enables *principial* economies that render entities to acquire different presence. The epochal principle *destines* the modes of intelligibility through a constellation of truth. Circumscribed by the mode of concealedness-unconcealment as manifested in the epochal economy of presence, our destiny (*Geschick*) and the mode of articulation of our experiences are shaped.

The temporal difference allows us to experience the impending caesurae between the epochs. With the withering away of the epochal principle, the era it governed comes to an end. As such, the *principium* loses its coherence, its intelligibility and practicality, its "matter-of-factness." Its ultimate referents become questionable. Here, we must heed the origin as plural — that is, as *arché*, the beginning that dominates an epoch; as *principium-princeps*, the foundation and authority; and as *Ursprung*, the coming into presence of entities under a given epochal order.[19] The "*turning*," remarked Heidegger, indicates that the metaphysical epochal economy of presence we now live in will come to its end. "If Enframing is a destining of the coming to presence of Being itself, then we may venture to suppose that Enframing, as one among Being's modes of coming to presence, changes."[20] With the exhaustion of the epoch of Enframing now *in reach of our finely attuned sensitivity*, it may be the case that "in these decades of ours, the principle is reversing that hitherto has managed a long epoch; that therefore *as a principle, it becomes thinkable because it is already farther away . . .*"[21] The prolonged, slow and gradual withdrawal of the epochal principle from the current economy of presence grants us the possibility of perceiving not only the principial economy under whose rule we have been and are still living, but also, in this specific point in time, the possible transmutation into a nonprincipial economy. During such times, current practices, namely, political action, begin to lose their intelligibility and new modes of action become plausible. We call *reversal* such interstices when a principial economy starts to recede into absence. Reversal, therefore, designates "where 'metaphysics' is drawing to a close and where 'the other beginning' is opening up."[22] Epochal reversals have their specific *community* (called *Menschentum*) from which man receives its being. Reversal, therefore, is always hegemonic. This tells us something important: "In expiring, a principle renders itself speakable."[23] At times of reversal the origin "comes back," showing us that it is *essentially* (with italicized *esse* [being] to emphasize the temporal character of being)[24] irreducible to all it has given rise to. The eventuating "touch" of presencing allows entities to reemerge differently. We become aware that all phenomena we have experienced can suddenly slip into a different modality and our experiences of phenomena are not and cannot be ultimate.

Deconstructing, radical phenomenology shows the ontological difference in reversals and in moments of inception. "But the difference as initiating is the 'event of appropriation' [or *enowning*], *Ereignis*. Access to the event is thus through history."[25]

The reversal between the epochs is one key element in the genealogy of epochal principles. The "turning" (*die Kehre*) is another. It designates, strictly, the end of our (metaphysical) epochal history. The hypothesis of closure begins by attending to the "turning." With the "turning," the truth of the essence of being turns homeward into all that there is. As such, "being may eventually be thought of in itself, for its own sake—as the event of presencing. The lineage of ideal entities promoted to the rank of principles would reach its end."[26] The event of presencing defies historical continuity, and as mentioned, introduces the idea of the *leap* as the mode of economic displacements. "No progression, no evolution, links one destiny to the other. Summer does not 'become' autumn. Suddenly it is autumn, the entities, old age," writes Schürmann. "Suddenly there is another way of thinking. . . . Suddenly the anarchic economy is ours. . . . Such disjunctive ruptures are in no way spectacular. They may go unnoticed for a long time. . . . To become thinkable, they demand of us an equally *decisive* leap."[27] While the epochal displacements that take place in the history of metaphysics are *principial*, the "turning" and the hypothesis of closure tell us, the displacement from a metaphysical epoch to the postmetaphysical and post-modern is *nonprincipial* and *anarchic*: in the postmetaphysical era, all supreme Firsts and ultimate referents lose their sway. *The post-modern, therefore, can be distinguished by non-principial, anarchic action*—in that the legitimation of *praxis* cannot proceed from *theoria*. The end of philosophy as the project of founding and securing principles and norms of action appears along with the end of practice as conforming to the norms and principles put forward by philosophy. Here, post-modern, anarchic action must be properly understood. Schürmann reminds us that presencing allows us to view practice as a response to the epochal constellations of truth. What follows is that insofar as there are transmutations from one metaphysical, principial epoch to another, human action is stranded between *arché* and *telos*. With the "turning," then, presencing no longer leaves behind any principle. "The turn beyond metaphysics thus reveals *the essence of praxis: exchange deprived of a principle*."[28] Anarchic action, therefore, denotes the precedence of action in relation to theory.[29]

Anarché is enabled through *Ereignis*. As mentioned, the atomization of the origin is *diachronic* in the sense that the principle arises, governs, and expires. But it can also be *synchronic*. *Ereignis* designates a synchronic event of *local* singular presencing, and not a *universal* economy of presence. As such, the "event of Appropriation" remains an event of radical singularity in which every presence of phenomena—to be specific, the relationship between the entity and its world—is always particular, local, individual, and therefore radically plural and unsubsumable under any universal hold or category. "This pluralization and localization of beings in time and space, of time and space themselves, is essential . . . to be able to describe and to perform not only the break with all traditional economies of presence, but the leap into a new 'anarchic' economy and into a possible 'other practice' or 'other acting'."[30] The other practice or the other acting: indeed *anarchic praxis*—along with the "other thinking"—is the postmodern acting proper. Anarchic *praxis* "un-does the rational paradigms of control and domination."[31] After the "turning" and into the postmetaphysical and post-modern, action, now free of principles, of *arché* and of *telos*, gives rise to thinking. Indeed, thinking undergoes a stepping back because rational thinking, a thinking that represents and *explains*, gives way after the "turning" to the "other thinking" (i.e., to a thinking that "*responds* and recalls"[32]). The *animal rationale*, therefore, cannot survive the "turning." Post-modern humans acquire a new name: "mortals"—those who "have renounced all ultimate holds. Only as mortals can we 'enter into the event' [*Ereignis*]. 'Rational animal' is an attributive-predicative-referential concept while 'mortal' is a systemic one."[33] "As 'rational animal', man rules supreme over the economies, but as 'mortal' he is one variable within them."[34] The mortal, for whom there are no holds more originary than natality and mortality, responds to the *anarchic* presence of phenomena in their own particular terms and contexts in their own particular *worlds*.

Now, if, as Schürmann acknowledges, epochal principles "requisition" a community of humans to engage in a finite mode of thought and action (*Menschentum*) and if, as such, these principles constitute the origins of the political, then it must be asked, what are the political consequences of *postmodern, anarchic praxis*? After all, we know that the politics of each *principial* era involves the confluence of things, words, and actions according to the regulatory economy of presence and the normative constellation of truth of that era. The answer is: anarchic action is inseparable from the place (*topos*) of *praxis*; therefore, such *praxis* by definition renounces all norms and their subjugative, regulatory frameworks. All categorial, all "accusatory" (*kategorein*: "to accuse"), denominations (indeed "stereotypes," as Schürmann calls them) that enforce upon humans presumed modes of being or acting such as gender or race lose not only their *authority* but also their *legitimation*. "By overturning structures of oppression and tyranny, the deconstructive play of anarchy retrieves the place (*topos*) of action and political decision (*polis*). The *polis* ceases to be merely a cultural construct, and instead defines specific ways by which human beings experience truth as unconcealment and cultivate the possibilities of dwelling."[35] With the technological "turning," *Ereignis* may finally be thought of, not under norm generating *principia*, but "in-itself." Since after the "turning" there remains no principial constellation of truth, no principial economy of presence to organize and "normalize" all present phenomena around its truth and intelligibility, truth shows itself in the strife between concealedness and unconcealment, between presence and absence. "The zone of strife is also the creative nexus to engender new meanings and reconfigure the loci of political engagement beyond conventional paradigms of domination."[36] Anarchic praxis is therefore inseparable from a post-modern topology of being—topology in the sense of preparing proper places for truth as *alétheia* (unconcealment). The term "topology," of course, is Schürmann's which he uses to refer to a certain approach to being in the later Heidegger. According to Schürmann, in *Being and Time*, Heidegger raised the question of presencing as the "sense of being" (his Existential Analytic), later as the "truth of being" (his historical analysis), and finally, as the "topology of being."[37] I adopt Schürmann's term "topology" here to designate a preparatory attention to and attitude toward current practices of social movements that may imply the possibility of modes of practice free from *arché* and *telos*—modes of practice that can only be perceived if we have come to understand the post-modern, nonprincipial event of presencing. Put simply, topology accompanies anarchic praxis because unlike principial economies in which presence has fixed loci, after the "turning" and in the anarchic economy the topos of each presence is to be prepared for in order to embrace the singularity of each presence. By virtue of *anarchic praxis*, the anarchic actor is to "respond" and prepare for *anarchic* economy. As such, "the subject in this sense of an actor in history . . . disappears with the hypothesis of closure."[38]

A thinking that prepares for the "turning" abandons all ultimate standards and is thus foreign to the metaphysical concepts of thinking as determining and identifying principles and norms of action. Nor is acting without *telos* an action the way we have conceived of it under metaphysical domination. Strategic to the "other thinking"—which may have a long time to find itself, as long as, perhaps, three-hundred years "to have an effect"[39]—and for the "other acting" is *feint*. *Feigning* is indeed a part of the deconstruction of epochs. Such thinking remains forever inceptive: it is to "think" the "turning." Thinking, therefore, is always an inceptive *experience*.[40] With the "turning," presence is *experienced* as presencing. Everyday experience of things in their always already givenness, as the *identity* between presence and entities, becomes inoperative in the technological *Kehre* because with the "turning," *difference* between presence and entities shows itself as difference. "If presencing—'being'—is grasped only through its difference from epochal presence, then our everyday experience of being is lost forever as soon as a new fold unfurls presence in a new constellation. Everydayness gives us immediate access to presencing, but that access remains momentary."[41] This means that in anarchic economy each phenomenon must be "thought" (and not "thought about" in the sense that it is "represented" cognitively) in its own terms, in its *singularity* as such. *Experiencing* phenomena in their own terms and situated in their own worlds is now called "thinking." We can have access to these phenomena through our everyday experiences only insofar as everyday experiences immediately expire and slip into a *genuine experiencing* of phenomena free from principial holds and pregiven paradigms. This experiencing always remains an inceptive, nonhegemonic experience. A genuine experience destines its articulators toward *topoi*, toward places of singular presences.

Awareness of the possibility of *Kehre* grants us, the children of this possibly transitional period, unparalleled attentiveness to the "new" modes of acting as well as "new" modes of thinking. It is in this relation that we may now adequately heed the question what is "new" in new social movements.

Utopia Unnamed: What Is "New" in New Social Movements?

A more original site of action can be determined through the "reversal" of dominant political paradigms. Such reversal occurs as a "turning" motion in which the vacillation between the withdrawal and arrival of truth subverts the emphasis on what is already present in conventional political structures.

Frank Schalow, "Revisiting Anarchy"[42]

Awareness of the hypothesis of metaphysical closure sheds new light on the question, "What is 'new' in new social movements?" We are now able to determine the "newness" of the new social movements out of their relation to modernity as the last epoch of our metaphysical history. Specifically, undermining ultimate referentiality enables a deconstruction of norms of acting in social movements. The first step in releasing practice from referential-theoretical holds, as Frank Schalow states in the epigraph above, is to subvert "what is already present" together with the theoretical representations of its ultimacy in order to let the play between withdrawal and arrival show us the possibilities current practices intimate.

To establish what is "new" in new social movements from the standpoint of Schürmann's epochal theory, one needs to show precisely how specific transformations in the realm of practice mark the shift from the older movements to the new ones in relation to the institution and destitution of modern social movement practices and thus modernity itself. This task necessitates that certain practices of social movements, older or new, be reexamined in relation to certain categories. This approach arises from the conceptual necessity of showing what constellations of truth have lost their intelligibility and what practices their plausibility. Therefore, in a radical phenomenological way, first I introduce a list of categories that show the two constellational poles, prospective and retrospective; these poles mark the beginning and end of the era dominated by modern principles of social movement practices. Acknowledging the loss of philosophical legitimation of ultimate representations, "radical phenomenology acts like a deconstructive higher court cancelling the justifications of authority issued by the constructive lower court of metaphysics."[43] Consequently, these categories not only *expose* the modern metaphysical dominance over practice, they also *subvert* them. For, to announce the end of referential thinking and acting leads to preparation for *Ereignis*. "Categorial phenomenology does not seek to formalize an object or some representable content. It seeks to set free the continuities according to which the many networks of epochal presence have differed from presencing."[44] The categories that the analytical gaze of the radical phenomenologist deciphers are *prospective* and *retrospective*. But looking at the inception and termination of an era is not enough. If we are experiencing the closure of the metaphysical era, then we need to account for the "turning" that takes us from the point of closure of modernity to the threshold of the post-modern. We are therefore in need of a third class of categories: *transitional* categories are the "'guiding' traits, providing direction, rather than 'founding', providing a base."[45] Aside from these radical phenomenological categories, we also need to identify certain aspects of social movement practices to demonstrate the possibility of a reversal in acting. While the three classes of radical phenomenological categories (prospective, retrospective, and transitional)—which I have adopted from Schürmann's deconstruction of western metaphysical epoch—seem exhaustive,[46] the number of aspects of social movement practices is not. Of course, here I use Schürmann's model to apply to the social movements that are strictly modern phenomena. Thus, as my *prospective* categories correspond to the principial foundation of modern epoch as manifested in modern social movements, so my *retrospective* categories refer to the exhaustion of the modern *principia* as manifested in certain practices of the *new* social movements. Finally, the Janus' face of *transitional* categories shows us the possibility of looking ahead in search of "*a possible rule for a possible non-principial play of presencing* to come," anticipating the "traits of the 'homecoming'"[47] from social movement practices that are anchored in various metaphysical ultimacies. Transitional categories are *bifocal* and thus consist of two terms. Of the two terms, only the first one is *deconstructive*. The second one is *commemorative* (of the ancient, presocratic, beginning when applied to the history of western metaphysics) and *preparatory* (for "the other beginning").[48] The first term in the *transitional* categories refers to the closure of a *principial* epoch, the second term to the opening of a *nonprincipial* era. Thus, *conceptually*, the first term is not applicable past the post-modern threshold. Thus, we need to elaborate on the second terms of transitional categories in the next section of this chapter.

As mentioned, the list of the aspects of social movement practices that I am about to enumerate in Table 1 is not by any standard exhaustive. However, I must also assert that they are the major aspects that would identify the exercise of modern principles over social movements. I intend to show what aspects of practice the weakening sway of these formerly dominant principles over movement practices, which addresses the question of the "newness" of the new social movements, may anticipate or render intelligible in relation to the possible transition to a post-modern era. In the categories below, I take liberalism and Marxism as the two major instituting moments of modern social movements (which amounts to saying that fascism and national liberation movements are not institutive of modern movements but only continuations, variations, or reactions to the institutive movements).

Table 1. Radical Phenomenological Deconstruction of Social Movements.

	Prospective Categories	Retrospective Categories	Transitional Categories
Social category of actors	The proletariat (Marx), the unitary individual (liberalism)	Subject positions (Laclau and Mouffe)	Articulated experiences /mortals, singulars (Heidegger, Schürmann)
Modality of practice	The revolution (Marx), warranting of the rights of the citizen (liberalism)	Identity politics (various new social movement theories)	Hegemonic relations of equivalence (Laclau and Mouffe)/anarchic action (praxis) (Schürmann)
Locus of practice	The factory and the state (Marx), civil society and the state (liberalism)	Information networks and civil society (Melucci, Touraine)	Regime (Lefort)/the pathway (Heidegger)
Social project	Utopian emancipation (Marx), individual Happiness and freedom from state intervention (liberalism)	Multiplication of identities vis-à-vis pregiven universalistic identities	Radical democracy and agonistic pluralism (Laclau and Mouffe)/ "letting-be" (Heidegger)
Knowledge	Totality (emergence of class-for-itself out of class-in-itself) (Marx), the rational individual and social contract (liberalism)	Hegemonic closure (Laclau)	Supplement as dislocated center (Derrida)/the "clearing" (Heidegger), topoi of presence (Heidegger and Schürmann)

Let us now explain each aspect of movement practices in light of the hypothesis of closure.

Social category

The institution of modern social movement practices posited a preconstituted social category of "privileged agents" through whose action the movement practice would comply with the pregiven, universal standards of social development. These agents are "privileged" precisely because they are endowed, by virtue of their respective hegemonic and theoretical-referential constitution, with a unique and irreplaceable capacity to fulfil a certain historical endeavour. This genus of "universal activist" has interesting characteristics. Since she or he receives her or his being from the universal logic of History, the universal activist always remains a *generic* subject, who is (mysteriously) predisposed with the ability to substitute for all particular subjects and their practices so long as the latter's particular demands can be brought into the universal project of historical fulfillment. The subject's uniqueness lies in that he represents the only class of humankind that bears knowledge about the Logic of History and its existing configuration(s). Such a compelling knowledge requires from the subject assuming the role of the privileged agent of History. He is a *unitary* agent who bears no internal differences, fragmentation, or conflict. Once achieved, the historical fulfillment will transform the subject and the agent into the *homogeneous* "new humanity." As Lyotard aptly articulated it, in the political narrative of legitimation, the "subject . . . is humanity as the hero of liberty."[49] Neither this heroism nor that homogeneous liberty survived the new social movement practices. In the Marxist discourse, the proletariat stood for such an *"ontologically* privileged agent," as Laclau and Mouffe described it, who was the sole class of activists endowed with the capacity to fulfill the historical mission of taking humanity in toto beyond the bourgeois society. The liberal discourse also posited the unitary conception of individual such as the citizen. The citizen is not only the subject to whom, and exclusively so, certain rights are guaranteed and protected by the state. The citizen is, more importantly, the agent that is capable of perpetuating the society founded upon the liberal principle of the rights of the individual. As such, the citizen views society as a social contract of one or another kind in which he or she participates. Both in Marxism and in liberalism, we can recognize the assumed presence of a unitary agent who, by virtue of its constitution, can guarantee the pace of society in the path "predestined" by an ordaining historical logic in the process of fulfilling itself. The difference between Marxism and liberalism, however, lies in the fact that agency in Marx is primarily *historical*, while in liberalism it is principally *structural* (hence the oppressive categorization of rights-bearing subjects).

With new social movements, the defeat of the revolutionary agent came first, as the unique logic of a unilinear History lost its intelligibility. The liberal democratic subject, however, retained its position, due to the prevailing hegemony as well as the structural-categorial flexibility of techno-logical liberalism. Nonetheless, the subject's unitary pretence sustained irre-coverable discredit, as his inevitable fragmentation was revealed at the crossroads of various subject positions. The identity known as the "citizen" is increasingly losing its once unquestioned primacy, giving rise to the un-precedented articulation of sexual, gender, ethnic, regional, ecological, la-bor, communal, aboriginal and numerous other identities. As such, the new movements' practices show the possibility of letting actors flourish out of the now inevitably fragmented hegemonic subject. Theoretically speaking, these actors receive their identities from the modes of action proper to their sub-ject positions. The increasing free play of the particular moments of resis-tance and antagonism may forecast the possibility of actors liberated from, firstly, the hegemonic inculcations that situate the subject within the existing regimes, and secondly, from the structural or historical mission(s) assigned to the agent. It can, theoretically speaking, also release *action* from the prison house of *activity*. I shall soon return to this point, but for now suffice it to say that *while activity receives its agenda from the hegemonic configuration of the social and has the subject as its performer, action is essentially anarchic. The actor is the incarnation of action.* The actor can never precede action. Thus, while *action* and subsequently *actor* are nonprincipled, *activity* and thereby the *subject* and the *agent* are always governed by principles.

The concept of *subject positions* subverts assumptions about the exist-ence of historically or structurally endowed unitary and privileged subjects. It signals a theoretical departure from the modern era of movement practices whose beginning was marked by Marxism and liberalism, and by the subject and the agent. The concept of subject positions indeed marks the springing of the *new* social movements out of the suffocating shell of the privileged, unitary, homogeneous, and universal subject or agent. Doing away with universal programs, the new movements seem to increasingly liberate them-selves from various forms of compliance with pregiven and normative struc-tural or historical logics. Through their practice, they acknowledge the "internal fragmentation" of the modern subject and refute many forms of subsumptive categorization. As such, the new movements intimate the *pos-sible* exhaustion of the modern principles that inform the social category that constitutes a movement. No deconstructive social movement theory has ever alluded to this possibility, for this possibility requires from us an abandon-ment of the habitual ways of thinking hegemony. While the performative approach of Laclau and Mouffe allows a radical rethinking of hegemony, it does not subvert the modern idea of hegemonic governance as such. Laclau

and Mouffe represent thinkers who provide a postmodern, pragmatic response to the modern question of governance, but they do not reformulate
the question itself and thus do not invite the possibility of social life free from
the hitherto known modes of governance as such (however hard to imagine
as it may seem from our present metaphysical stance).

As the first term of transitional categories, the *genuine* (i.e., nonhegemonic) articulation of experiences, which set in motion destinal movements,
anticipates the possibility of life in nonhegemonic politics in which particularities dwell in a political realm while retaining their irreducible difference.
In this relation, the concept of *experiential hegemony*—which demystifies
the question of democratic governance as inherited from liberalism—indicates our radical awareness about the *hegemonic articulation of experiences*
and thereby *hegemonic, principial destiny*. Because of the condition of life
under a principial economy, a clandestine but powerful inceptive experience
perpetually haunts our articulations. So much so that the allusive possibility
of nonhegemonic articulation of experiences necessitates the subversion of
hegemony back to its instituting moment. Therefore, high among the strategies of nonhegemonic articulated experiences is the ever so new rearticulation
of the past. In this sense, *remembering* as such is the most subversive political
act of all. Thus, by virtue of its conceptual relationship of hegemony and
destiny, the concept of articulated experiences deconstructs the performative
and pragmatic approach to the question of hegemony. Genuine articulated
experiences refer to the *subjects* who stand at the threshold of becoming
*actors. Once this bold step is taken, genuine articulation of experiences can
take us beyond the principial destinies* that are legitimized by channelling our
experiences through certain hegemonic worldviews and social categories of
subjects and agents. In our time, articulation of experiences that disrupt
hegemony can take us to the threshold of anarchic destiny. Therefore,
genuine articulated experiences indicate a preparation for nonhegemonic
sociality. This enormous leap into the post-modern entails the removal of
all ultimacies, of forms of legitimation through normative standards, and of
the *injustice* (*hubris*) of the "enforced residence under principial surveillance—whatever form it may take."[50] The removal of modern, metaphysical principles over practice will allow politics as the confluence of speech,
deeds, and things to reappear in a totally different way. This confluence is
the politics of mortals (i.e., the actors proper of the posttechnological era).[51]
Thinking action in terms other than referentiality, to which anti-humanism
summons our caring attention, will be the strategy of mortals who no
longer reign over the world as supreme but are simply one variable among
the many.[52] It is with mortals that *phenomenal democracy* can also include
humans as players, instead of having them as rulers. To the category of mortals
belong those who have rid themselves of preoccupation with fundaments and

warrants, goals and finalities. "Once that preoccupation is undone, the extended family of woodcutters, forest rangers, poets, and thinkers comes to include all actors."[53] In an anarchic economy of presence, phenomena stand as *singulars* in relation to one another, and therefore, not subsumable under any universal hold (as may particulars). Mortals live in this world of singulars; indeed, each one of them becomes a singular. These actors are all, like woodcutters and forest rangers, frequenters of the wood paths.

The modality of practice

Recall, from Chapter 3, how for revolutionary Marxism the moment of the workers' strike is not merely a particular event (i.e., strike in the strict sense of the term) but also the moment of the universal emancipatory Revolution. The strike is, in other words, a metonymy for the Revolution (a part standing for the whole). As the universal moment of the dialectical consummation of the existing conflicts, the Revolution incarnates itself in every particular conflict. So much so that any particular moment that does not fall within the boundaries of the revolutionary discourse, and thus is not a metonymy of the Revolution, will be treated as a nonmoment (hence, the late and uneasy recognition of women's, gays, ecological, and many other movements by certain variations of the Left). For a long time, the Revolution imposed on all social movements certain practices that conformed to its *teleological norms of activity*. The exhaustion of the revolutionary model of movement practice allowed the new movements to "liberate" the particular moment from the pregiven, universalistic (revolutionary) discourse of resistance. It has led to "the decline of the unifying and legitimating power of the grand narratives of speculation and emancipation," as Lyotard commented on a strikingly analogous matter (science).[54] Once the universal moment of the Revolution loses its subsumptive grip over heterogeneous movement practices, a free play of the particular moments of resistance and a plurality of modes of antagonism become possible. Emphasis on group particularity (identity politics) marks the exhaustion of the prospective category informed by the principle of Revolution over movement practices and thus the reversal of the modern sway in this respect. New social movements have shown that not only do they dwell in these particular moments, but also, they problematize the entire teleological discourse of revolutionary practice by multiplying and plurifying their particular moments.

The emergence of particularities as we witness in the new social movements also shows the fundamental failure of the liberal state in championing the expansion of the rights of the citizen. The citizens enjoy rights and the possibility of expansion of those rights precisely so long as they unproblematically identify with this regime and its self-image. Under the sway of liberalism, the expansion of rights in fact requires from citizens to give their consent to further categorization—one that hides the violence of "pressing-near" with unparalleled gestures of freedom and rights. This is how the technological liberalism portrays it rights-bearing subjects as free acting individuals. Herein lies the paradox the new social movements actors find themselves facing: without appealing to their citizenship, the new movements' actors cannot legitimize their particularistic rights. But these rights, as mentioned, undermine the liberal notion of unitary subject called the citizen. Furthermore, identity politics demystifies, to varying degrees, the all-embracing category of the citizen and shows the structural handicap of technological liberalism in subsuming genuine practices under its oppressive categories. The new movements have indeed radicalized the entire modern project of citizenship and their struggles to expand rights have mostly aimed at the recognition of the rights that are particular to specific groups. Consider the example of the gay movement: it never stood *as* the particular moment *in relation to* the universal moment of the Revolution. However, once the normative grip of revolutionary practices slackened and as a result new social movements' entry into politics became possible, the political yielded, to a certain extent, to the play of differences. But at the same time, the practices of various gay movements have been increasingly undergoing self-radicalization and multiplication, producing several particular moments (gay, queer, etc.) without the prospect that these particular moments can ever converge based on the pregiven logic of a universal moment. The convergence of these movements now entirely depends on the modes of articulation in the political. The gay movement struggles for certain rights that cannot be expanded to all citizens (e.g., the right to legal same sex marriage). Particularistic rights have indeed made many of us question the liberal notion of universal categories of the subject. The recognition of one's particular rights no longer necessarily or directly strengthens one's identification through citizenship. That is why identity politics defines our retrospective category.

The first term of the transitional category in relation to the modality of practice is the hegemonic relations of equivalence (Laclau and Mouffe), a concept that entails the deconstruction of the relationship between universality and particularity. The hegemonic relations of equivalence show how a particular becomes universal through hegemonic articulatory practices that bring several particularities together in a hegemonic formation. As such, universality derives its legitimacy from practice, and not from an impending metonymic presence that forces itself onto particular practices (Revolution). The modern, universalistic *teleocracy* is thus subverted. Both the Revolution and citizenship lose their normative-regulative power over movement practices.

Relations of equivalence indicate the convergence of several horizons into one hegemonically inclusive imaginary. With the "turning" and the ensuing possibility of nonhegemonic configuration, *anarchic* action, an action free from founding inception and normative ends, becomes the modality of practice proper to the post-modern society—one in which universality, in all its expressions, gives way to the endless play of particularities that with the former's self-exhaustion will become *singulars* in the event of Appropriation.

The locus of practice

In the Marxist discourse, the revolutionary practice of the proletariat has its roots in the economism of the factory and its objective in the capturing of the state power as the locus through which society could transcend capitalism. The idea that movement practices must have certain preconstituted loci is a distinguishing characteristic of modern social movements. Indeed, the pregiven loci of movement practices belong in the same package as the ontological privilege of the historical agent and the inevitable mode of practice. From this locus, the agent delivers its historic mission. But such pregiven loci of movement practices must not be understood of exclusively Marxian origin. In the liberal discourse, the origins of movements are much harder to identify, because demands emerge precisely out of the hazy sphere where the distinction between civil society and the state no longer holds (in spite of the liberal gestures to the contrary). The conflictual relations between, on the one hand, the new struggles that have their roots in the experiential plains which many uncritically attribute to the civil society, and on the other, the existing rights recognized by the state and guaranteed by laws show that the articulation of every new demand indeed represents a moment of problematization of the long held distinction between the state and civil society. Characteristic of the modern era, institutional politics has engendered party politics, and party politics by definition always involves engagement with the state as the unique locus of dissemination of politics. It is from this locus, and this locus alone, that an activity can acquire its political quality. In other words, an activity is political because it engages, directly or indirectly, in party politics to affect the state—or even subvert the state power in case of insurgent parties. This in turn means that modern liberal politics is rigidly organized around the distinction between civil society and the state, in which the former sphere represents the decisions made in and by the latter, and the demands of the former are represented and responded to in the latter. The collapse of representational politics by modes of activity of new social movements has problematized the distinction between civil society and the state. The new movements undermine the privileged pregivenness of the state as *the* locus of struggle or institution of society. This has become possible through the increasing involvement of the new movements in such loci of social life as information networks (Melucci) and civil society (Touraine). The new movements disturb the clear-cut distinctions between production and consumption or between state and civil society. With the loci of movement practices so widely dispersed across the field of action and so unpredictably emerging anew or renewed ever more frequently, no pregiven locus of practice can sustain its privileged stance. More importantly, the struggles of the new movements for the recognition of the rights that particularly address specific identities, the long held and cherished liberal distinction between state and civil society also loses its intelligibility. In short, the pregivenness of the loci of practice, which makes our prospective category, now meets its exhaustion in the face of the increasing multiplication of the new movements and their practices.

This point deserves closer attention. The new movements engage in various forms of struggle, thereby showing the originally political character of all spheres of life and all loci of struggle, exposing the illusory distinction between the state and civil society by pointing out, implicitly or explicitly, the hegemonic institution of the social and by unveiling the construction of consent by the regimes of technological liberalism. New social movements are rightly characterized by their identity politics, but the term *identity politics* does not adequately capture the vast stretch of action from the state to civil society and thus does not problematize the long presumed modern binarisms of public-private, politics-society, or the state-civil society. The new movements' practices do away with all kinds of rigidly formative and circumscribing preconstituted loci and appear wherever identities and demands for new rights are claimed. The locus of practice, in other words, follows the possible itineraries of the expansion of rights. It must be acknowledged that this ongoing expansion has been made possible by the liberal principle of rights. Although to this day, the liberal state has retained its position as the sole granter and guarantor of rights, it has clearly lost vision and leadership in regard to the generation of new rights. One can clearly observe that new social movements are so creatively and unpredictably ahead of the state in demanding the reformulation of rights that the state can only significantly lag behind in response. The gay movement exemplifies this point: it has always put forth demands before the state (e.g., legal marriage of gays and the subsequent rights: legal parenthood, adoption rights, partner benefits) that to this day any decision of the state can only signify the latter's unjustified belatedness.

These great achievements become possible through the abolition of "representation" (a metaphysical operation). For Melucci, the multiplication of loci of emergence of new social movements indicates the "democratization of everyday life."[55] The radicality of the new movements lies in that they democratize everyday life precisely through their democratization of politics as given by the hegemonic regime. Insofar as the new movements' practices allude to the inadequacy of party and institutional politics, insofar as they reveal and challenge, in practice, the hegemonic institution of the existing regime, and insofar as they refuse to be subsumed under categories of practice assigned to the hegemonic subject and agent, *they may bear within them the seeds of anarchic action.* The real prospect that the new movements are eventually "pressed-near" into the categories of rights-bearing subjects of technological liberalism does not refute the point I made about the possibility of *anarchic* action: *I refer not to the new movements as we investigate them here and now, but to what will possibly emerge out of new social movements (i.e., through their transmutation), past the post-modern threshold.* Speculations about the co-optation of the new movements truly reinforce my argument by attesting to the real threat of the domination of technological liberalism. Technological liberalism imposes itself as a challenging force that new social movements are to face head-on, should the epochal "turning" eventuate the proper phenomenal possibility.

Accordingly, the first term of the transitional categories (i.e., Lefort's concept of regime), remains a powerful critique of the invisible domination of technological liberalism that is founded upon the state-civil society binary. The concept of regime becomes a radical deconstruction of technological liberalism, showing that it hides and suppresses internal aporias through its celebration and upholding of the principle of rights. The ramifications of the concept of regime are so far-reaching that once one becomes aware of the three-fold operation of the regime, one can no longer perceive of any known form of governance, including liberal democracy, as genuinely democratic. Therefore, the concept of regime always points toward *anarché*. The second transitional category is the "pathway," a metaphor Heidegger used to refer to *anarchic* action and thought. The pathway is the place in which action is free from *arché* and *telos*. As we shall soon see, only in the pathway can we conceive of nonhegemonic existence.

The social project

The presupposed privileged agent of the transparent logic of History rendered modern movement practices *teleocratic.* Communism exemplifies the Utopia that dominated over some of the greatest revolutionary movements of the twentieth century. Utopia is indeed the name for the normative-regulative force of a *finality* that in fact constitutes the *origin* of social movement. In this regard, modern revolutionary movements (socialist or national liberation) show their continuity with the history of metaphysics in reminding us of Aristotle's normative notion of *telos* which in fact comes to determine the *arché*. However, Utopia lost its sway over movement practices as new social movements gave up the promised future for the uncertainty of the present, disregarded utopian visions in favour of individual and group identity, and replaced regulative powers of such visions with rather pragmatic struggles for the recognition and exercise of the rights of diverse identities. It is in this respect that the liberal conception of rights exhibits the possibility of closure of the prospective category of Utopian emancipation. Struggles for the recognition of identity and for warranting the rights necessary for upholding and perpetuating such identities indicate the "unnaming of utopia" that perhaps has had the most subversive effect on modern, *teleocratic* movement practices. With *Utopia unnamed*, actors can rid themselves of the obsessive-compulsive desire for warranting in advance the type and extent of, as well as assuring continuity in, change. The word Utopia indeed is the Achilles' heel of the domination of modern metaphysics over the practices of social movements.

The liberal discourse obviously lacks the Marxian type of grandiose utopian project primarily because its project does not have to wait until after the revolutionary transformation. We are, as Francis Fukuyama believes, living the triumphant liberal utopia at the "end of history," in which, with the collapse of all its rivals, liberal society is now destined to flourish. At the pinnacle of the liberal discourse stands the principle of the individually defined Happiness, which requires a certain guaranty that such definition should not be disturbed by the state's definition. One must not overlook the normative-regulative character of the principle of Happiness. As the arch principle of liberalism, the individually defined Happiness bears an inherent political character. Happiness, thus, becomes the name of a normative-regulative arch principle toward which the society is presently moving. The power of the principle of Happiness, however, lies in that in our day it does not need to wait for a dramatic passage (e.g., revolution). The universal principle of Happiness is represented here and now every time a particular right is achieved, such that the achieved new rights or greater freedom would not be possible without this normatively operative utopian principle of Happiness. As such, the defenders of liberalism refer to particular identity claims as the examples of the flourishing of individually defined notions of Happiness without the state intervention. Precisely thus, they subsume all particular movements under their universalistic principle of Happiness and conceal its teleocratic, regulative hold.

The deconstructive terms of the transitional categories with respect to social project are the radical democracy and agonistic pluralism of Laclau and Mouffe. With the subversion of the positivity of the social, the abolition of the liberal notion of the unitary individual, the recognition of the plurality of actors and demands, the metaphoric character of all social practices, the primacy of the political, the original particularity of universals, the operative chain of equivalence in democratic politics of the new movements, and finally, with the radical contingency of hegemony, Laclau and Mouffe rightly arrive at the agonistic characteristic of a radical democracy that by definition consists of plurality of actors and multiplicity of visions that inevitably fill the political realm with diverging practices. As a deconstruction of modern politics, radical democracy, theoretically speaking, invites a departure from institutional and party politics the way we know it. My critique of Mouffe's affirmation of basic liberal institutions and principles stems from my argument that radical democracy may represent the possible anticipatory politics that looks forward to the epochal transmutation. However, *radical democracy cannot become the post-modern political configuration of society because it has not done away with the very concept of hegemony*. After the "turning" and with the withering away of *principial* economies, the *anarchic* action of mortals become manifestations of what Heidegger called *letting-be*. That is to say, now action yields to things and mortals that present themselves in a multitude of ways as presencing as such lets them be. In letting-be, with the *anarchic* economy, presencing lets entities flourish time and time again in new modes of presence.

Knowledge

Let us return to the example of the strike: if the particular moment of the strike always represents the universal moment of the Revolution, then the revolutionary consciousness is nothing but the expression of the universal moment. In other words, one's knowledge about his or her position in the society, and subsequently the position she or he takes, is always measured against a totality. *Totality* is the realm in which a universal reigns: due to the preconstituted domination of the universal, the free play of particulars is constantly suppressed. Therefore, the particular is not conceivable qua particularity as such within totality. If the subject cannot recognize the totality as represented in the particular moment, the subject suffers from "false consciousness." The particular is therefore always a channel through which the universal reveals the laws of societal development and thereby the practices proper. The task of the particular is then to discover those laws by mooring its own particularity in the universal and thus becoming the latter's representation. Older movements, revolutionary or otherwise, all appealed to a universal knowledge about the *totality* of history, development, the autonomous individual, and the like, and channelled movement practices in order to conform to those laws. In modern social movement discourses, knowledge refers to awareness about totality. In fact, all configurations of modern politics—Marxist, liberal, national liberation, or any other—posit classes of subjects whose knowledges do not notably surpass the idle confirmation of to-tality of one kind or another. Consider Marx's theory of revolution: in order to become the vanguard revolutionary class, the proletariat must transcend class-in-itself (its being) and grow into a class-for-itself (its agency). It must become aware of social totality out of which it emerges as a universal class. Therefore, the universality of the revolutionary agent is not possible without knowledge of the totality of society and the moment of revolution.

In spite of important internal variations, the liberal discourse assumes that ultimate knowledge about society can be acquired. The citizen, this unitary subject, is also a rational individual who is able to calculate the costs and benefits that may arise from the individual's participation in the social contract. The concept of society as a social contract enables the liberal discourse to connect the rational subject to the rationally founded society. Thus, at any given time, society is viewed as the crystallization of inherited social contracts. Such ideas as John Rawls' "veil of ignorance"—that curtains the judgment of two agents about their possible losses and gains, should they enter a social contract—do not really undermine the liberal assumptions about the rationality of the individual and the rational foundations of society. Here, society itself, presented as social contract, represents the totality of knowledges. The role of the hegemonic subject of liberal regimes is precisely to acknowledge that totality and act according to its preconstituted rational logic.

New social movements refuse to represent such overarching universal-ity and show that totality is a modernist phantasm. Once the universal loses its omnipresence (i.e., its power over the particular loci out of which it can represent itself) it becomes inexpressible. That is to say, in the absence of particular expression, the universal consciousness becomes mute and loses its grip. This is probably one of the greatest lessons that the study of new social movements has for us: *since there is not, and has never been, any universal language of action, the universal can never speak universally.* This amounts to saying, with Laclau, that every universal is in fact a dominant particular. By bringing other particulars into its language, the hegemonic particular becomes universal. The prospective category that measures the knowledge of the agent against the yardstick of a pregiven totality comes to an end with the retrospective category that shows every totality is merely a *closure.* A contribution of Laclau to political theory, the concept of closure indicates that the class actor is never fully present. Therefore, the metaphoric charac-ter of the strike undermines the universal moment of Revolution and the subsequent totalistic social transformation. The necessary character of total-ity gives way to the contingency of closure. The refusal of the particular moment of strike to lend its speech to the universal moment of the Revolu-tion subverts the latter and liberates the particular from the burdensome universal terms that incline to reduce and regulate the playfulness of the particular as witnessed nowadays in the practices of new social movements. The universal loses its monopolized concession over the articulation of experiences of its particulars. This offers another important lesson: *the particular knowledge cannot be delegated, for it cannot precede action*. It is always action (*praxis*) that determines what direction the play of particular consciousness should take. Since action can only be properly understood in relation to its context, the emergence of knowledge out of action must be dealt with through the study of each particular new social movement as its practices unfold.

The deconstructive term of transitional category as regards knowledge is the Derridean concept of "supplement" as dislocated center. It teaches that every totality is in fact the *effect* of a dislocation by an outside that brings a system to a closure. As such, an actor's knowledge about her or his particular identity as a decentered identity is also always knowledge about the particularity of her or his constitutive outside, of her or his *other*. Now, antagonisms are to be understood to take place between two particularities with one of the particularities questioning the universal gesture of another, thereby fracturing its pretence of totality. "Supplement" observes a society in which phenomenal conflicts are imposed upon particular phenomena by the grip of universal gestures. Nevertheless, by exposing that no totality is ever truly total and no universality universal, supplement also bears the *possibility* of moving beyond such conflicts and their corresponding violence. The final withering of all universals, which can only become possible past the post-modern threshold, allows knowledge to submit itself to the Heideggerian concept of *clearing*. Poets and thinkers, forest rangers and woodcutters of nonhegemonic phenomenal arrangements and of an *anarchic* economy of presence now heed the *topoi* of presence and acquire knowledge from each *singular* phenomenon as it discloses itself.

Informed by the hypothesis of closure, these five categories of social movement practices highlight the abandonment of the principle of *Utopia* as the crux of what is "new" in new social movements. The abandonment of the powerful sway of a normative *telos* is key in understanding the radical newness of new social movements. In various modern political practices, the term *Utopia* has been referring to the principle, governing action and thought, that society systemically involves a projected universal horizon which legitimizes, in fact requires, certain modes of practice and intelligibility—a universal horizon towards which society as a whole is deemed to normatively progress. Utopia has been the prime characteristic of all modern, universal models of the socio-historical development of human governance. As discussed, in the contexts set forth by the principle of Utopia, any particular demand or attainment is necessarily and inevitably a step toward, and therefore inseparable from, the universal. Various Marxisms, for example, considered socialism, the labour movement, women's rights movements and national liberation as stances representing the moments of a monistic movement toward the classless society. In liberal democratic regimes of our day, these movements are *not* treated as threats against the existing liberal model of governance, but as evidence for the flourishing and expansion and for the functionality of liberalism. Under the normative grip of Utopia, any particular remains particular insofar as it signifies the universal direction that Utopia will generate. All the categories I discussed above indicate that in practice new social movements have resisted the subsumption of particulars (and their actions proper) under the universal principle(s) of a totalizing Utopia. Thus, the particular demand and attainment no longer reinforces Utopia; quite the contrary, the particular problematizes and delegitimizes the universal.

By using the imprecise term "identity politics," what we refer to nowadays is the twilight of modernity, which raises the question about our being situated differently today through a different mode of unconcealment. The mode of unconcealment *may* allow the individual's identity to no longer signify identification with a pregiven principle such as citizenship or a utopian historical project. The individual's identity *may* now appear, with this new mode of unconcealment, as penetrated by a *temporal difference* between an actual mode of insertedness (identity) and the possible reinsertedness (identification) which defies, in this case, universal norms. Utopia unnamed signifies the ontological difference between the way one currently *is* and the way one can *be*, should the normative grip of the modern, *principial* economy recede onto itself. For, in a possible nonprincipled unconcealment, the social imaginaries are *essentially* differential in that they designate the destinal distance between one's existing place and one's possible place(s) of arrival in an irreducibly plural fashion.

In practice, new social movements have subverted Utopian principles and totalistic models. Their practices attest to the fact that Utopia has lost its intelligibility and plausibility. They do not allow Utopia to articulate their experiences in universal terms or to im-pose upon their movements a certain totalizing and normative horizon. Stated precisely, the new social movements resist such forms of destinal enframing as Utopia represents. Therefore, new social movements allow a multiplicity of destinal movements to arise, a plurality of social imaginaries to capture their actors' imaginations, a broader and embracing horizon to summon their enthusiasms, and their identities to recede further and further as they move on the destinal path. With Utopia unnamed, put out of play and possibly operatively out of existence, new social movements seem to be in the process of liberating their practices from those impositions (in prospective categories) as mentioned in the five aspects of movement practices. It is precisely in this respect that the present investigation does not regard right-wing social movements as "new":

despite their seemingly "non-utopian" agendas, right-wing movements entail a dangerously utopian tendency toward the universal models taken from the past or from certain moral doctrines that violently exclude various minorities, sexual orientations, the poor, and so on. Right-wing movements suppress all particularities that do not conform to their universalistic models. The danger of right-wing movements lies in their relative success in hiding their violent and suppressive tendencies behind their grassroots popularity as well as their democratic and reformist gestures and self-acclaimed "reasonable" and "practical" agendas.

Utopia derives from metaphysics due to the operative determination of *arché* by *telos*. In the study of social movements, this reminds us of the fact that almost all *revolutionary social movements had their origins in the goals they sought to achieve*. "Utopia unnamed" signifies the death of *teleocracy* and thus suggests the weakening of the principle of reason and its foundationalist expressions. Moreover, it implies that there is a possibility of nontotalistic and nonteleocratic articulation of experiences. Once the economy of presence slips into this nonprincipial modality, the actor is able to articulate experiences without the burden of a normative *telos*, a superior reason, a binding logic, a mysteriously privileged agent, a definitive place of arrival, or a suffocating totality. Utopia unnamed, the fall of teleocratic normativity, with its tremendous ramifications for political life (of which I discussed five aspects) is precisely what is new in new social movements. The emergence of particularities as particularities has now become possible: the particular no longer has to reside from the outset under the overarching arcade of the universal. However uneasy, it can now emerge as a particularity. Whether a particular will or will not eventually be subsumed under the universal does not refute the fact that new social movements demonstrate the possibility of nonuniversalized emergence of particularities. That is why the new movements allude to an initial break in the hegemonic, universal project of political modernity.

Thus, as Frank Schalow suggests in the epigraph to this section, we must come to acknowledge an important shift in "dominant political paradigms"—a turn in the epochal constellation of truth that allows certain modes of action to be no longer intelligible, a transition we are only beginning to experience, if we have salvaged our sensitivity from numbing monotony that is symptomatic of *principial* holds to the extent of paying heed to the possible *anarchic* epochal unconcealment.

Before attending to anarchic acting, I should clarify two points regarding my approach to the new social movements. These points are intended to cancel certain theoretical attitudes toward the study of social movements. The first point regards the investigation of newness in the study of social movements. In Chapter 4, I drew on the Zapatistas of Mexico to offer a theory of articulation of experiences. Let us now situate the Zapatista movement in the context of the inceptive shift in political practices that the new movements represent. In addition to the unnaming of Utopia, what qualifies the Zapatista movement as a *new* social movement is their resistance against the hegemony of liberal discourse. By refusing to become an institutionalized party or to seek power, the Zapatistas signify the beginning of a new era in revolutionary politics. The era of revolutionary Left in Latin America is marked by the 1959 Cuban revolution, which founded an era dominated by the triumphant utopia of socialism, a *telic* imaginary that kindled a new ray of hope among Latin American masses that suffered from malnutrition, poverty, dictatorships, coups, and corruption. Cuba also literally *assigned* a specific mode of political action (i.e., armed, guerrilla struggle), to achieve that imaginary. The 1994 Chiapas uprising marked the end of the era formerly instituted by Cuba. When the Zapatistas abandoned their initial allegiance to Maoist doctrines and learned to *listen* (be "obedient," in Marcos' words) to the indigenous communities, and as they transformed into an armed movement for peace and for a "new world," the grip of the principle of utopian revolutionary Left had already expired. The mode of unconcealment had slipped into a presence of political practices that were not *teleocratic*. However, between these two outermost signposts of that era of Latin American revolutionary practice, there sparked an agonizing moment of interstitial undecidability: the Sandinista revolution of 1979 in Nicaragua. The fact that after a decade of bloody civil war against the US-backed Contras, the Sandinistas accepted their electoral defeat to the Nicaraguan right in 1990, shows, in a commentator's words, that "the idea of revolution has withered and virtually died because its outcomes ha[d] become either unwanted or unimaginable."[56] It is against this background that the Zapatista movement shows its significance as standing at the threshold of a radical shift in Latin American politics.

Furthermore, the Zapatistas also denote the beginning of a new era of political praxis. It is in this relation that the Zapatistas represent one of the most vivid examples of new social movements, even though they have not emerged in Western postindustrial societies, do not express middle class radicalism, are not identity claims taking place in a liberal democratic polity, and even though they are, in their core, an armed guerrilla movement. The novelty of the Zapatista movement cannot be understood through superficial categorizations of many European "sociological" new social movement theories. What matters to the radical phenomenologist is to investigate how certain principles that govern action in an era suddenly cease to be intelligible or to seem plausible. What is important is to heed the loci *(topoi)* in which the certain practices manifest their presence without making reference to the existing principles of action. What is essential is to see how unconcealment addresses us from behind the concealedness of the everyday and what possibilities that unconcealment entails.

The specific forms or practices of each social movement are to be studied in relation to changes in eras and times. In the example of the Zapatistas, their unnaming of Utopia even led to what some observers called a "reinvention of revolution."[57] It may well be the case that the Zapatistas of Mexico offer to the world its first *nonteleocratic* revolutionary practice. With Utopia unnamed, their concept of "dignity" calls for a radical transformation of society. "Dignity" is the Zapatista social imaginary, a receding signified, a horizon that retreats in itself, for it "implies a constant moving against the barriers of that which exists, a constant subversion and transcendence of definitions."[58] With Utopia unnamed, we can expect further radical redefinitions or subversions of current movement practices to take place. And that is precisely what renders a movement to be a new social movement. This point essentially refutes many characteristics that the "sociological" new social movement theorists identify to distinguish between older and new movements.

The second point regarding my approach to social movements involves the categorization of movements based on historical periodizations. The question whether new social movements are *historically* "new" phenomena has been the topic of debates. Lorna Weir, for example, has pointed out that some of the movements identified to be "new" had already emerged as early as the late nineteenth century.[59] The point that Weir makes forces new social movement theories to establish what exactly constitutes "newness" in the new movements. Her criticism of new social movement theory eventually leads her to call for the elimination of the term from the language of the Left. But in her call for such abandonment, she shows that she has not really grasped the newness in the new movements. It is true, as she claims, that some of the new movements (women's, sexual minorities, urban social struggles) were present as long ago as the late nineteenth century. However, she misses the point that, due to the constellation of truth in modernity, these movements had emerged and functioned within the dominant paradigm of politics of their time, which, in the West, was constructed around the liberal public-private distinction and organized around the unitary citizen. These movements were from the outset subsumed under the political configurations of their time and did not offer any alternative politics. This is an example of how an analyst misses the fact that the "same" phenomenon can appear differently in different periods in time. The movements Weir refers to could not have appeared as new movements then. But they *can* — in fact, they do — now. For a radical phenomenologist, the statement that the new movements had already appeared almost a century ego amounts to implying a temporal difference: entities such as civil society and the state present themselves in a different mode of unconcealment, for now the new movements' practices indicate that a new confluence of things, speech, and action have emerged. In other words, certain practices become unintelligible and appear differently. Now, it is the task of the social *movement study to see precisely how this difference occurs*. The specific modality of presence of the late nineteenth century politics subsumed the constituents of the so-called new movements under its terms of principled economy of presence. The newness of the new movements does not arise *solely* from their own actions or agendas, but *primarily* from the *economic constellations of truth* in which the experiences of the new actors are articulated. One cannot analytically objectify action (as does Weir). In retrospect, the nineteenth century movements could not have moved in the paths opened by the destinal social imaginary as do new social movements today, because a century ago the horizon of politics did not allow the plurification of social imaginaries as we witness today. This criticism entails an important point about my approach to the study of social movements: by themselves, abstract historical periodizations can hardly say anything intelligible about practice and its transformations. Rather, it is by heeding *practice* and the extent to which practices of an era disclose and problematize the metaphysical and referential principles governing eras that we can attend to the *new* and *prepare* our thoughts and our selves for the possibility of a radically different era.

Perceived as a preparatory thinking free from metaphysical holds, articulated experiences intimate the possibility of new horizons. The new social movements place before our waiting eyes the possibility that destiny (*Geschick*) may eventually be articulated out of particular sites and allude to the proper loci of arrival free from normative holds. "Utopia unnamed" is the name of the situation we are currently experiencing: the situation in which the normative grip of teleocracy is giving way to a play of destinal unconcealments. "Action in the strict teleocratic sense . . . shows itself to be born with the principial economies over which a supreme end reigns," remarks Schürmann. "But when the representations of some ultimate end fade, action as the pursuit of goals appears as a 'humanist' delusion. With the withering away of the principles that generate *telé*, action metamorphoses along with the economies. That is the hour when . . . principial dispositions yield to anarchic ones."[60] If this indeed is the case, if new social movements' practices represent the *incipient* forms of practice in the time of long and stealthy "turning" when principial holds are increasingly slackened, then we should explore, in a preparatory spirit, what post-modern, postmetaphysical action reveals to us. We must, in other words, prepare ourselves for the astonishing moment of a new beginning, a moment that, ironically, does not expressly announce its arrival and thus passes unnoticed by untrained eyes. Let us just remind ourselves that this is no easy endeavor. "A beginning," remarks Heidegger, "always contains the undisclosed abundance of the unfamiliar and extraordinary, which means that it also contains strife with the familiar and ordinary."[61] Presencing may well abolish all existing theorizations. Here, then, we are tied to the realm of preparatory theorization whose new horizons Martin Heidegger opened—a theory that will prospectively place new social movements in the context of a possible postmetaphysical, post-modern epochal inception.

Heidegger's "Pathway": Toward a Preparatory Theory of Post-Modern Action and Thought

[Non-teleocratic acting and being] lack an assignable end.
In other words, such an existence is already misunderstood when it is pressed to produce reasons for its behaviour.

Schürmann, "Political Thinking in Heidegger"[62]

In his short but tremendously significant essay, "The Pathway" ("*Der Feldweg*"), written in 1947 and 1948, Heidegger introduces the metaphor of "wood paths" or the "country path" (*Feldweg*) that grants us the possibility of conceiving anarchic and nonteleocratic action. Here, I submit a reading of Heidegger's concept of "pathway" that explicates the elements of his epochal philosophy. My intent is to provide the conceptual avenue for understanding action in terms other than referentiality, one that accords with the radical phenomenological inquiry that prepares thought and action for a possible passage into the post-modern era. I will go about this task by outlining the elements of a *pathway theory of action and thought*.

　　(1) The wood paths are always there "whether at Easter *when the path shines bright* between growing crops and waking meadows, or at Christmas *when it disappears* in snowdrifts behind the nearest hill."[63] The path is always there, whether it is unconcealed or concealed. The shining or dimming of the pathway is possible by the epochal unconcealment. Every mode of unconcealment (*alétheia*) has within it concealedness (*léthe*). Every actuality veils possibilities. Therefore, the concealment of possible wood paths, those that are not seen and therefore not taken, does not mean their nonexistence. The present modes of acting and thinking, therefore, indeed render all possible modes of acting and thinking invisible. If they are rendered manifest, these possibilities channel our lives into different destinies. Destiny (*Geschick*) is, as mentioned, epochally articulated. Thus, it "can no longer designate an individual's or a collectivity's appointed lot and its reception. It designates rather, the way the modalities address us, as if they were emitted. To be 'destined' or bound for a particular place is to have committed oneself

to it," writes Schürmann. "To commit, emit, transmit all imply a sending, *schicken*. *Geschick* has therefore been translated as 'mittence'. At stake are the ceaseless arrangements and rearrangements in phenomenological inter-connected-ness that 'bring everything where it belongs.' To speak of destiny is, then, to speak of places and of placing."[64] The wood paths *destine* the actors to different *places* by *sending* to them, through shining, *prospect places of arrival of being*. This implies that, as regards our contemporary political insertedness, the possibility of breaking with the existing hege-mony of technological liberalism rests on the unconcealment of concealed modes of acting and thinking. This requires from us an acute attentiveness to the possible modes of governance other than technological liberalism as they disclose themselves.

(2) The pathway "*remains just as ready* for the thinker's steps as for those of the farmer who goes out to mow in the early morning."[65] The *path* stretches before anyone who walks its way. It does not designate a priori a specific ontologically privileged agent. Nor is it of great significance whether it is the thinker or the layman who steps in it. Once the pathway discloses itself, it becomes "something everyone is familiar with, however poorly; it will have to be a knowing that is not episodic, not contingent; a knowing whose seat is everydayness."[66] For it *sends* the prospect of possible places. The thinker only experiences to greater extent or with esoteric sophistication what the farmer experiences rather poorly and through commonsense. Knowl-edge about this modality of acting can only be adequately acquired through (anarchic) *praxiology*. Anarchic praxis falls in the category of what Schürmann, following Heidegger, called "the other acting": it is the nonmetaphysical, *nontelic* acting. The "essence of praxis: exchange deprived of a principle," remarks Schürmann.[67] "It cannot be confused with the *praxis* assigned its goal by reason and sustained by the will."[68] After the closure of metaphysics, "the other acting" as preparation for *Ereignis*, will bring things to places where they belong and leave them there. Every pathway releases a course of action proper. The actor is he or she who takes the action that is proper to the pathway. In other words, *now destinal action defines the actor* and not vice versa (anti-humanism). Here a clarification is in order: the pathway's proper action viewed from out of our metaphysical stance is already misun-derstood. Taken under the hypothesis of closure, a pathway cannot be a "pathway," strictly speaking, if it is not open, multiplying, and "letting." Schürmann's reading of Heidegger, which informs my approach, does not allow any kind of relativism and has an unequivocally anarchic overtone. Thus, the pathway receives its measure from Schürmann's seemingly oxymo-ron: *le principle d'anarchie*.[69]

(3) "When deep in the forest an oak would occasionally fall under the axe's blow, my father would immediately go looking *throughout the woods*

and sunny clearings for the cord allotted him for his workshop. There he *labored thoughtfully* during *pauses* from his job of seeking the tower clock and the bells, both of which maintain *their own relation to time and temporality*."[70] Man's relationship to *time* in the pathway is revealed through the "*clearing*" (*Lichtung*). The clearing *lets* beings glow in their phenomenal sites, where they belong and in the soil where they have their homes, and not through making ultimate references to other beings. Schürmann reminds us that according "to the mainstream of the metaphysical tradition, acting follows being; for Heidegger, on the other hand, a particular kind of acting appears as the *condition* for understanding being as time. This kind of acting he calls 'letting'."[71] It is the *clearing* that allows the actor to pause episodically from the ordinary to "labor thoughtfully" her or his way through the woods. The cord allotted to the actor, the actor's undertaking which links her or his being to temporality, is found by the actor's *journey* in the woods at times of clearing. Action receives its content, the allotted cord, from the clearing, the letting, of being. Action is not "founded" and no longer bound by grandiose historic plans of humans. "The chosen path, in retrospect and in prospect, appears at every juncture in a different light, with a different tone, and stimulates different interpretation."[72] In the pathway the relationship of actor to time is revealed through the *clearing* of being and *letting* is its action proper. The actor, liberated from preoccupation with *arché* and *telos*, becomes a poet—one who " 'sings' for no end or purpose. He is of the family of woodcutters and forest rangers, a frequenter of woodpaths."[73]

(4) Acting now embraces certain playfulness. "On these *journeys of play* you could still easily get to your *destination* and return *home* again. The *dream-element* in such voyages remained held in a then hardly perceptible luster which lay over everything."[74] The clearing grants the anarchic and nonteleocratic action a "dream-element": in the absence of *arché* and *telos*, it is still possible to arrive after a "journey of play" at a destination and to return home safely. For Heidegger, the safe return to home is always "to save"—that is, "to fetch something home into its essence, in order to bring the essence for the first time into its genuine appearing."[75] The clearing, therefore, saves the actor by permitting his or her safe journey back to the *essence* of action, an *essence* that disregards the im-positions of *arché* and *telos* and thus remains forever nonreferential. *The clearing nestles in the everyday praxis*, in the "hardly perceptible luster which lay over everything."

(5) *Homecoming*, however, does not amount to groundedness as such. The Oak tree's growth "is there grounded what lasts and fructifies; *to grow* means to *open* oneself up to the expanse of heaven and at the same time to *sink roots* into the darkness of earth."[76] The growth of the actor comes as he or she, while constantly returning to the *essence* of his or her action, strives for the *open*. The "right measure" of openness and rootedness now defines

"everything genuine."[77] The clearing does not render the familiar everyday superfluous or irrelevant. Nor does it create out of the open a utopia for the sake of which everything here and now must be transcended. Destiny is nonutopian. The clearing allows the actor to be at home and out in the open at the one and the same time. As the movement from one phenomenal locus to another, destiny does not primarily rely on man. In other words, "it is not man's destiny that counts, but the destiny that sends fields, epochs, 'clearing' of possible life and thought."[78] This is the life and thought of experience as peregrination. Removing the burden of metaphysical constrains off the shoulders of action, the clearing grants action the shift into a playfulness that allows the actor to *grow* as he or she stays in here and soars out there at every given moment. *Praxis* is indeed the playful bringing together of actuality and possibility without arriving at a point of reconciliation or stoppage. *Praxiology*, therefore, is the art of thinking the *pull* between actuality and possibility in their own *terms*.

(6) These terms are not, however, thinkable independent of the pathway. "The pathway gathers in whatever has its Being around it; *to all who pass this way it gives what is theirs*."[79] Action summons all *beings* around it to take part in it, to walk the pathways. By calling the beings of actors, action gives them what is theirs and theirs alone: action itself. All beings around the pathway, all beings somehow influenced by it, receive the gift of acting from the pathway. Action renders possible the actor—that is, *the actor receives his or her being from acting*. But in acting, the actor does not "incorporate" some foreign being into his or her own; rather, he or she receives the being that is his or her's. The pathway summons our attention to the *gift of being that we receive while acting*; a gift that at all times reminds the actor of temporality.

(7) "[A]lways and everywhere the call [*Zuspruch*] of the pathway is the same": it is "the simple."[80] The genuine call always addresses the actor in a simple way. Anarchic and nonteleocratic action is not complex in the sense of having to abide by the normative principles of metaphysical dogmas. No longer must action be the submitting of practice to the principles put forward by theory. The call of the pathway is in this sense simple. Acting becomes its own presence and not the representation of a principial First. The simple is indeed the fecund soil for the growth of the actor.

(8) Growth is not an exclusive feature of the actor. The open expanse (*Gegnet*[81]) is wide, and as such, it lets everything grow along the pathway. It is, in other words, a phenomenal expanse whose unconcealment is free of the technological posture. The actor is not privileged in any sense in this nonprincipial phenomenal arrangement; she or he is only a member of the phenomenal community. "The wide expanse of everything that grows and abides along the pathway is what *bestows world*."[82] By virtue of its nonprincipial

"giving" (in the sense of *Es gibt*; as opposed to principial and archic, and thus always hegemonic, instituting), the world of the pathway allows each member of this phenomenal community to be what it is as they return safely home to their *essences*, while at the same time, letting them explore in the open the phenomenal community. The actor, now, alternately moves between the home and the open. With the exhaustion of principial grips, the actor who receives his or her being while walking in the pathway becomes a player (and not a practitioner, which defines the subject) and an explorer (and not a conqueror, which is the agent's assignment). The anarchic actor is a traveller without fixed itinerary, a wanderer indeed in an ever more expansive world.

(9) The call of the pathway can only reach those who can hear it. To hear the call of the pathway initially requires a change of attitude. The grip of principial economies and their hegemonic configurations in each era, which always reveal themselves in political regimes, initially breaks once the subjects and the agents of these regimes are no longer protected by normative, regulative armors and are now penetrated by the internal aporias of a system at times of principial exhaustion. But the change of attitude immediately surpasses itself. For, now, the actor receives his or her being along the way from the pathway—a being that nonetheless is specifically his or hers. Letting, as the mode of action that links being to time, allows actors to thus receive their beings. As such, "the call of the pathway speaks only as long as there are men, *born in its atmosphere*, who can hear it."[83] To receive the *gift* of being, the actor must *give* him- or herself to the pathway. This is an event of rebirth. The gift of being takes the actor to his or her *origin*. Anarchic actors, therefore, "*are servants of their origin, not slaves of machination.*"[84] The anarchic actor refuses the rule of technicity, the reductive categorization and standing-reserve of *Ge-stell*, in all its manifestations (specially the "pressing-near" of technological liberalism). Only those who have released themselves from Enframing and its isomorphic contextualizing can hear the call of the pathway. The actor's refusal to become the subject or the agent of technological regimes rests precisely in his or her rebirth into the "atmosphere" of the pathway. To serve one's origin requires that one heeds the origin and act accordingly. Thought and action are not separate domains of performance in the pathway. We contemplate as we travel through the pathway and we travel as we contemplate. Now, everything may initially be conceivable with a change of attitude, but the shift from the mode of thinking that is governed by the principle of reason (i.e., *nihil est sine ratione*— this *principium* of modernity) to a thinking that heeds the call of the pathway requires more than attitude. It calls for the vigilant "step back from the thinking that merely represents—that is, *explains*—to the thinking that *responds* and recalls." "The step back from the one thinking to the other is no

mere shift of attitude."[85] The shift is not conceivable without the epochal "turning."

(10) The actor gains the ability to recognize the simple qua the simple, a recognition that has virtually faded away under the rule of technicity. Here reiteration seems inevitable. The simple is precisely that: the simple. "To the disoriented, the simple seems monotonous. The monotonous bring weariness, and the weary and bored find only what is uniform."[86] The calculative rationality that *Ge-Stell* im-poses upon all phenomena "accuses" the simple of monotonousness (the "accusatory" violence of categorization is the basis of calculative rationality and the levelling mechanism of technological liberalism). Action falls within the simple because it now receives its direction and meaning (*Sinn*) from the pathway and time and thus constitutes the actor.

(11) Under the rule of technicity, the "simple has fled. Its *quiet power* is exhausted."[87] Enframing, with the atomic power representing the extent of its devastating calculation, overpowers the "*gentle force of the pathway.*"[88] In the pathway, a principial economy can no longer violently force action into certain phenomenal domains to carry out assigned tasks. The *gentle power* of the pathway is "a sense which loves the free and open."[89] As such, it is alien to the violence of all reductive categorizations. The pathway's power stems from its quality of letting all phenomena around it receive in the clearing what are *essentially* theirs. In other words, the power of the pathway rests precisely in that it does not coerce. The expanse into the open alludes to that now there are "fewer and fewer arch-present standards to be observed and ideals to be contemplated, many new injunctions—ever new injunctions—to be listened to."[90] The gentle power of the pathway comes from the call into the open. No longer fettered by *arché* or *telos*, action becomes contemplating every phenomenal site in the open to which the actor pays a visit. "Here praxis determines thinking."[91]

(12) The "serene wisdom" that accompanies life in the pathway "is at once 'playful and sad, ironic and shy.' "[92] Melancholy seems inevitable. This wisdom does not "claim" knowledge: it is a "serene melancholy which says what it knows with veiled expressions."[93] Thinking in the pathway always remains carefully sober not to veil the open through its predicates. Hence, the serene wisdom's "veiled expressions," lest its knowledge obscures learning. The serenity is the gift of pathway. The actor, having already renounced metaphysical ultimacies, finds his or her being in this serenity.

(13) Finally, the call of the pathway "makes us at *home* in the arrival of a *distant origin*."[94] With the "turning" (*Kehre*), the metaphysical im-positions that dominated us for two and a half millennia, the posure whose contemporary configuration is technological Enframing, expires through an irrecoverable self-destitution. The ancient question of being returns. The

"distant origin" now becomes our home. In homecoming, acting and think-ing, practice and theory, acting and being belong together.

A caveat is in order. It is clear that the pathway theory does not legis-late or legitimate a course of action according to the dictates of a normative goal. Against possible accusations of utopian thinking, I must explicitly point out that the pathway theory refuses the violence of utopian thought. To us, the children of this technological era, any statement about the future seems Utopian at first glance because our views are so tainted by "the metaphysical essence of modernity"[95] that in any such statement we automatically seek the compelling logic of a goal. Utopia is possible only under principial econo-mies. If the pathway theory seems Utopian to untrained eyes it is because under principial economies destinal movements are organized according to the legislative logic of the point of arrival. Obviously, the anarchic concepts of open expanse and homecoming abolish the utopian view altogether. This tells us that so long as we live under the rule of modernity, we cannot totally exclude utopian impulses from our driving force. Conditioned by the meta-physical sway of modernity, we will inevitably remain motivational beings. What is important is that we channel these impulses toward the subversion of monotonic, teleocratic and archic utopias and prepare to conceive of nonprincipial economies. What will become of the utopian impulses and motivational rationalizations of the children of modernity after the "turning" will only be known by the posttransmutational generations.

Now, let us arrive at some final remarks about anarchic acting. The pathway theory of thought and action provides us with a preparatory guide for understanding post-modern acting and thinking. If we were passing from one principial economy to another (epochal reversal), then the hegemonic subjects and agents would only transmute into new hegemonic subjects and agents. We would not be significantly able to offer new reflections on action and thought. The hypothesis of closure, however, allows us to think that the shift in acting and thinking that we are now experiencing *may* signify a passage from a principial economy to an anarchic one. From this very pos-sibility arises the ability to perceive of the demise of subjects and agents, a demise that would allow the actor—one who receives his identity not by the principled politics of a principial era but by the non-principled action of an imminent anarchic epoch. Hegemony as such becomes a vestige of the past.

As post-modern, action and thought are now nonfoundational, nonreferential, in short, postmetaphysical. This guide, however, is only pre-paratory, and as such, should by no means be read as a normative prescrip-tion. That would go against the spirit of Heidegger's metaphor, for "under the metaphor of 'woodpaths', he challenges the declarations of faith in final-ity."[96] This is an important caveat because so long as we live in a principial economy and engage in the activities that are hegemonically assigned to us, there is a danger of turning any preparatory thought into a binding normative law. As a preparatory theory of acting and thinking, the pathway theory *prepares* us, literally, for the situation in which anarchic destinal unconcealments, which are *essentially* different from those im-posed by technicity's rule, summon us in the pathway. Nonreductive by definition, postmetaphysical destiny, which the pathway theory prepares for, will indeed appear before the actors who have been challenged by various kinds of violence and domination whose scars they still bear. Since this destiny is not ruled by a First Principle, it belongs to an anarchic economy—one in which the actor's acting and thinking becomes possible through the call of, and responses to, the phenomena that are "touched" by *presencing* and thus have their presence as *singularity*.

The pathway theory of action and thought, then, necessitates the distinction between *action* and *activity*, and in a parallel way, *actor* and *activist*, two classes of terms that have been treated as equivalent under modernity's sway. Metaphysical thought has treated practice as an activity toward a *telos*. Activity, therefore, belongs to the realm of teleocratic practice. Moreover, unlike action, activity belongs to the domain of the will. Action, on the contrary, signifies nonteleological practice, for as we saw in Heidegger's "The Pathway," action is a *response* to the epochal unconcealment which in the post-modern era acquires anarchic and nonteleocratic modality. Action, strictly speaking, is by definition political—that is to say, it always refers to things and speech.[97] As such, *action*, or *praxis*, is *the* post-modern practice proper. It refuses to be measured by standards of Reason; it resists being probed from the standpoint of calculative rationality. While any action has a "because," it does not have a "why."[98] The "because" of every phenomenon lies in its worlding phenomenality—that is, in the way, through *presencing*, the entity's *presence* in its phenomenal site acquires its *singular* modality.

In the nonhegemonic governance of anarchic economy, which makes the domination of universalistic holds impossible, the proper conditions for the emergence of *singularities* are provided. In the absence of all modes of phenomenal violence, including all forms of systemic violence, produced by the domination of universals, *singulars* indicate the post-modern modes of existence: *singular* beings are no longer, like particulars, subsumable under a universal legislation. Only *singulars* can venture into the "open expanse" and experience a safe "homecoming." A proper understanding of particularity always points out the *possibility* of the springing of singulars out of the actual particulars. And this springing cannot be realized without the sudden, but silent, leap from modernity to post-modernity. As the adventurers into the "open expanse" with safe "homecoming," *singularities* must be understood in relation to *hubris* (i.e., phenomenal injustice, or strictly, the enforced residence under principial economies). The possibility of emergence of *singulars* is at the same time the possibility of overcoming the *archic, systemic violence* and its derivatives. It is with *singularity* that phenomenal communities can be formed free from imposed utopian, regulative norms, return to traditional values, attempts at showing the greatness of a nation, the status quo, or any other perpetuative practice of phenomenal injustice. *Singularity is not a return to an ancient myth*—which is ultimately impossible—but to *let* beings be in an anarchic mode of concealment that was made impossible by twenty-five centuries of violent metaphysical rule. Community now is formed on the basis of homecoming as a nonground and action in an open expanse. Communities are therefore loose, voluntary, and overlapping.

It is in this relation that paying heed to the articulation of experiences in the time of epochal transmutations finds its momentous significance.

Articulated Experiences and the "Turning"

This shift to another order of experience, out of experience that is driven by the same impulse that founds metaphysics, is difficult to put into words. Indeed, a shift in language, a shift in the operations of the word in experience, is demanded and must be addressed.

Dennis Schmidt, *"Solve et Coagula"*[99]

Earlier in this text, I proposed a theory of social movements based on the concept of "articulated experiences." By linking together experience, identity, destiny, and social imaginary (or horizon), this concept enables us to do away with various kinds of ultimate referentiality while also avoiding a purely differential and performative approach. Now, in light of Heidegger's hypothesis of metaphysical closure, the concept of articulated experiences shows it theoretical merits. Let us conclude this chapter by revisiting this concept in the context of a possible epochal "turning" towards postmetaphysical, postmodern acting and thinking.

Since "articulated experiences" reveals the operation through which identity is linked to social movement, it is not conceptually restricted to certain economy of presence. As in the case of utopian social movements such as proletarian or national liberation movements, articulated experiences can take place under principial economies and their normative sway. Because the articulation of experiences in these cases occurred under the principial economy in which phenomenal *presence ruled as ultimate identity* (between presence and entity), it would inevitably take the form of conformity with the *teleocratic* social imaginary and its totalistic horizon. A teleocratic social imaginary always has a specific epochal community (*Menschentum*) as its receiver. As such, the articulation of experiences links the identity of the proletariat to the socialist imaginary or the identity of a colonized people to the national liberation imaginary. Both of these cases involved suppression of the play of internal differences in order to protect the façade of a united front (universal) of like individuals (participants). Such individuals converged on the basis of homogenized elements of past experiences and were galvanized by a monolithic imaginary and therefore had their allegiances in a (fixed) futuristic Utopian horizon. What is precisely metaphysical about this mode of articulation of experiences rests in the fact that in this modality "action requires a principle to which words, things, and deeds can be related."[100] This was, and to some extent still is, the typical social movement practice of modernity whose twentieth century exemplars include the Russian revolution of 1917 and the heightened national liberation movements in the 1960s and 1970s, as well as the postwar dream of ideal liberal democratic citizen.

With the post-modern anarchic *presencing* the above vista is to change dramatically. *Presencing marks phenomena with irreducible difference* (between presence and entities). The articulation of experiences, then, manifests itself in myriad ways. In an anarchic economy, unconcealment discloses at any given moment the "touch" of *presencing* such that the *difference* between what a phenomenon *is* and what it *becomes* appears as an *irreducible* and integral feature of phenomenality. Every mode of presence quickly recedes into absence; the familiar incessantly turns into a stranger; the commonplace becomes astonishing; and knowing gives way to learning. *In anarchic economy, the continual influx of novelty occupies our experiences.* It is here that *genuine* articulation of experiences takes place: in the absence of normative holds and teleocratic principles, the articulation of experiences leads identities of various actors, through infinite play of differences, to the movements of individuals with heterogeneous stocks of past experiential elements. Such individuals are animated by fascination toward a multiplicity of imaginaries and therefore can conceive of several paths before themselves at any given time. These actors are destined to a plurality of places as they prepare for *Ereignis*. Such articulations of experiences are *genuine* in the sense of belonging to the "true stock" or the "true genus" of phenomena; that is to say, they prepare places for the phenomena unconcealing themselves in their *singularity*, and not subsumed or subsumable, by force, under a universal. In short, it is *genuine* in the sense that it is *nonhegemonic*. Thanks to the temporal difference, experience is now articulated nonhegemonically because the economy of presence slips into a new modality in which the singular entities do not constantly receive their presence from, and thus represent, the universal. That is why the articulation of experiences is not primarily a human act of consciousness; rather, the possibility of articulation is given epochally, as the elements that are summoned by experience appear anew with each modality of presencing and its corresponding modes of intelligibility. After the "turning," articulated experiences would be nonhegemonic and anarchic because the elements they summon are no longer subsumed under universal principles. They thus manifest themselves in their singularity, making possible, inevitably, an irreducible plurality of horizons. In the absence of normative holds, the power of nontelic horizons rests in that they do not compel but fascinate. In the absence of points of arrival, every movement toward horizon, every acting and thinking, becomes feigning.

The hypothesis of closure allows us to view the new movements in light of the possible "turning" beyond metaphysics. The point here is that it has been through the *praxis* of these movement, and the shift it marks with its precedents, that today we can ask the question of post-modernity. This is an important point, because it tells us something essential about *praxis: in the events that may imply the epochal "turning," in an inceptive way, praxis is the first to slip away from principial domination.* Indeed, praxis is such inceptive event. Paying heed to *praxis, praxiology*, receives its significance from this characteristic. "[U]nder the anarchy principle, as yet only on the threshold of closure, thinking remains merely preparatory and the other destiny, a potential," writes Schürmann. "Similarly, preparatory acting must be distinguished from the 'other' acting. The only action capable of preparing an economy without principles is that which contests their vestiges in today's world and confines them to their site: as remnants of a closed destiny."[101] New social movements show an *inceptive* allusion toward the possibility of an open destiny. The true challenge, then, for new social movements is to save actors from the veiled systemic oppression that is characteristic of the hegemony of technological liberalism. The liberal regime indeed challenges actors as it imposes upon them, by oppressive (pressing-near) categorization of the rights-bearing subjects, a closed destiny. The danger of the "pressing-near" of the subjects under technological liberalism is properly understood when we consider how "pressing-near" appears as an impediment to *the leap from particularity to singularity*—a leap which corresponds to the epochal "turning" from modernity to post-modernity. Insofar as the systemic oppression of technological liberalism violently and reductively holds particularities together under universal categories, and insofar as the hegemony of such a categorization is not fully challenged through the practices of new social movements, technological liberalism prevents the possible leap of particularities into singularities that can, by definition, only emerge in a nonhegemonic mode of governance. But the greatest threat to the making of the leap by the actors stems not from oppressive categorization: it arises out of the lack of awareness that allows technological liberalism to hegemonize the illusion of an open destiny by recognizing new identities and opening new categories. An awareness so radical renders life, and thereby actors, forever and increasingly political. The sober, genuine actor resists all pretense to open destiny and measures open destiny by attunement to the temporal difference. Thus, saving is now *the* concern. As Heidegger states, "Saving does not only snatch something from a danger. To save really means to set something free into its own presencing."[102] Whether the new movements will *move* toward a saving so genuine will show where we may be headed. But one thing is clear, new social movements are modern phenomena, although they have been actualized through the crisis, and possible self-exhaustion, of certain principles of modernity. Therefore, they cannot be deemed as agents of any historical shift. What will become of the new movements past the possible "turning" we cannot know. We are aware that nothing will be "overcome," as the new movements never really overcame the older movements. Attunement to the temporal difference means that we should witness an irreducible plurivocality of actors to the extent that *all* categories such as gender, race, ethnicity, nationality, sexuality, and others lose their sway over our acting and thinking. And from our stance today, this seems the politics that attends to *Ereignis*.

We witness today a civilizational crisis with all kinds of systemic violence and the injustice of being forced to live under the principial economies that thus far have brought us wars, poverty, hunger, dictatorships, imprisonment, dire human conditions, ecological degradation, media inculcation, digital instantiation, technological objectification, capitalist exploitation, machination, nation-states, ethnic and racial domination, gender inequality, right-wing popular movements, and last but not least, the expanding hegemony of technological liberalism. Now, it is *time*, manifesting itself through the temporal difference, that brightens our lips into the genuine articulation of experiences, intimating the possibility of phenomenal freedom, indeed of *freedom as such*, in which all singulars receive their presence from the "touch" of presencing, are their own sovereigns, and enter a phenomenal community by expanding into the open and returning safely home. The question is, are we attuned to time as temporal difference and prepared to act and respond to it?

CHAPTER 7

Radical Phenomenology and the Sociology of Possibilities

A phenomenology that deconstructs the epochs "changes the world"
because it reveals the withering away of these principles.

Schürmann, *Heidegger on Being and Acting*[1]

For quite some time now, it seems, we have been standing at a historic threshold in which our response to the radical shift in social movement practices as insinuations toward the possible epochal transmutation into a postmetaphysical, post-modern world of anarchic acting and thinking has become decisive. How sociology responds to this radical shift will decide whether it intends to save its self-aggrandizing disciplinary privilege as the "science of modern society" (August Comte), or whether it is ready to surrender its self-acclaimed centrality in the study of society and humbly submit itself to the possibilities that current modes of practice may release for theory. That sociology needs to adapt to the situation that is generally called the "end of modernity" is not new. Zygmunt Bauman has already raised the issue in a compelling fashion. Articulating the societal shift that has resulted from the advent of postmodernity, Bauman rightly calls for the abandonment of the view of sociology as a universal knowledge about a presumed transparent, rational entity called society and thus as an instrument for human emancipation, a view that emerged in the period of Enlightenment. The play of differences that is characteristic of postmodernity, Bauman argues, repudiates any totalistic knowledge or universal project. The modern concerns about human betterment, however, have not disappeared. Postmodern strategies suggest that the object of sociology has changed and now sociology involves new purposes and procedures. So Bauman argues that the human concerns can bring modern sociology under postmodern conditions. "In other words, this strategy points toward a sociology of postmodernity, rather than a postmodern sociology."[2] Sociology, in Bauman's view, can still retain its theoretical and methodological approaches to apply to the new issues and new conditions.

From the standpoint of the hypothesis of metaphysical closure, Bauman's sociological perception, while addressing the issue, will at best remain parochial since it is bound by the established practices of sociology and can therefore only follow shifts in action and thought to a limited extent. His "sociology of postmodernity" can only address those issues that indicate continuity with the modernity. To be specific, his approach addresses the questions that have arisen under the postmodern condition by using concepts and ideas that belong to modernity. His notion of postmodernity has no implication for the theoretical determination of sociology as an enterprise; nor does it call for a reflective sociological shift in relation to the possibilities of praxis. Thus, his approach to the issue suffers from inattentiveness to how the hegemonic-epochal operations disguise their im-posed issues and concerns with the veneer of people's creativity. This approach also stems from Bauman's lack of a specific concept of the "post-modern." Radical phenomenology enables us to see these problems and adapt in a preparatory way to the possible new situations. It allows us to release ourselves from disciplinary dictates and prepare to *respond* to both the issues *and* practices that disclose themselves during a possible epochal "turning." Only by modestly *responding* to the "surfacings" of issues and practices can we *responsibly* release ourselves from the hegemonic principles that govern the thoughts and practices of the modern era and into the anarchic unconcealment and the possibilities that the prospect of *Kehre* releases for acting and thinking.

In this chapter, I invite the reader to heed a brief outline of what I call the *sociology of possibilities*—a practice of sociology that specifically *prepares* itself for the "turning," and, as the epigraph to this chapter suggests, participates in "changing the world" by explicating the withering away of the dominant principles.

Discursive Topologies/Experiential Strategies

Thinking these strategies through to the end, we may learn something about our own times, about where we come from and where we may be going. To me, tracing the transmutations that philosophical topics undergo through the ages, with the intent of clarifying our own topos, is the most fruitful way of doing philosophy today. Looking with one eye to the sequence of past epochs, and with the other to the potential that this sequence yields for our own age amounts to more than a mere history of concepts. . . . It consists rather in treating the cultural fluctuations as a phenomenon in the strict sense.

Schürmann, "Neoplatonic Henology As an Overcoming of Metaphysics"[3]

Once again, Reiner Schürmann's epochal theory provides a guideline that inspires the sociology of possibilities. Schürmann identifies the major consequences of Heidegger's thinking for action as: (1) abolishing the primacy of teleology in action; (2) abolishing the primacy of responsibility in the legitimation of action; (3) action as a protest against the administered world; (4) a certain disinterest in the future of humankind, due to a shift in the understanding of destiny; and finally, (5) anarché as the essence of what is "doable."[4] The sociology of possibilities prepares for these consequences, watchfully seeking to identify the places, *topoi*, in which these consequences may arise. It prepares itself for ways of perceiving how present practices "move" toward anarchic and nonteleocratic action. In that sense the main approach of sociology of possibilities to the study of acting and thinking is *topological*: it *heeds* the *places* in which the "touch" of *presencing* allows a different *presence of entities*. Topology, therefore, "delivers us to a place that is as a possibility. For this reason Schürmann describes topology as the 'phenomenology of the possible' . . . it draws us toward the future, our coming singularization."[5] Politics is the foremost milieu to which this topology attends, for the unconcealed principles always have their most vivid expressions in politics. Since the political is the confluence of things, speech, and deeds, and since discourse is constitutive of human experience, *topology is primarily discursive.*[6] Topology is discursive because it heeds discourse as the *site* and mode of articulation of experiences within the political. In my discursive-topological approach to the Zapatistas, I attended to the EZLN discourse to demonstrate how a new modality of action has disclosed itself and to which possibilities it alludes. Using the concepts of "destiny" and "articulated experiences," I briefly showed the "peregrination" between possible places the Zapatistas might have embarked on. These possible places appear with utmost lucidity in the study of the destinal paths of social movements. Destiny, as established, comes with, and is inseparable from, the articulated experiences that link identity to a social movement. Therefore, *discursive topology* always at the same time aims at identifying *experiential strategies*: it points out the horizons, social imaginaries, and identifications that, due to the articulation of experiences, set certain "strategies" for the movement actor. Together, *discursive topology* and *experiential strategies* identify the possible nontotalistic destinies that anarchic unconcealment may release.

As a radical and reflective departure from the dominant practice of sociology, the sociology of possibilities comes with certain distinctive characteristics. It is informed by the epochal mode of concealedness-unconcealment—by *alétheia*. It takes every actualization (i.e., unconcealment) as concealing other, possible, modes of phenomenal disclosing. The sociology of possibilities investigates these possibilities in order to seek the ways out of the technological Enframing and its products: hegemonic political systems and rationalist, objectivist social sciences. As such, it tries to attune to the modes of acting and thinking in the light of the hypothesis of metaphysical closure.

Thus, the sociology of possibilities studies the *present* entities and phenomenal arrangements primarily in order to unveil the operations of epochal principles. It seeks to identify the principles governing the economy of *presence* that have given rise to the current phenomenal configurations. As such, in heeding what is present it regards the *motility* that the verb *to be* (or the participle *being*) connotes as opposed to the *sedimentation* that the noun *entity* denotes (the ontological difference). In this relation, *the sociology of possibility does not categorize practices according to some abstract common denominators, let alone imposing rules upon them.* It remains *descriptive* and avoids the lures of *prescriptive* gestures. It receives practices as they manifest themselves, but shows what possible modes of practice the *motility* of *being* may give to the presently manifest practices. This attitude toward *being* allowed me to view new social movements' practices as *possible*, inceptive intimations toward anarchic action.

The sociology of possibilities tends to search for the *original* moment of institution. As such, historical ruptures, whether these ruptures are dramatically marked by historical events or whether they take place unnoticed, are of utmost importance to this practice of sociology. The sociology of possibilities challenges the amnesia about *Urstiftung* as well as inattentiveness toward the epochal unconcealment. By *remembering* the moments of original institution, it opens itself to what is concealed and their possible unconcealment, that is, to the possible opening of what seems closed. Insofar as the current norms governing action are manifestations of the existing principial economy of presence, the sociology of possibilities seeks to identify the origins of these governing norms in order to show that they are temporally bound. It, therefore, searches for the principles of *anarché* which the existing economy of presence conceals. With certain disinterestedness in the future, it seeks to *release* these concealed *anarchic principles* from the violent grip of the technological Enframing. My approach to the "pressing-near" of technological liberalism in relation to new social movements and the concept of rights was an attempt in that direction.

The sociology of possibilities begins by a *radical transgression*. It subversively undermines all existing disciplinary boundaries and analytical paradigms that have established through their theoretical postulates the laws that govern society. The designation *sociology* in the "sociology of possibilities" does not restrict it to what Heidegger called the "the compartmentalization of sciences"[7]; rather it only points out its *place* of surfacing in an academic world that is already compartementalized. In other words, the sociology of possibilities is interdisciplinary. It takes the presumed laws, sociological or otherwise, of social life simply as academic expressions of the dominant economy of presence. For the sociology of possibilities all *actualities*, all laws known to govern action, are subject to topological deconstruction and to the radical phenomenological *epoché*, and consequently, to the subversion of principles of which theoretical, disciplinary rules are nothing but expressions. Transgression, however, is not a product of the creativity of the sociology of possibilities. In its transgressiveness, the sociology of possibilities merely *responds* to the places from which *transgressive* modes of action — played by *genuine* actors in destinal paths — spring out of the existing hegemonic activities of the subject and the agent. In acknowledging the radical *transgression* of action, the sociology of possibilities humbly submits itself to action and tries to free action from all ascribed theoretical rules that express the existing principial economies of presence. It vigilantly seeks to identify the modes of action that seem no longer plausible as well as the modes of action that emerge and become dominant. Thus, it heeds the way closure and opening may anticipate anarchic action. This sociology, therefore, always remains *anticipatory*. In no respect does the sociology of possibility stand higher than the actor. In fact, anyone who submits him- or herself to this modest practice of sociology becomes a "knowing actor . . . who takes his sole measure from what discloses itself."[8]

In the absence of modernist ambition of theorizing the foundations of practice, the sociology of possibilities entails a *feigning* of knowledge, and as such, it takes all its methods, concepts, and theories as *preparatory*. *Feint* is the modality of thinking in the "intermittent" times of epochal transmutation when one principial epoch is withdrawing (and the constellation of truth loses its intelligibility) and another epoch is yet to reveal to its principle(s). To *feign* is to abandon philosophy for *thinking* — a task that is not that of philosophers but poets. The sociology of possibilities is strictly "today's" practice: "Today has its origins in what has happened and is at the time disposed to what comes towards it."[9] It is resolutely conscious and cautious about the likelihood of falling prey to its own "sociologizing" — that is, of turning what discloses itself to it into an ultimate referentiality. It lets go of all ultimacies, especially of the positivity of the social that has dominated the practice of sociology ever since its inception. Therefore, the sociology of possibilities perpetually "steps back" from its own postulates. It seeks openness rather than closure, unfixity rather than fixity, denial rather than affirmation. It relinquishes the modern longing for overarching paradigms and totalizing categories and acquires concepts as it encounters phenomena and actions in their particularities.

This brief outline indicates that the sociology of possibilities follows the *anticipatory* thrust of deconstruction along with the *preparatory* thrust of radical phenomenology.[10] Thinking, then, is a task of preparatory, not of founding, character. "The preparatory thinking in question does not wish and is not able to predict the future."[11] Having adopted preparatory thinking, the sociology of possibilities no longer posits man as "as the measure for discourse in the sciences called *social* and *human*."[12] In order to address the possible "*turning*" toward the post-modern era, sociology needs to take a bold, hospitable *turn* toward incorporating the idea of anti-humanism. As Schürmann reminds us, "Without anti-humanism, there can be no metaphysical closure."[13] The epochal "turning" decenters man, and as such, takes away from it the anthropocentric privilege of originating objectivity.[14] Preparatory thinking takes away all such privileges from the practice of sociology and calls for its openness toward *Ereignis*—the event of the self-establishing of an epoch. The sociology of possibilities, therefore, remains openly and finely attuned to "the thoughtfulness of present and future actors. Any other reference game would constitute pure speculation, pure dogmatic construction."[15]

Notes

Chapter 1. What Can New Social Movements Tell about Postmodernity?

1. Reiner Schürmann, " 'What Must I Do?' at the End of Metaphysics: Ethical Norms and the Hypothesis of a Historical Closure," in *Phenomenology in a Pluralistic Context*, ed. William L. McBride and Calvin O. Schrag (Albany: State University of New York Press, 1983), 53.

2. Reiner Schürmann, "Adventures of the Double Negation: On Richard Bernstein's Call for Anti-Anti Humanism," *Praxis International* 5 (3): 290 (1985).

3. Reiner Schürmann, *Heidegger on Being and Acting: From Principles to Anarchy*, trans. Christine-Marie Gros (Bloomington: Indiana University Press, 1990), 1.

4. Ibid., 10.

5. Schürmann quotes Heidegger to suggest that his reading him "backward" accords with the way Heidegger himself viewed his own work. Heidegger states in a 1969 seminar: "After *Being and Time*, [my] thinking replaced the expression 'meaning of being' with 'truth of being'. And so as to avoid any misapprehension about truth, so as to exclude its being understood as conformity, 'truth of being' has been elucidated as 'locality of being'—truth as the locus-character of being. That presupposes, however, an understanding of what a locus is. Hence the expression *topology of being*" (Heidegger as quoted in ibid., 12).

6. Schürmann, *Heidegger on Being and Acting*, 63.

Chapter 2. Identity and Contemporary Social Movements

1. Karl Marx and Friedrich Engels, *The German Ideology*, ed. C. J. Arthur (New York: International Publishers, 1995), 59–60.

2. Alberto Melucci, "Getting Involved: Identity and Mobilization in Social Movements," *International Social Movement Research* 1 (1988): 330.

3. Ibid., 336. Also see Alberto Melucci, *Nomads of the Present: Social Movements and Individual Needs in Contemporary Society*, ed. John Keane and Paul Mier (London: Hutchinson Radius, 1989), 18, 19, 25, 28, 204.

4. For example, the exclusion of the "question of political economy" as criticized in: Barry D. Adam, "Post-Marxism and the New Social Movements," *Canadian Review of Sociology and Anthropology* 30 (3): 316 (1993).

5. Alain Touraine, "Social Movements, Revolution and Democracy," in *The Public Realm: Essays on Discursive Types in Political Philosophy*, ed. Reiner Schürmann (Albany: State University of New York Press, 1989), 275.

6. Alain Touraine, "Beyond Social Movements?" *Theory, Culture, & Society* 9 (1992), 143.

7. Alan Scott, *Ideology and the New Social Movements* (London: Unwin Hyman, 1990), 16–19.

8. Ibid., 30. For the organizational features of new social movements see ibid., 34.

9. Enrique Laraña, Hank Johnston, and Joseph R. Gusfield, "Identities, Grievances, and New Social Movements," in *New Social Movements: From Ideology to Identity*, ed. E. Laraña , H. Johnston, and J. R. Gusfield (Philadelphia: Temple University Press, 1994), 6–9.

10. This is the prime feature of all mainstream social movement theories, namely, the resource mobilization theory of John McCarthy and Meyer Zald, as well as Charles Tilly (see Charles Tilly, "Models and Realities of Popular Collective Action," *Social Research* 52 (4): 718–47 [1985]); the "master frames" theory of D. A. Snow and R. D. Benford (see David A. Snow and Robert D. Benford, "Master Frames and Cycles of Protest," in *Frontiers in Social Movement Theory*, ed. Aldon D. Morris and Carol McClurg Mueller [London/New Haven: Yale University Press, 1992], 133–55). Jean Cohen advocates the convergence of the "identity paradigm" (which I called the "sociological" new social movement theories) and the "resource mobilization paradigm" (see Jean L. Cohen, "Strategy or Identity: New Theoretical Paradigms and Contemporary Social Movements," *Social Research* 52 (4): 663 [1985]; see also William K. Carroll, ed., *Organizing Dissent: Contemporary Social Movements in Theory and Practice* [Toronto: Garamond Press, 1992]). For the distinction between the two approaches also see Scott, *Ideology and the New Social Movements*; Laraña, Johnston, and Gusfield, ed., *New Social Movements*; and Tilly, "Models and Realities of Popular Collective Action."

11. Reiner Schürmann, "A Brutal Awakening to the Tragic Condition of Being: On Heidegger's *Beiträge zur Philosophie*," trans. Kathleen Blamy, in *Martin Heidegger: Politics, Art and Technology*, ed. Karsten Harries and Christoph Jamme (New York/London: Holm & Meier, 1994), 98.

12. See: Reiner Schürmann, "On Self-Regulation and Transgression," *Social Research* 49 (4): 1036 (1982); Reiner Schürmann, " 'What Can I Do?' in an Archaeological-Genealogical History," *The Journal of Philosophy* 82 (10): 545 (1985); Reiner Schürmann, "On Constituting Oneself an Anarchistic Subject," *Praxis International* 6 (3): 305 (1986).

13. Schürmann, *Heidegger on Being and Acting*, 30.

14. Alain Touraine, *Return of the Actor: Social Theory in Postindustrial Society*, trans. Myrna Godzich (Minneapolis: University of Minnesota Press, 1988), 8.

15. Alain Touraine, *The Voice and the Eye: An Analysis of Social Movements*, trans. Alan Duff (Cambridge: Cambridge University Press/Paris: Editions de la Maison des Sciences de l'Homme, 1981), 6.

16. Ibid.

17. Ibid. Italics added.

18. Touraine, *Return of the Actor*, 118.

19. Touraine, *The Voice and the Eye*, 135.

20. Touraine, *Return of the Actor*, 125.

21. Ibid., 8.

22. Ibid., 118.

23. See Alain Touraine, *Can We Live Together?* trans. David Macey (Cambridge/Oxford: Polity Press, 2000), 106, 111.

24. Touraine, *The Voice and the Eye*, 7.

25. Alain Touraine, "Democracy: From a Politics of Citizenship to a Politics of Recognition," in *Social Movements and Social Classes*, ed. Louis Mahen (London: Sage Publication, 1995), 267.

26. Alain Touraine, "The Idea of Revolution," *Theory, Culture, & Society* 7 (1990), 130. Italics in original.

27. Alain Touraine, *What Is Democracy?* trans. David Macey (Boulder: Westview Press, 1997), 10.

28. See Alberto Melucci, "An End to Social Movements? Introductory Paper to the Sessions on 'New Movements and Change in Organizational Forms,' " *Social Science Information* 23 (4/5) 826 (1984).

29. Melucci, *Nomads of the Present*, 19. Also see Alberto Melucci, "Social Movements and the Democratization of Everyday Life," in *Civil Society and the State*, ed. John Keane (London: Verso, 1988), 245–46.

30. See Alberto Melucci, "The New Social Movements: A Theoretical Approach." *Social Sciences Information* 19 (2): 218–21 (1980).

31. Melucci, "Getting Involved," 330; see also Melucci, *Nomads of the Present,* 19.

32. Melucci, "An End to Social Movements?" 826. Melucci takes as synonymous the terms postindustrial, complex, advanced capitalist, "post-material" (ibid., 831) and "late capitalist" (Alberto Melucci, "New Movements, Terrorism, and the Political System: Reflections on the Italian Case," *Socialist Review* 11 (2): 99 [1981].

33. Melucci, *Nomads of the Present,* 45.

34. Ibid., 171.

35. Alberto Melucci, "Liberation or Meaning? Social Movements, Culture and Democracy," *Development and Change* 23 (3): 69 (1992).

36. Ibid., 73.

37. See Melucci, "Social Movements and the Democratization," 258–59.

38. Touraine, *Return of the Actor,* 38–39, 56.

39. See Alain Touraine, "An Introduction to the Study of Social Movements," *Social Research* 52 (4): 773 (1985).

40. Touraine as quoted in Alan Scott, "Action, Movement, and Intervention: Reflections on the Sociology of Alain Touraine," *Canadian Review of Sociology and Anthropology* 28 (1): 42 (1991).

41. Touraine, *Can We Live Together?* 89.

42. Melucci, *Nomads of the Present,* 80, n. 2.

43. Ibid., 73.

44. Melucci, "New Movements, Terrorism, and the Political System," 100.

45. Melucci, *Nomads of the Present,* 20.

46. Melucci, "New Movements, Terrorism, and the Political System," 113. On the new movements and modernization see ibid., 104–17; on resistance see 110–11.

47. Touraine, *The Voice and the Eye,* 9.

48. Ibid., 140, 168–70. For Touraine's principles of sociological intervention see ibid., 213–14; for his detailed outline of sociological intervention see ibid., chapter 9.

49. Ibid., 216.

50. Melucci, *Nomads of the Present,* 240. Italics in original.

51. Melucci, "Liberation or Meaning," 51.

52. See Alain Touraine, *Critique of Modernity,* trans. David Macey (London/New York: Blackwell, 1995), 24, 27.

53. Ibid., 165–67. On rationalization and subjectivation see ibid., 38, 165, 205–6.

54. Ibid., 240. For his characterization of the Subject see: ibid., 234.

55. Ibid., 374.

56. Ibid., 167.

57. Ibid., 242, 292.

58. Touraine, "An Introduction," 781–82. Italics in original.

59. See Touraine, *The Voice and the Eye*, 10.

60. See Escobar and Alvarez, ed., *The Making of Social Movements in Latin America*; David Slater, ed., *New Social Movements and the State in Latin America*; and John Holloway and Eloína Peláez ed., *Zapatista! Reinventing Revolution in Mexico* (London/Sterling, VA: Pluto Press, 1998).

61. See Touraine, *What Is Democracy?* 28–29, 56–57.

62. Fernando Calderón, Alejandro Piscitelly, and José Luis Reyna, "Social Movements: Actors, Theories, Expectations," in *The Making of Social Movements in Latin America*, ed. Escobar and Alvarez, 32.

63. Arturo Escobar, "Culture, Economics, and Politics in Latin American Social Movement Theory and Research," in *The Making of Social Movements in Latin America*, ed. Escobar and Alvarez, 71. Italics added.

64. Klaus Eder, *The New Politics of Class: Social Movements and Cultural Dynamics in Advanced Societies* (London/New York/New Delhi: Sage, 1993), 145.

65. See Claus Offe, "New Social Movements: Challenging the Boundaries of Institutional Politics," *Social Research* 52 (4): 831–32 (1985).

66. Ibid., 833. Italics in original.

67. Ibid., 857–58.

68. Alberto Melucci, "A Strange Kind of Newness: What's 'New' in New Social Movements," in *New Social Movements*, ed. Laraña, Johnston, and Gusfield, 103.

69. Melucci, "Getting Involved," 344. See also Melucci, *Nomads of the Present*, 52–53.

70. Alberto Melucci, "The New Social Movements Revisited: Reflections on a Sociological Misunderstanding," in *Social Movements and Social Classes*, ed. Louis Maheu (London: Sage Publications, 1995), 117.

71. Alberto Melucci, *Challenging Codes: Collective Action in the Information Age* (Cambridge/New York: Cambridge University Press, 1996), 233.

72. Eder, *The New Politics of Class*, 45. Italics in original.

73. Ibid., 1–2, 5. Eder argues that in postindustrial society capital and labor (class) are defined independently of culture or political traits (collective action). Thus, one cannot apply the Marxist base-superstructure model to analyze postindustrial societies (26).

74. Ibid., 10. Italics in original.

75. Ibid., 170.

76. Ibid., 67.

77. Ibid., 64.

78. Klaus Eder, "The 'New Social Movements': Moral Crusades, Political Pressure Groups, or Social Movements?" *Social Research* 52 (4): 873 (1985).

79. Eder, *The New Politics of Class*, 160. Italics in original.

80. Ibid., 93. Italics in original.

81. Ibid., 173.

82. Ibid., 109.

83. Ibid., 101. Post-Fordist and postmaterialist (Ibid., 186) are Eder's terms to refer to what Touraine and Melucci call the postindustrial society.

84. Ibid., 159. It is worthy to note that Eder still takes new social movements as single issue movements. This is in fact the idea that gives rise to what Eder criticizes. Logically, only when we conceive of new social movements as single-issue movements (of marginalized groups), will we be able to view them seeking the inclusion of their single issues.

85. Ibid., 86.

86. Eder, "The 'New Social Movements'," 888; see also ibid., 875.

87. Eder, *The New Politics of Class*, 134.

88. Melucci, *Nomads of the Present*, 46.

89. Touraine, *Return of the Actor*, 40. See also Touraine, "An Introduction," 766.

90. See Touraine, *The Voice and the Eye*, 33, 60.

91. Alain Touraine, "Economic Reform and Democracy: A New Social Contract?" *Labour and Society* 16 (4): 474–75 (1991).

92. Touraine, "An Introduction," 772.

93. Touraine, *The Voice and the Eye*, 60.

94. Ibid., 62; see also Touraine, *Return of the Actor*, 8.

95. Touraine, *Return of the Actor*, 68; Italics in original. See also Touraine, *The Voice and the Eye*, 77; Touraine, "An Introduction," 760.

96. Touraine, "An Introduction," 778.

97. This assertion comes from Touraine's distinction between the actor (e.g., worker) from the agent (e.g., the proletariat) (ibid., 773); Touraine, "The Idea of Revolution," 125.

98. Touraine, *Return of the Actor*, 42. Italics in original.

99. Touraine, "An Introduction," 778–79.

100. Touraine, *Return of the Actor*, 9, 18.

101. Ibid., 79–80.

102. Touraine, *Return of the Actor*, 80.

103. Ibid., 81.

104. For Touraine, these elements "belong to the same universe [and] express the central conflict of a societal type" (Touraine, "An Introduction," 761). On the distinction between social and political movement see also Touraine, *The Voice and the Eye*, 80–81.

105. Touraine, "Economic Reform and Democracy," 475.

106. Touraine, *What Is Democracy?* 131.

107. Alain Touraine, "What Does Democracy Mean Today?" *International Social Science Journal* 43 (2/128): 263 (1991).

108. Melucci, *Challenging Codes*, 83.

109. Melucci, "Getting Involved," 332–33. See also Melucci, "Liberation or Meaning?" 49; Alberto Melucci, "The Symbolic Challenge of Contemporary Movements?" *Social Research* 52 (4): 793 (1985). For Melucci's conception of identity as a product of negotiation see Melucci, *Nomads of the Present*, 35. For his usage of the *personnage* and other theatrical metaphors see Melucci, "An End to Social Movements?" 825.

110. Alberto Melucci, *The Playing Self: Person and Meaning in the Planetary Society* (New York/Cambridge: Cambridge University Press, 1996), 35.

111. Melucci, *Challenging Codes*, 159.

112. Melucci, "Getting Involved," 340.

113. Ibid., 344; see also Melucci, *Nomads of the Present*, 136.

114. Melucci, *Nomads of the Present*, 34; Italics in original.

115. Melucci, "Getting Involved," 342; see also Melucci, *The Playing Self*, 51–53.

116. Melucci, "The Symbolic Challenge," 793.

117. Melucci, "An End to Social Movements?" 825.

118. Melucci, *Nomads of the Present*, 49.

119. Melucci, "The New Social Movements," 202; Italics in original.

120. Melucci, "The Symbolic Challenge," 792.

121. Melucci, "The New Social Movements," 218.

122. See Melucci, "New Movements, Terrorism, and the Political System," 98–99; Melucci, "The New Social Movements," 219–20.

123. Melucci, "Social Movements and the Democratization," 247–49.

124. Melucci, *Nomads of the Present*, 46.

125. Melucci, "Social Movements and the Democratization," 245. Also see Melucci, *Nomads of the Present*, 25.

126. Melucci, "Getting Involved," 337–38. For his notion of "political reductionism" see Melucci, *Nomads of the Present*, 43; see also Leonard Avritzer and Timo Lyyra, "New Cultures, Social Movements and the Role of Knowledge: An Interview with Alberto Melucci," *Thesis Eleven* 48 (1997), 101.

127. Melucci, "Social Movements and the Democratization," 253.

128. Melucci, *Nomads of the Present*, 71. Italics added. For the concepts of latency and visibility see Melucci, "An End to Social Movements," 829; Melucci, "Social Movements and the Democratization," 248; Melucci, "The Symbolic Challenge," 800–801.

129. Melucci, "Social Movements and the Democratization," 247.

130. Schürmann, "On Constituting Oneself an Anarchistic Subject," 305.

131. Touraine, "Beyond Social Movements?" 136–37. Italics added.

132. Ernesto Laclau and Chantal Mouffe, *Hegemony and Socialist Strategy: Toward a Radical Democratic Politics* (London: Verso, 1985), 93.

Chapter 3. Identity, Experiental Hegemonies, *Urstiftung*

1. Schürmann, "Adventures of the Double Negation," 290.

2. Jacques Derrida, "Structure, Sign, and Play in the Discourse of the Human Sciences," in *Writing and Difference*, trans. Alan Bass (Chicago: The University of Chicago Press, 1978), 278–81.

3. Jacques Derrida, "Remarks on Deconstruction and Pragmatism," in *Deconstruction and Pragmatism*, ed. Chantal Mouffe (London/New York: Routledge, 1996), 83.

4. Laclau and Mouffe, *Hegemony and Socialist Strategy* 98.

5. See Chantal Mouffe, "Toward a Theoretical Interpretation of 'New Social Movements,'" in *Rethinking Marx*, ed. Sakari Hännien and Leena Paldán, (New York: International General/IMMRC, 1984), 139–40. Also see Ernesto Laclau and Chantal Mouffe, "Interview," conducted by Ian Angus, in *Conflicting Public Series* (Vancouver: The Knowledge Network, 1998). Website transcript is available at: http://www.knowtv.com/primetime/conflicting/mouffe.html (viewed January 1999).

6. Laclau and Mouffe, *Hegemony*, 159.

7. Ibid., 1. See also Mouffe, "Toward A Theoretical Interpretation," 141.

8. Laclau and Mouffe, *Hegemony*, 164.

9. Ibid. 65. Italics in original.

10. See Ernesto Laclau, "Subject of Politics, Politics of the Subject," *Differences* 7 (1): 151 (1995).

11. Ernesto Laclau, *New Reflections on the Revolution of Our Time* (London. Verso, 1990), 180.

12. Laclau, "Subject of Politics, Politics of the Subject," 151–52.

13. See Ernesto Laclau, "Deconstruction, Pragmatism, Hegemony," in *Deconstruction and Pragmatism*, ed. C. Mouffe, 47–48. See also Laclau, *New Reflections*, 35.

14. Laclau, "Deconstruction, Pragmatism, Hegemony," 54.

15. Laclau, *New Reflections*, 21.

16. Ernesto Laclau, "The Death and Resurrection of the Theory of Ideology," *MLN* 112 (1997), 310–11.

17. Laclau, "Deconstruction, Pragmatism, Hegemony," 54

18. Ibid. Also see Laclau, *New Reflections*, 60–61.

19. Laclau, "Deconstruction, Pragmatism, Hegemony," 55.

20. Laclau and Mouffe, *Hegemony*, 161.

21. Chantal Mouffe, *The Return of the Political* (London: Verso, 1993), 76.

22. Chantal Mouffe, "Democratic Politics Today," in *Dimensions of Radical Democracy*, ed. C. Mouffe, 10–11.

23. Chantal Mouffe, "Post-Marxism: Democracy and Identity," *Environment and Planning D: Society and Space*, 13 (1995), 264.

24. Ernesto Laclau, "Metaphor and Social Antagonism," in *Marxism and the Interpretation of Cultures*, ed. Cary Nelson and Lawrence Grossberg (Urbana/Chicago: University of Illinois Press, 1988), 254.

25. See ibid., 250.

26. Laclau and Mouffe, *Hegemony*, 105. Italics in original.

27. See ibid., 113.

28. Ibid. Italics in original.

29. See ibid., 97–105.

30. Ibid., 125. Italics in original.

31. Laclau, "Metaphor and Social Antagonism," 256.

32. Antonio Gramsci, *Selections from the Prison Notebooks*, ed. and trans. Quintin Hoare and Geoffrey Nowell Smith (New York: International Publishers, 1971), 245. Italics added.

33. Ernesto Laclau, "Totalitarianism and Moral Indignation," *Diacritics* 20 (3): 95 (1990).

34. Ernesto Laclau, "The Time Is Out of Joint," *Diacritics* 25 (2): 93 (1995).

35. Laclau and Mouffe, *Hegemony*, 134.

36. Ernesto Laclau, "Why Do Empty Signifiers Matter to Politics," in *The Lesser Evil and the Greater Good: The Theory and Politics of Social Diversity*, ed. Jeffrey Weeks (London: Rivers Oram Press, 1994), 169.

37. See ibid., 169, 174–75.

38. Chantal Mouffe, "Democratic Politics and the Question of Identity," in *The Identity in Question*, ed. John Rajchman (New York/London: Routledge, 1995), 40.

39. Ernesto Laclau, "Universalism, Particularism, and the Question of Identity," *October* 61 (1992), 87.

40. Laclau, "Deconstruction, Pragmatism, Hegemony," 60.

41. Mouffe, "Post-Marxism: Democracy and Identity," 263.

42. R. B. J. Walker, *One World, Many Worlds: Struggles for a Just World Peace* (Boulder/London: Lynne Rienner/Zed Books, 1988), 109.

43. See Mouffe, "Post-Marxism," 261–63.

44. For studies of the 1996 electoral victory of the Left in Italy see Lucio Magri, "The Resistable Rise of Italian Left," *New Left Review* 214 (Nov./Dec. 1995), 125–33; Michele Salvati, "The Crisis of Government in Italy," *New Left Review* 213 (Sept./Oct. 1995), 76–95; and Tobias Abse, "The Left's Advance in Italy," *New Left Review* 217 (May/Jun. 1996), 123–30.

45. Salvati, "The Crisis of Government in Italy," 89.

46. Laclau, "Deconstruction, Pragmatism, Hegemony," 55.

47. Ibid.

48. Ibid., 50. In this respect, see Laclau's discussion about the phenomenological concepts of sedimentation and reactivation in his *New Reflections*, 34. Also see his take on Heidegger via Reiner Schürmann in Ernesto Laclau and Lilian Zac, "Minding the Gap: The Subject of Politics," in *The Making of Political Identities*, ed. Ernesto Laclau (London/New York: Verso, 1994), 27–31.

49. See Laclau, "Why Do Empty Signifiers Matter to Politics?" 167–78.

50. Gramsci, *Prison Notebooks*, 365–66.

51. Ibid., 276.

52. Ibid., 325.

53. See Antonio Gramsci, *Selections from Political Writings 1921–1926*, trans. & ed. Quintin Hoare (London: Lawrence and Wishart, 1978), 441–62. See also Gramsci, *Prison Notebooks*, 165, n. 64.

54. Gramsci, *Selections from Political Writings 1921–1926*, 443.

55. Ibid. Italics added.

56. Gramsci, *Prison Notebooks*, 55. In *Hegemony and Socialist Strategy*, Laclau and Mouffe utilize this Gramscian conception of subalternity by using the term "relations of subordination" (153–54).

57. As Gramsci implies in his discussion about Americanism and Fordism: "the subaltern forces, which have to be 'manipulated' and rationalized to serve new ends, naturally put up a resistance" (*Prison Notebooks*, 279).

58. Ibid., 52.

59. See ibid., 334.

60. Ibid., 52.

61. This separation appears in Perry Anderson and his so-called "scenarios" of hegemony. See Perry Anderson, "The Antinomies of Antonio Gramsci," *New Left Review* 100 (1977), 5–78.

62. Gramsci, *Prison Notebooks*, 52. Italics added.

63. "The dialectical nexus between the two categories of movement, and therefore of research, is hard to establish precisely" (ibid., 178). In the same vein, Gramsci uses the term *inorganic* to designate peripheral or occasional, where the necessary (organic) relationship is mostly absent.

64. Ibid., 12. The "definitional" problem persists where the multilayered nature of Gramscian texts is not understood. For instance, see Anne Showstack Sassoon's definition of civil society in "A Gramsci Dictionary," in Anne Showstack Sassoon, ed., *Approaches to Gramsci* (London: Writers & Readers, 1982), 12. An illuminating point in this respect is made by Norberto Bobbio who discusses that

Gramsci's notion of civil society is not a borrowing from Marx, as is commonly believed, but from Hegel. Gramsci writes in a passage that he refers to civil society "as Hegel understands it, and in the way in which it is often used in these notes." Then he defines civil society as "the political and cultural hegemony which a social group exercises over the whole of society, as the ethical content of the State" (in Norberto Bobbio, "Gramsci and the Concept of Civil Society," trans. Carroll Mortera, in *Civil Society and the State*, ed. John Keane (London: Verso, 1988), 83–84.

65. Ibid., 337.

66. Gramsci as quoted in Bobbio, "Gramsci and the Concept of Civil Society," 85–86.

67. Antonio Gramsci, *Letters from Prison*, vol. 2 ed. Frank Rosengarten, trans. Raymond Rosental (New York: Columbia University Press, 1994), 169.

68. Gramsci as quoted in Bobbio, "Gramsci and the Concept of Civil Society," 86.

69. Mouffe, "Democracy, Power, and the 'Political,'" 245.

70. See Gramsci, *Prison Notebooks*, 366.

71. Antonio Gramsci, *Selections from Cultural Writings*, ed. David Forgacs and Geoffrey Novell-Smith, trans. Willian Boelhower (Cambridge: Harvard University Press, 1985), 104. Italics are mine. See also Gramsci, *Letters from Prison*, vol. 2, 171–72.

72. Gramsci, *Prison Notebooks*, 367.

73. See ibid., 149, 159, 232–34, 325, 365, 388. On the state and dictatorship see Gramsci, *Selections from Political Writings 1921–1926*, 209–12.

74. Gramsci, *Prison Notebooks*, 323–24.

75. Ibid., 416, 423.

76. Ibid., 324.

77. Ibid.

78. Ibid., 421.

79. Ibid., 324.

80. Ibid., 419.

81. Ibid., 388.

82. Ibid., 350.

83. See Ibid., 147–48.

84. Ibid., 149.

85. Ibid., 161, 245.

86. Ibid., 157.

87. Ibid., 418. Note that the distinctions between feeling, understanding, and knowing are made by Gramsci in this passage.

88. Ibid., 360. Italics added.

89. See ibid., 445.

90. Claude Lefort, *Democracy and Political Theory*, trans. David Macey (Minneapolis: University of Minnesota Press, 1988), 217. Italics in original.

91. Ibid., 2.

92. Ibid.

93. See ibid., 217–19, 230.

94. See Edmund Husserl, *The Crisis of European Sciences and Transcendental Phenomenology*, trans. David Carr (Evanston, Ill.: Northwestern University Press, 1970), 354.

95. Reiner Schürmann, "Technicity, Topology, Tragedy: Heidegger on 'That Which Saves' in the Global Reach," in *Technology in the Western Political Tradition* ed. Arthur M. Melzer, Jerry Weinberger, and M. Richard Zinman (Ithaca/London: Cornell Universtiy Press, 1993), 204.

96. Husserl, *The Crisis of European Sciences*, 72.

Chapter 4. Articulated Experiences: The Epochal (Trans-) Formations of Identities and Social Movements

1. Reiner Schürmann, "Symbolic Difference," trans. Charles T. Wolfe, *Graduate Faculty Philosophy Journal* 19 (2/20): 13 (1997).

2. EZLN (Zapatista Army of National Liberation) communiqué as quoted in John Holloway, "Dignity's Revolt," in *Zapatista! Reinventing Revolution in Mexico*, ed. Holloway and Peláez, 159.

3. Laclau, *New Reflections on the Revolution of Our Time*, 65.

4. Reiner Schürmann, "Conditions of Evil," trans. Ian Janssen, in *Deconstruction and the Possibility of Justice*, ed. Drucilla Cornell, Michel Rosenberg, and David Gary Carlson (New York/London: Routledge, 1992), 388.

5. All references and excerpts of the play are taken from Samuel Beckett, *Waiting for Godot* (New York: Grove Press, 1954).

6. See Edmund Husserl, *Cartesian Meditations*, trans. Dorion Cairns (London/Boston: Kluwar Academic Publishers, 1950), 92.

7. See Husserl, *The Crisis of European Sciences*, 281.

8. See Martin Heidegger, *The Question Concerning Technology and Other Essays*, trans. William Lovitt (San Francisco: Harper & Row, 1977), 121.

9. Martin Heidegger, *Basic Concepts*, trans. Gary E. Aylesworth (Bloomington and Indianapolis: Indiana University Press, 1993), 77.

10. Reiner Schürmann, "The Ontological Difference and Political Philosophy," *Philosophy and Phenomenological Research* 40 (1): 115 (1979).

11. See Reiner Schürmann, "Situating René Char: Hölderlin, Heidegger, Char and the 'There Is,'" *Boundary–2* 4 (1976), 513.

12. See Jacques Derrida, *Of Grammatology*, trans. Gayatri Chakravorty Spivak (London/Baltimore: John Hopkins University, 1974), 61.

13. See Martin Heidegger, *Being and Time*, trans. John Macquarrie and Edward Robinson (San Francisco: Harper & Row, 1962), 41. To render the etymological kinship between the verb *geschehen*, to happen, and the word *Geschichte*, history—a kinship stressed by Heidegger—the translators of *Being and Time* coin the verb "historize"—that is, a happening in a historical way. Historizing is not what the historian does. It is rather a property of Dasein (ibid.). At the same time, *Geschichte* contains within it *Geschick*, or "mittence" or "sending" which, as Schürmann argues, refers to the horizon in which humans may dwell in a given epoch (Reiner Schürmann, "Heidegger and Meister Eckhart on Releasement," *Research in Phenomenology* 3 [1973], 110–11).

14. Schürmann, *Heidegger on Being and Acting*, 270.

15. Heidegger, *Basic Concepts*, 77.

16. The concept of the "immanent time" is, of course, a borrowing from Husserl. Once we severed the link to the metaphysical subject, we would come to appreciate Husserl's theory of internal time consciousness that makes possible what he calls "the universal synthesis" of phenomena. Immanent time now stands as the "constant infinite horizon" before experience, a horizon that makes the articulation and rearticulation, the surfacing and ruptures of experience possible. See Husserl, *Cartesian Meditations*, 43.

17. And imitation, Derrida remarks, always intends to present the "idea" and the "idea" is the "presence of what is." See Jacques Derrida, "The Double Session," in *Disseminations*, trans. Barbara Johnson (Chicago: University of Chicago Press, 1981).

18. Paul Ricoeur, "Phenomenology of Freedom," in *Phenomenology and Philosophical Understanding*, ed. Edo Pivcevic (London/New York: Cambridge University Press, 1975), 184. Italics in original.

19. Melucci, *Nomads of the Present*, 114.

20. The attentive reader will recognize that the ideas of past, present, and future presented here show my debt to Heidegger's thrownness, projection, and fallenness, in *Being and Time*, as the conditions of *Dasein* in relation to time.

21. In this respect see Martin Heidegger, "A Dialogue on Language," in *On the Way to Language*, trans. Peter D. Hertz (San Francisco: Harper San Francisco, 1971), 3–5.

22. Schürmann, *Heidegger on Being and Acting*, 81. Italics added.

23. Reiner Schürmann, "Questioning the Foundation of Practical Philosophy," in *Phenomenology: Dialogues and Bridges*, ed. Ronald Bruzina and Bruce Wilshire, (Albany: State University of New York Press, 1982), 16.

24. Subcomandante Marcos and EZLN, *Shadows of Tender Fury: The Letters and Communiqués of Subcomandante Marcos and the Zapatista Army of National Liberation*, trans. Frank Bardacke, Leslie López, and the Watsonville, California, Human Rights Committee (New York: Monthly Review Press, 1995), 214.

25. "Declaration of the Lacandon Jungle: Today We Say 'Enough,'" in ibid., 51.

26. Ibid., 108.

27. Ibid., 116.

28. Ibid., 50.

29. Ibid., 228.

30. Jacques Derrida, *The Gift of Death*, trans. David Wills (Chicago: University of Chicago Press, 1995), 8.

31. See George A. Collier, *Basta! Land and the Zapatista Rebellion in Chiapas* (Oakland, Calif.: Food First Books, 1994), 36, 84–85.

32. Jacques Derrida, *Speech and Phenomena, and Other Essays on Husserl's Theory of Signs*, trans. David B. Allison and Newton Garver (Evanston, Ill.: Northwestern University Press, 1973), 67.

33. Subcommandante Marcos and EZLN, *Shadows of Tender Fury*, 138.

34. Collier, *Basta! Land and the Zapatista Rebellion*, 36.

35. Here, of course, I follow Derrida's critique of metaphysical parallelism which holds that a signified always already functions as, and is in the position of, a signifier. See Jacques Derrida, *Of Grammatology*, 7. See also Jacques Derrida, *Positions*, trans. Alan Bass (Chicago: University of Chicago Press, 1981), 20.

36. Subcomandante Marcos and EZLN, *Shadows of Tender Fury*, 109. In this respect also see John Holloway and Eloína Peláez, "Introduction: Reinventing Revolution," in *Zapatista! Reinventing Revolution in Mexico*, ed. Holloway and Peláez, 4.

37. Reiner Schürmann, "Principles Precarious: On the Origin of the Political in Heidegger," in *Heidegger: The Man and the Thinker*, ed. Thomas Sheehan (Chicago: Precedent Publishing, 1981), 250.

38. Subcomandante Marcos and EZLN, *Shadows of Tender Fury*, 167.

39. Quoted in Holloway and Peláez, "Introduction: Reinventing Revolution," 10.

40. See David Ronfeldt and John Arquilla, *The Zapatista Social Netwar in Mexico* (Santa Monica, Cal.: RAND, 1998), 61. Readers must be aware that these authors produced the study as a project on "Stability and the Military in Mexico," funded by the RAND Corporation for the US military. On-line version is available at: http://www.rand.org/publications/MR/MR994/MR994.pdf/ (viewed in January 1999).

41. Jacques Derrida, *Aporias: Dying—Awaiting (one another at) the "Limits of Truth,"* trans. Thomas Dutoit (Stanford: Stanford University Press, 1993), 15. Italics in original.

42. Ibid., 8.

43. Ibid., 20–21.

44. Schürmann, "Conditions of Evil," 389.

45. Schürmann, *Heidegger on Being and Acting*, 122.

46. David Slater, "Social Movements and A Recasting of the Political," in *New Social Movements and the State in Latin America*, ed. Slater, 5.

47. See Andreas Huyssen, "The Inevitability of Nation: Germany after Unification," in *The Identity in Question*, ed. Rajchman 83, 86. Based on a pre-World War I law, German citizenship is decided by blood lineage not by the place of birth.

48. Martin Heidegger, "In Memory of Max Scheler," in *Heidegger: The Man and the Thinker*, ed. Sheehan 159.

49. Reiner Schürmann, "On Judging and Its Issue," in *The Public Realm: Essays on Discursive Types in Political Philosophy*, ed. Reiner Schürmann (Albany: State University of New York Press, 1989), 15.

Chapter 5. Technological Liberalism and the Oppressive Categorization of "Transgressive" Actors

1. Schürmann, *Heidegger on Being and Acting*, 60.

2. Derrida, *Of Grammatology*, 154.

3. Mouffe, *The Return of the Actor*, 77.

4. Claude Lefort, *The Political Forms of Modern Society: Bureaucracy, Democracy, Totalitarianism*, trans. David Macey (Cambridge: MIT Press, 1986), 303.

5. Laclau and Mouffe, *Hegemony and Socialist Strategy*, 153.

6. Ibid., 154.

7. Derrida, *Of Grammatology*, 145.

8. Laclau and Mouffe, *Hegemony*, 154.

9. Derrida, *Of Grammatology*, 142. On supplement see ibid., 141–64.

10. Ibid., 143. For Derrida, the logic of supplement follows the logic of *différance*. Producing what is forbidden is then the feature of all relations dislocated through *différance*.

11. Ibid., 145. Derrida does not miss the opportunity to remind that although the subaltern is surplus to presence (domination), it can replace the latter. See also 149.

12. Lefort, *The Political Forms of Modern Society*, 198.

13. Schürmann, "Questioning the Foundation of Practical Philosophy", 18. See also Schürmann, *Heidegger on Being and Acting*, 97.

14. Schürmann, *Heidegger on Being and Acting*, 90. Italics in original.

15. Derrida, *Of Grammatology*, 149.

16. For a discussion on the place of agency in Laclau and Mouffe see Paul Smith, "Laclau's and Mouffe's Secret Agent," in *Community at Loose Ends*, ed. Miami Theory Collective (Minneapolis/Oxford: University of Minnesota Press, 1991), 99–110.

17. Schürmann, "On Constituting Oneself an Anarchistic Subject," 305.

18. Schürmann, *Heidegger on Being and Acting*, 27.

19. Ibid., 110.

20. See Heidegger, *The Question Concerning Technology*, 65.

21. In regard to this paradox see Lefort's perceptive observation in *The Political Forms of Modern Society*, 256–57.

22. See Schürmann's discussion in *Heidegger on Being and Acting*, 78–93.

23. Schürmann, "Principles Precarious: On the Origin of the Political in Heidegger," 250.

24. Schürmann, *Heidegger on Being and Acting*, 84.

25. Offe, "New Social Movements: Challenging the Boundaries of Institutional Politics," 826.

26. Derrida, *Of Grammatology*, 73. Italics in original.

27. Jacinthe Michaud, "The Welfare State and the Problem of Counter-Hegemonic Responses within the Women's Movement," in *Organizing Dissent*, ed. Carroll, 205–6.

28. Reiner Schürmann, "On Self-Regulation and Transgression," *Social Research* 49 (4): 1038 (1982).

29. See Max Weber, "Politics As Vocation," in *From Max Weber: Essays in Sociology*, ed. and trans. H. H. Gerth and C. Wright Mills (New York: Oxford University Press, 1946), 78.

30. Ibid., 90.

31. Ibid., 121.

32. Max Weber, "Bureaucracy," in *From Max Weber*, ed. Gerth and Mills, 224.

33. Ibid., 226.

34. Ibid., 242.

35. Jerry Weinberger, "Technology and the Problem of Liberal Democracy," in *Technology in Western Political Tradition*, ed. Arthur M. Mezler, Jerry Weinberger, & M. Richard Zinman (Ithaca & London: Cornell University Press, 1993), 257.

36. Ibid., 270.

37. Martin Heidegger, *Introduction to Metaphysics*, trans. Geoffry Fried and Richard Polt (New Haven and London: Yale University Press, 2000), 40.

38. Martin Heidegger, "On My Relation to National Socialism." Semiotext(e) 4(2): 253 (1982).

39. Martin Heidegger, "Only A God Can Save Us: *Der Spiegel's* Interview with Martin Heidegger," *Philosophy Today* 20 (4): 282 (1976).

40. Schürmann, " 'What Must I Do?' at the End of Metaphysics," 51.

41. Schürmann, *Heidegger on Being and Acting*, 81.

42. Schürmann, "Questioning the Foundation of Practical Philosophy," 14. Italics added.

43. Heidegger, *The Question Concerning Technology*, 137.

44. Ibid., 4.

45. Ibid., 12.

46. Ibid., 23.

47. See Veronique M. Fóti, *Heidegger and the Poets: Poiésis, Sophia, Techné* (Atlantic Highland, N.J.: Humanities Press, 1992), 13, 112.

48. Heidegger, *The Question Concerning Technology*, 19.

49. Ibid., 18.

50. Ibid.

51. Schürmann, "Questioning the Foundation of Practical Philosophy," 17. Italics in original.

52. Schürmann, "On Self-Regulation and Transgression," 1040.

53. Ibid.

54. Schürmann, "Technicity, Topology, Tragedy," 209.

55. Weinberger, "Technology and the Problem of Liberal Democracy," 255.

56. Schürmann, "Technicity, Topology, Tragedy," 210.

57. Martin Heidegger, "Homeland." *Listening* 6 (1971), 235.

58. Schürmann, "Technicity, Topology, Tragedy," 210. Isomorphic contextualization is accompanied by "dispersive decontextualization" as the dual character of technicity. Technicity singularizes phenomena. "Be they phenomena of nature or of culture, subjective or objective, encountered outside or inside, they have lost their respective world. Natural resources, neuroses, archaeological or literary curiosities *are* inasmuch as they answer the question: What can be made with this?" (ibid., 211).

59. Schürmann, *Heidegger on Being and Acting*, 37.

60. Schürmann, "Technicity, Topology, Tragedy," 210.

61. Ibid.

62. See Mouffe, "Post-Marxism: Democracy and Identity," 262.

63. Chantal Mouffe, "On the Itineraries of Democracy: An Interview with Chantal Mouffe," *Studies in Political Economy* 49 (Spring 1996), 135.

64. Chantal Mouffe, "Politics, Democratic Action, and Solidarity," *Inquiry* 38 (June 1995): 101.

65. Mouffe, "On the Itineraries of Democracy," 145.

66. Ibid. Italics added.

67. Ibid. Italics added.

68. Ibid., 137. Italics in original.

69. Chantal Mouffe, "Democracy, Power, and the 'Political'," in *Democracy and Difference: Contesting the Boundaries of the Political*, ed. Seyla Benhabib (Princeton, N.J.: Princeton University Press, 1996), 246–47.

70. Mouffe, "On the Itineraries of Democracy," 144.

71. Claude Lefort, "1968 Revisited: A French View; Not Revolution, but Creative Disorder," *Dissent* 35 (Summer 1988): 345–46.

72. Weinberger, "Technology and the Problem of Liberal Democracy," 256.

73. Heidegger, *The Question Concerning Technology*, 28; see also ibid., 34, 42.

74. Reiner Schürmann, "Heidegger and Meister Eckhart on Releasement," *Research in Phenomenology* 3 (1973): 98.

75. Schürmann, "On Self-Regulation and Transgression," 1040.

76. Lefort, *The Political Forms of Modern Society*, 258.

77. Ibid.

78. Schürmann, "Technicity, Topology, Tragedy," 210.

79. Hans-Georg Gadamer, *Philosophical Hermeneutics*, ed. and trans. David E. Linge (Berkeley: University of California Press, 1976), 9.

80. The more originative pulls are nothing but "coming-to-being" and "ceasing-to-be," or as Schürmann cites Hannah Arendt (in *The Life of Mind*), "natality" and "mortality." All other originative ultimacies are subject to this ultimate double pull. See Schürmann, "Technicity, Topology, Tragedy," 204–5.

81. Martin Heidegger, "Only a God Can Save Us," 276.

82. Ibid.

Chapter 6. An Epochal Theory of Action

1. Schürmann, *Heidegger on Being and Acting*, 81.

2. Schürmann, "On Self-Regulation and Transgression," 1036–37.

3. Schürmann, *Heidegger on Being and Acting*, 1. Italics added.

4. Ibid., 82.

5. Schürmann, "'What Must I Do?' at the End of Metaphysics?" 51.

6. Ibid.

7. Schürmann, *Heidegger on Being and Acting*, 81.

8. Schürmann, "'What Must I do?' at the End of Metaphysics?" 51.

9. Schürmann, *Heidegger on Being and Acting*, 29.

10. Michel Haar, "The Place of Nietzsche in Reiner Schürmann's Thought and in His Reading of Heidegger," *Graduate Faculty Philosophy Journal* 19(2–20:1): 230 (1997).

11. Schürmann, *Heidegger on Being and Acting*, 170.

12. Ibid.

13. Ibid., 171.

14. Schürmann, "Adventures of the Double Negation: On Richard Bernstein's Call for Anti-Anti Humanism," 289.

15. Schürmann, "Principles Precarious: On the Origin of the Political in Heidegger," 245–46.

16. Schürmann, *Heidegger on Being and Acting*, 122.

17. Schürmann, "Principles Precarious," 246.

18. Schürmann, "Adventures of the Double Negation," 288.

19. Schürmann, *Heidegger on Being and Acting*, 25.

20. Martin Heidegger, "The Turning," in *The Question Concerning Technology and Other Essays*, 37.

21. Schürmann, *Heidegger on Being and Acting*, 31. Italics added.

22. Ibid., 183.

23. Schürmann, "Principles Precarious," 248.

24. Following Veronique Fóti, by italicizing the *esse* in "essence" or "essential" I mean to signify the temporal character of Being (as Heidegger's term *Wesen* designates); therefore, by "essence," I do not designate the metaphysical concept of essence. See Fóti, *Heidegger and the Poets*, xi. The attentive reader heeds that the word "essential" (from the Latin *essentia*, "being") is composed of two segments: "*esse*" means "being" and "*ens*" refers to "a being" or "entity." Such ontological difference manifests itself in the English word "essence."

25. Schürmann, *Heidegger on Being and Acting*, 124. The translator's of Heidegger's recent English title, *Contribution to Philosophy (From Enowning)*, have made an astute argument about the inadequacy of any existing translation of the German word *Eregnis* (such as the "event of appropriation" or simply the "event") to make a case for the term they suggest, *enowning*. *Enowning* denotes in an active sense (through the prefix "en-") the "non-possessive owning" that is characteristic of *Ereignis*. See Parvis Emad and Kenneth Maly, "Translators' Foreword," in Martin Heidegger, *Contribution to Philosophy [From Enowning]*, trans. Parvis Emad and Kenneth Maly (Bloomington and Indianapolis: Indiana University Press, 1999), xx.

26. Schürmann, *Heidegger on Being and Acting*, 34.

27. Ibid., 273–74.

28. Ibid., 18. Italics added.

29. Haar, "The Place of Nietzsche," 239.

30. Ibid., 233.

31. Frank Schalow, "Revisiting Anarchy: Toward a Critical Appropriation of Reiner Schürmann's Thought," *Philosophy Today* 41 (4): 556 (1997).

32. Martin Heidegger, "The Thing," in *Poetry, Language, Thought*, trans. Albert Hofstadter (San Francisco: Harper and Row, 1971), 181. Italics added. See also Reiner Schürmann, "Anti-Humanism: Reflections of the Turn Towards the Postmodern Epoch," *Man and World* 12 (2): 165–66 (1979).

33. Schürmann, "Adventures of the Double Negation," 289–90.

34. Schürmann, *Heidegger on Being and Acting*, 60.

35. Schalow, "Revisiting Anarchy," 555.

36. Ibid., 556.

37. Schürmann, *Heidegger on Being and Acting*, 17. Schürmann refers to Heidegger's 1969 Le Thor Seminar to show the truth of his periodization of Heidegger.

38. Ibid., 46–47.

39. Heidegger, "Only A God Can Save Us: *Der Spiegel's* Interview with Martin Heidegger," 279.

40. Schürmann, *Heidegger on Being and Acting*, 123.

41. Ibid., 157–58.

42. Schalow, "Revisiting Anarchy," 556.

43. Schürmann, *Heidegger on Being and Acting*, 156.

44. Ibid., 160.

45. Ibid., 203.

46. See ibid., 161.

47. Ibid., 205.

48. Ibid., 232.

49. Jean-François Lyotard, *The Postmodern Condition: A Report on Knowledge*, trans. Geoff Bennington and Brian Massumi (Minneapolis: University of Minnesota Press, 1984), 31.

50. Schürmann, *Heidegger on Being and Acting*, 281.

51. Ibid., 225.

52. See Schürmann, "Adventures of the Double Negation," 290. See also Schürmann, *Heidegger on Being and Acting*, 60.

53. Schürmann, *Heidegger on Being and Acting*, 259.

54. Lyotard, *The Postmodern Condition*, 38.

55. See Melucci, "Social Movements and the Democratization of Everyday Life".

56. Jorge G. Castañeda, *Utopia Unarmed: The Latin American Left After the Cold War* (New York: Vintage Books, 1993), 241.

57. Holloway and Peláez, "Introduction: Reinventing Revolution," 1–18.

58. Holloway, "Dignity's Revolt," 169.

59. See Lorna Weir, "Limitations of New Social Movement Analysis," *Studies in Political Economy* 40 (1993): 73–102.

60. Schürmann, *Heidegger on Being and Acting*, 85.

61. Martin Heidegger, "The Origin of the Work of Art," in *Poetry, Language, Thought*, 76.

62. Schürmann, "Political Thinking in Heidegger," 202–3.

63. Martin Heidegger, "The Pathway," in *Heidegger: The Man and the Thinker*, ed. Thomas Sheehan (Chicago: Precedent Publishing, 1981), 69. Unless noted otherwise, all italics in the excerpts from Heidegger's "The Pathway" that I quote in this section are mine.

64. Schürmann, *Heidegger on Being and Acting*, 270.

65. Heidegger, "The Pathway," 69.

66. Schürmann, "Conditions of Evil", 388.

67. Schürmann, *Heidegger on Being and Acting*, 18.

68. Ibid., 83.

69. "Thinking Heidegger further," Werner Marx shows that the abandonment of principles is not the same as abandonment of measures. He, therefore, advocates post-metaphysical "nondeterminant measures." See Werner Marx, *Is There a Measure on Earth? Foundations for A Nonmetaphysical Ethics*, trans. Thomas J. Nenon and Reginal Lilly (Chicago and London: University of Chicago Press, 1987).

70. Heidegger, "The Pathway," 69.

71. Schürmann, "On Self-Regulation and Transgression," 1039.

72. Martin Heidegger, "A Recollection" (1957), in *Heidegger: The Man and the Thinker*, ed. Sheehan, 21.

73. Schürmann, *Heidegger on Being and Acting*, 258.

74. Heidegger, "The Pathway," 69–70.

75. Heidegger, *The Question Concerning Technology*, 28.

76. Heidegger, "The Pathway," 70.

77. Ibid.

78. Schürmann, "Questioning the Foundation of Practical Philosophy," 18.

79. Heidegger, "The Pathway," 70.

80. Ibid. Here "call" translates the German *Zuspruch* with connotations that include message, appeal, and address (see the translator's note in ibid., 72).

81. For this translation of the archaic German word *Gagnet* as "open expanse," see: Martin Heidegger, *Discourse on Thinking*, trans. John M. Anderson and E. Hans Freund (New York: Harper and Row, 1966), 66. It is also translated as "that-which-regions" (ibid.) to refer to *the* region of horizonal openness—indeed a radical movement in non-"re-presentational" thinking which I must leave to another study.

82. Heidegger, "The Pathway," 70.

83. Ibid.

84. Ibid.

85. Heidegger, "The Thing," in *Poetry, Language, Thought*, 181.

86. Heidegger, "The Pathway," 70.

87. Ibid.

88. Ibid.

89. Ibid., 71.

90. Schürmann, *Heidegger on Being and Acting*, 232–33.

91. Schürmann, "On Self-Regulation and Transgression," 1039.

92. Heidegger, "The Pathway," 71.

93. Ibid.

94. Ibid.

95. Heidegger, *Basic Concepts*, 14.

96. Schürmann, *Heidegger on Being and Acting*, 255.

97. My distinction between action and activity is rather different from Schürmann's. For him, the distinction goes back to the political as the locus of coming together of action, words, and things. "[I]f action remains deprived of speech and of reference to other actions, a new domain opens itself: not that of action but of activity with utensils" (*Heidegger on Being and Acting*, 36). In other words, activity is not political; action, on the other hand, always is. For me, however, action and activity are both political, but the first is nonhegemonic and anarchic and the second hegemonic and principial.

98. Schürmann, "Political Thinking in Heidegger," 204.

99. Dennis J. Schmidt, "*Solve et Coagula*: Something Other Than an Exercise in Dialectic," *Research in Phenomenology* 28 (1998): 362.

100. Schürmann, *Heidegger on Being and Acting*, 6.

101. Ibid., 274–75.

102. Heidegger, "Building Dwelling Thinking," in *Poetry, Language, Thought*, 150.

Chapter 7. Radical Phenomenology and the Sociology of Possibilities

1. Schürmann, *Heidegger on Being and Acting*, 11.

2. Zygmunt Bauman, "Is There A Postmodern Sociology?" in *Intimations of Postmodernity* (New York/London: Routledge, 1992), 111.

3. Reiner Schürmann, "Neoplatonic Henology as an Overcoming of Metaphysics," *Research in Phenomenology* XIII (1983), 26.

4. See Schürmann, "Questioning the Foundation of Practical Philosophy," 15–18.

5. Reginald Lilly, "The Topology of *Des Hégémonies brisées*," *Research in Phenomenology* 28 (1998): 241.

6. Schurmann identifies three types of topology: recapitulative, critical, and anticipatory (see Schürmann, "Technicity, Topology, Tragedy," 196–200). While the study of the implications of these topologies for the sociology of possibilities cannot be even initiated in these pages, for the purpose of clarification of terms, let us identify these sorts of topology. Recapitulative topology designates the topology of the historical movement of a discourse as normative from its institution to its destitution. Critical topology refers to the topology of what we are but can no longer be, and as such, what we are is always only a possibility. Anticipatory topology denotes the topology of historical sites as given but not yet occupied, literally a topology of possibilities (see Lilly, "The Topology of *Des Hégémonies brisées*," 240–42). Discursive topology, and the sociology of possibilities, for that matter, can engage in all three sorts of topology.

7. Heidegger, "Only a God Can Save Us: *Der Spiegel's* Interview with Martin Heidegger," 269.

8. Schürmann, *Heidegger on Being and Acting*, 93.

9. Martin Heidegger, "Homeland," *Listening* 6 (1971): 234.

10. In Schürmann's words, "Deconstruction is anticipatory in its entire thrust. Radical phenomenology 'prepares' for another, a possible, economy" (*Heidegger on Being and Acting*, 228).

11. Martin Heidegger, *On Time and Being*, trans. Joan Stambaugh (New York: Harper and Row, 1972), 60.

12. Schürmann, " 'What Must I Do?' at the End of Metaphysics," 61.

13. Schürmann, *Heidegger on Being and Acting*, 58.

14. See ibid., 50.

15. Ibid., 208.

Index